PAUL CARBERRY
The Autobiography

with Des Gibson

Paperweight

A CIP catalogue record for this book
is available from the British Library.

ISBN 978-0-9569134-4-9

ISBN e book 978-0-9569134-5-6

Printed and bound by
CPI Group (UK) Ltd, Croydon, CR0 4YY

Paperweight Publishing Group, Level 4, Building 5,
Dundrum Townhouse Centre, Dublin 16, Ireland.

www.paperweightpublications.ie

CONTENTS

Dedication
John O'Meara
A good friend, lost too early

Foreword

By Noel Meade

There are two things that have often been said about Paul Carberry. First is always that he is a bit of a hell-raiser. The second, and the more important of the two, is that he is the most naturally gifted and talented jockey in racing. And there's a lot of truth in both. However, I hope what shines through in this book are the other sides of Paul Carberry. Paul, the brutally honest and shy gentleman. A man full of integrity, who would do anything he could to help anyone he could.

I know Paul most of his life and we have been involved in racing together for almost 20 years. Paul's father Tommy was a bit of a hero of mine and I am proud to say he became a close friend. Tommy rode for me when I first started out training and I have got to know Pamela and all the Carberrys very well through the years. Their love of life and their family is infectious and they are loved by all who know them.

Paul was always destined to be a great jockey. I suppose when you look at a horse, you examine its pedigree. Well Paul's pedigree is second to none. He is the son of a champion jockey, and his mother is the daughter of a champion jockey. I guess with that kind of racing royalty in your blood he was always going to be good. But Paul exceeded all expectations and I can honestly say that he is exceptionally gifted in the saddle. He is both talented and fearless in equal measure and that is a potent combination for any young aspiring jockey. To put it simply, it is easier for Paul to do the right thing on a horse than the wrong one. It's almost a subconscious reaction, a natural gift. Within days at my yard I knew I had someone very special on my hands.

Part of Paul's natural talent lies within his unique bond with horses. He loves being around them and they respond to him in a way that I have never seen with any other rider. He would never punish or mistreat a horse or ask them to do anything they weren't capable of. I remember after watching Paul finishing second on one of my horses, Harchibald, in a Christmas Hurdle at Kempton and I thought Paul had been a bit soft on him. When I later asked Paul why he hadn't given the horse a crack of the whip, he looked at me with almost tears in his eyes and said: *'Sure why would I? Wasn't he already giving me everything he had.'* And that's just Paul. He is brutally honest, and always with the interest of the horses at heart. I suppose Paul is most comfortable when he is riding and that is why he is often withdrawn and overly shy when in a crowd.

However, his friends and those close to him know a different Paul. Ever the joker, Paul is sharp-witted and enjoys his life to the full. He is great company and enjoys winding people up too. There was one year over at the Cheltenham Festival that always comes to mind. We were all at the Cheltenham racecourse hours before racing began to give our horses a bit of a practice run on the track and let them have a proper look at the fences. It gives the trainers a chance to assess their horses' chances and to meet up with other trainers and chat about the week ahead. Likewise, for the jockeys, it's a chance to school the horses before the big event and look for the best ground. They would meet up with the other jockeys in the centre of the course to shoot the breeze and talk up their chances. That morning, Paul was schooling Sausalito Bay and he met Ruby Walsh at the track and Ruby asked him what horse he was riding. *'I haven't a clue... just one of Noel's,'* Paul said, before galloping off, leaving a dumbstruck Ruby shaking his head. Paul knew well what horse he was on but he just enjoyed the wind-up and always liked to let on that he knows much less than he does.

That horse went on win the Supreme Novices' Hurdle, the opening race of the meeting, giving me my first ever Cheltenham Festival win after many years of trying.

We have had our ups and downs through the years. You will read about them in this book. At times he's taken me to the pin of my collar and driven me crazy but he's also responsible for some of my greatest days in racing. Whichever the case, Paul always remained loyal and this loyalty and generousity of spirit was not confined to me. Paul would never speak of it, but he has often put the needs of others ahead of his own, both in terms of his time and finances.

To try and sum up Paul, it would be fair to say that horses are in his blood. They are the centre of his universe. Paul's story, like his talent, is unique and it will be a long time before you see his kind in racing again.

-August 2011

CHAPTER 1

Just Plane Madness

How in God's name did it come to this?

I was there, sitting in an airport police room, trying to talk my way out of a real nightmare. Beads of sweat occasionally stung my eyes and my head was beginning to hurt. I was like a bold schoolboy, being told that I was lucky not to be in handcuffs and locked in a cell for a while. *'That would be the normal procedure, you know'.* But the garda officer said that it didn't seem necessary at the time because I didn't 'give them any hassle' and I was making a full statement. I sat in the chair for what seemed like hours, going over and over what had happened in Row 18 of that Aer Lingus flight 583, explaining why I had done it, and the policeman explaining what was going to happen next. I had fallen at the last hurdle, crashed and burned.

After a week of relaxing with friends in Spain, I was now being grilled in a back room at Dublin Airport, with the threat of jail looming over me. Mam and Dad and all the family would hear about this. So would my trainer Noel Meade who had stuck by me for almost 20 years. In fact, every trainer and owner in Ireland and Britain would hear about this if I end up in court. Or worse, I end up banged up in jail.

"Starting a fire on an airplane is a serious offence and endangered lives".

1

Oh shit. I could go down for this.

****

A week before at the same airport in Dublin, the mood was very much different. It was the last week of September 2005, and a good gang of about 15 of us headed off for a lads' holiday in Puerto Banus in Spain, just as we had done for the past few years. We stayed at the Pyr Hotel, a high-rise hotel in the middle of the Costa del Sol resort overlooking the Mediterranean. It was also right in the thick of it as far as the local nightlife was concerned, perfect for us to wind down and blow out before the new national hunt season kicked off. A friend Pat Healy used to arrange it, and a good few jockeys including Davy Russell, Mark Grant, Robbie 'Puppy' Power and Davy Condon would come along. Some friends of mine like Alan 'Horsebox' Egan, who was a fireman, Fresh, Maurice 'Sneaky Boo' Sheehy, Michael 'Chips' Gannon, Justin Flood and a few bookmaker pals would come over as well. I'm not too sure of where most of the nicknames came from, but I know Alan was christened Horsebox by Tucker Geraghty, jockey Barry Geraghty's dad, because every time he came down to his yard he was looking for a horsebox so the name stuck. Most of them were all fairly good drinkers, not a lightweight between the lads who drank.

This was a week to relax, get some sun during the day, drink most of the night, and generally just have a laugh. I was single at the time, as were most of the lads on the trip. We used to go after the Listowel races and before the new national hunt season got off properly. I remember ringing Noel Meade and telling him that I'd be away for a week, and that I was heading off with the lads. I guess that call put the mockers on me because I remember Noel warning me: *'Now don't do anything stupid!'* I told him that I'd try my best not to.

That night a load of the lads who lived further down the country came up and stayed at my place so we could go to Dublin Airport together the next morning. We had a few pints in the local and ended up in The Attic, a disco bar in Dunshaughlin. My younger brother Mark joined us for the night as well and I got stuck into the vodka to get the ball rolling. I was never really a man for beer and ever since I started on the vodka and orange or 7up it was the drink for me. I hadn't been drinking at all for the week of Listowel, I'd been fairly good so I deserved a proper blow-out.

The flight the next day was about eight o'clock in the morning so we barely made the bed before heading off to the airport. After dropping the bags at check-in, we had a quick drink in the airport bar and boarded the two-and-a-half-hour flight to Malaga. As soon as we hit the hotel we headed down to the beach to take in some sun and hit the bar. Like most lads our age we would drink Sangria and shorts until the evening when some of the lads would head out for something to eat. I was never one for having big meals, in fact I don't think I ate at all for that week. I tended to stay back with a couple of the lads around the beach bar and enjoy the music there in the evening, before meeting up with the rest of the lads at a bar down the town later on.

Generally the days would all end the same, drinking at the beach for the day, acting the maggot by whipping the shorts off and jumping into the water to cool down and sometimes head back to the room for a siesta before going out for the night and not returning until the early hours. Sneaky Boo was a friend of Pat Healy's, a bit of a character, and he'd be up telling jokes all night having us in stitches. I was wasted most days and the lads even found me asleep in a chair at a hairdressing salon down the town one afternoon. The Spanish girl working there had thought I was dead.

3

It was Davy Condon's first time away with us and he was in a room with me and Horsebox. Condon was a bit mad and we were a bit worried about him because he's a lunatic at home but he certainly wasn't the wildest in the group on that holiday and it actually made him seem a bit quiet and shy compared to the other lads. Anyway, Condon was younger than the rest of us so he was a bit afraid to step out of line.

However, one night he did get up to a bit of messing and shaved a sideburn and half an eyebrow off a drunken Horsebox so when Alan woke the next morning he was hopping mad and was out to get him back. So every night Condon would be bricking it about the retaliation and he'd leave the bar before us to head back to the hotel alone. By the time we got back to the room Condon had moved his mattress and duvet into the bathroom and slept in the bath with the door locked. He was afraid of his life of waking up with no eyebrows or something even worse. In the end Condon shaved off his own sideburns, fearing that Alan would have done much worse a job.

While I thought that was the end of the messing and Condon was behaving himself, it turned out he was on my phone every time my back was turned. Every feckin night he was texting my trainer Noel Meade from my phone at all hours of the night without me knowing. Noel has always been a loyal boss and friend to me despite all my messing but that week he was about to reach breaking point and blow a gasket. And who could really blame him.

Condon would grab my phone at all hours, three or four in the morning, and send texts to Noel saying 'Harchibald needs blinkers, he needs blinkers' or 'Harchibald's a dog'. Harchibald was a horse I was riding for Noel and we had just missed out on the Champion Hurdle at Cheltenham earlier that year. He was a special horse for us, but everyone seemed to have an opinion on how best to ride him. At one stage he even rang Meade in front of the lads pretending to be me. After months of listening to people talking complete rubbish about how Harchibald should be trained and ridden, this was the last thing Noel wanted to be hearing.

At the end of our week in Spain, just before we were heading home I got a text on my phone from Noel. He was going mad. When I say there was a text from Noel, it was actually more like an essay. It started out with the words: *'Paul, the elastic band that holds our bond of friendship together is about to snap'*. And it went on to say that if he got any more texts or calls in the middle of the night, then *'the bond will be broken'*. I could tell that Noel was fairly serious, but of course the lads got a great laugh about it when they heard. I was raging but I could still see the funny side. But from that moment I had Condon's card marked and I knew I would get him back.

Setting fire to someone's newspaper was something I'd done lots of times. If ever I was out with the lads, or on a stag night or anything and one of them opened up a newspaper, I'd come up behind them with a cigarette lighter and light the bottom of it. It was just something I did when acting the maggot, a natural reaction. Looking back now, I guess it wasn't the greatest idea to do it on an airplane. In fact, it was bonkers.

I looked at my ticket, 18D, and we shuffled down to our seats. I was in the aisle seat, Davy Condon beside me in the middle with Mark Grant on the inside fast asleep, with all the boys sitting around us. We were only about twenty-five minutes into the flight when Davy took out his newspaper and quick as a flash, I set it on fire at the bottom. It went up, Davy banged it together and scrunched it up to put it out and dropped it to the floor. It all lasted about two seconds in total, but that's when the trouble started.

A stewardess came down to me and asked what happened. I told her I hadn't a clue, but then I later told her something like *'the paper had gone on fire'.* There had been some smoke and I guess a smell of burning and some other passengers weren't happy at all. The stewardess came back down and asked me for the cigarette lighter which I gave to her. She then said we were to stay in our seats and there was to be no messing for the rest of the flight.

That's when the slagging really started. The rest of the boys were all saying *'You're going to jail this time Carbs'.* I suppose it was only a few years since 9/11, and any kind of messing on an airplane just wasn't the thing to do. Timmy Murphy had just been jailed for causing hassle and assaulting a stewardess on a plane from Japan to Heathrow just a couple of years previously. For the rest of the flight home to Dublin the lads were saying *'Timmy Murphy didn't do half of what you did, you're fucked'.* I was putting on the bravado and while I thought there might be a bit of trouble, inside I was just hoping that would be the end of it. I sat with my hands sweating for the rest of the flight, trying to keep calm, while all the time listening in the background to the lads speculating about how much shit I was in. Condon and Grant weren't saying much though, as they were convinced that they were going to be questioned by the guards as well. Maybe, just maybe that will be the end of it. Perhaps the doors will open, I'll get off and be in the clear.

But when we landed, the intercom came on and a voice asked everyone to be patient and remain in their seats for a few minutes after the plane had stopped as a member of the police force would be boarding the airplane. Shit, that's it, I'm done for now. Sure enough the door of the airplane was opened and there were two gardai at the door. I knew it was for me. They didn't board the plane or come down to me, so in one last attempt to escape the grief I put on one of Davy Russell's jumpers hoping to confuse them. Looking back now it was a pretty desperate and pathetic effort at a disguise, but I was hoping that all this would just go away.

But sure enough as I went to get off the airplane I was pulled to one side. A garda told me that they needed to talk to me and I was led to the station, a room they had for questioning at the airport. I was led into the room and told to sit down at the table where I spent ages going over and over what had happened in the past three hours or so. I made a statement and was asked to sign the bit of paper which I did. I wasn't even sure at that point if I was under arrest but I guess I was. I was being charged with breaching the peace, and possibly endangering lives. It was all going by in a blur. I couldn't believe this was happening to me. Starting a fire on an airplane... Mid-flight... Full of passengers. This wasn't sounding very good. I was told I would have to appear in court on Tuesday, three days away, and I was told I could leave and go home in the meantime.

The lads had already picked up my bags, so when I left the police station, Condon, Russell and Mark Grant were waiting for me in a car driven by Jules, who was working with me. I don't think I said a word during the trip back to Meath and wasn't that pushed when Condon said that the rest of the lads were waiting for us back in a local pub, The Forge near Trim, to finish off the holiday. I just wasn't in the humour but the lads were insistent. When we got to the pub, I was in no kind of mood and I was standing alone at the bar ready to head home. Just then Alan Egan went over and stuck some coins into the jukebox. Billy Joel's *'We Didn't Start The Fire'* blasted out and the lads went wild, cheering and banging their glasses.

It was black humour and I just had to laugh and go with the flow. It lifted the spirits for a while, but much worse times lay ahead...

CHAPTER 2

The Early Years

A lot of what has been written or said about me throughout the years has been untrue. Well, some of it has anyway. Yes I enjoy my life and, while I don't like to talk about the lows, I don't exactly shout about the highs either. I know I'm quiet and tend not to talk that much when in a group. And anybody who knows me will tell you that in a car journey I'll be asleep by the first corner, when I'm not driving of course. It rarely ever happens when I'm in the driving seat. I guess I'm a little shy at times, which may sound strange given some of my antics over the years. But this would make perfect sense to anyone who has spent time in my company. That said though, I do enjoy having people around me and I have kept the same group of friends for most of my life. I'm lucky that way. There have been lots of laughs, some bad times, plenty of messing and damn lunacy along the way. It's been some ride.

****

I had been surrounded by horses growing up. I had a simple goal in life and that was to make it as a jockey, and I knew from very early on in my life that I wanted to be a jump jockey. I was born on February 9, 1974 at Dad's Ballybin yard in Ashbourne, not far from Ratoath in Ireland's County Meath, the second child of Tommy and Pamela Carberry. My brother Thomas was born just over a year before and Mark followed a year later. Three more children would come, but there was a bit of a wait for the younger set, with Philip born in 1980, Nina four years later and finally Peterjon in 1989. So back then it was me, Thomas and Mark against the world. Well, our world that is, which was fields, horses and school. Where we lived was quite remote so our adventures were kept largely to around the yard. I wouldn't imagine that it was a normal childhood as such. We were three lunatics, and we ran off more baby-sitters than I can remember.

Growing up as a Carberry, there was nothing else I ever wanted to do except to ride horses. And that suited Dad, who was a bit of a legend around the area. When I had just turned one year old, Dad had won the greatest race in the world, The Aintree Grand National on L'Escargot. The horse was trained by Mam's father, the great Dan Moore. It would be 24 years before an Irish horse would win the English Grand National again, but that's another story.

Mam had met Dad when he was working as stable jockey at her father, my grandfather, Dan Moore's yard up in Fairyhouse and they married in 1970. Dad went on to be Irish champion national hunt jockey five times while Dan was a famous champion trainer. L'Escargot was the jewel in Dan Moore's yard, running in four English Grand Nationals and finishing third and second before finally passing the post in front of the mighty Red Rum in the 1975 Aintree showpiece. Red Rum was trying for his third successive victory in the race that day, but L'Escargot thumped him by 15 lengths, with Dad brilliant in the saddle, and grandad Dan the successful trainer, adding the National crown to L'Escargot's two Gold Cups of 1970 and 1971.

Dad had also been the jockey for L'Escargot's 1970 and 1971 Cheltenham Gold Cup triumphs, and made it an incredible four Gold Cup wins when he won on Ten Up in 1975 and then on Tied Cottage in 1980. However, Tied Cottage was later disqualified along with two other Irish horses after an illegal substance was found in their system. This was believed to have been accidentally caused by the feed they were given from contaminated containers, but despite what the record books might show, I know Dad passed the post in front in four Gold Cups. That 1975 year was a golden one for the family as Dad added the Irish Grand National with Brown Lad, to become the only jockey in history to win the Cheltenham Gold Cup, English Grand National and Irish Grand National in the same year.

I guess I never really fully appreciated how good Dad was as a jockey until I was much older and started riding myself. It was only then that other people involved in racing told me so much that I hadn't even known about. It takes so much discipline and fitness to get on in racing and Dad's record is incredible. He also had sixteen winners at the Cheltenham Festival through the years, an incredible achievement in itself. He rode professionally until he was 40 years old, when he had a career-ending fall, ironically during a flat race when riding at the Listowel Races.

Dad's also quite shy and modest and would never be harping on about what he did or what he won. I'd always have to hear how much he had done from others, that is just the way he is. He's been one tough act to follow.

Dad's family have a long history in the area. There are mentions of Thomas Carberrys right back to the early 1800s. His great grandfather Thomas is believed to have lived in Garristown in North County Dublin over 200 years ago. His son Thomas, my Dad's grandfather, moved to Ratoath in Meath around 1907 and had four children, one of them being Thomas

11

of course, my Dad's father. He married Monica White and they had six children, with the second child born in 1942 and being named Thomas, who later became simply known as Tommy, my Dad.

Dad's family have long been involved in the local Ward Union hunts, and his younger brother John became Master of the Fingal Hounds, while his sister Anna's husband Oliver later became Secretary of the Stag Hunt.

Mam's family also had a long history immersed in horseracing. Mam's grandfather, Thomas Levins Moore, was Trinity College educated and was later the Director of the National Bank. He was also involved in the Ward Union Hunt almost all of his life and was Secretary of the Ward for over 20 years and Master for five. He married Florence Smithwick and they had five children, the second of which being Dan, my Mam's father.

Dan was born in 1910 and had a very successful career as an amateur jockey before turning professional very late in his career, when he was aged 28. He won the Irish Grand National twice in 1943 and 1947, and was just pipped for the Aintree Grand National when Royal Danieli finished second in the 1938 race. He was Irish champion jockey five times before turning his incredible experience to training. He and his wife Joan had three children, Arthur, my mother Pamela, and then Dan Jonathon (DJ) who was a good deal younger, just a few years older than myself.

Mam's brother Arthur Moore followed their father into racehorse training and would later become very successful in his own right. Indeed, his knack for getting horses right would bring both myself and my younger sister Nina great days in the future.

Uncle DJ was also involved in racing until a horrific accident over ten years ago. Tragically DJ ended up paralysed from the waist down for doing the right thing, the cruellest twist of fate.

Having driven a long distance, he felt tired and decided to pull into the side of the road to rest, to shut his eyes for a few minutes. Moments later his car was smashed by a passing truck and Jonathon ended up paralysed.

****

I guess with that kind of racing pedigree I was always going to be heading to the racetrack. And I had the good luck as a young lad to be small, and fairly thin, growing up.

In fact, I just couldn't seem to put on weight and didn't eat that much and always seemed to be getting sick. Mam was worried and took me to a doctor and it eventually turned out I was a coeliac. It wasn't that big of a deal but it just meant that I had to eat certain things and couldn't eat others. Thankfully that eventually passed and I grew out of it before my teenage years.

School just wasn't my thing. I was never exactly top of the class but the interest just wasn't there from the very first day in Ratoath National School. Again, I knew that it wasn't for me. It was a distraction, something that got between me and being at home riding horses. I did a bit of long distance running while at school but I never really had any interest in other sports. I had started riding when I was just three or four years old. We had a few ponies and Mam was hunting at weekends and I'd go along. We'd all set off on the hunt at the same time with the adults out front and we would follow behind on a set course with gates if you weren't confident enough to jump.

Me and Thomas would go out and ride any time we could. Mark would join us a lot, but his heart just wasn't in it like it was for us. Mark was always doing his own thing and he ended up doing very well in carpentry, but he just wasn't pushed on horses like the rest of us were. When it came close to a big hunt or pony camp Mark would get back out riding for a while to get back up to speed but then he could leave it again for months. I guess myself and Thomas were different, we were always a bit wild and lived for the horses. Dad had racehorses out the back of the house but my first real pony was a rat of a thing called Jack that just wandered into the yard from the road one day and we took him in. He was an old mine pony and he basically just did what he wanted. He would let you trot around on his back for a while and then he'd just stop dead and stick his head down and he'd send you over the top. He may have been a stray but he seemed to know who was on his back. If you put someone up on him that couldn't really ride, he'd basically stay still, but if you could ride he would duck and dive and give you a spin. Philip and Nina would get plenty of use out of Jack in later years so I suppose it was a good thing we took him in. Then one day my Dad went off to the sales with his friend Tommy Gallagher and came back with a proper pony called Spiddal, even though Mam went mad, saying that it was far too big for a first pony. But myself and Thomas loved him and used to take turns on his back.

Soon afterwards Dad was up at a big schooling day at Fairyhouse after races at the Easter meeting and ended up in Ratoath with friends of his, Timmy Jones and Francis Kiernan. Francis had a decent pony called Buckley Boy but his son James had moved on to showjumping horses at that stage and Timmy said to Francis that he should give Dad the good pony Buckley Boy for Thomas to use at home. So from then on Thomas had his own horse, and I had Spiddal. We'd take them out the back and compete as if we were at the races.

Myself and Thomas lived for the hunts and pony club. Mam would take us with our ponies in the trailer at the weekends, mostly Sundays, and showjump, and then during the summer months we would go to pony camp at Fairyhouse racecourse, which was really what it sounded like. It was a holiday for a week or two just riding horses and meeting others who felt the same way. Guys like Mick Foley and Gavin Cromwell, who lived just down the road and is now training some horses and working as a farrier. Also there, Adam and Niall Lord, who are still my friends today, and Fergus Galvin, who owns a few nice horses such as Salford City which he owned with Adam. He is based out in Kentucky in America now, where he has a breeding establishment after a stint working with Coolmore. Simon Fay and Ronan O'Dwyer were there too. We are all around the same age and they are all still close to me now. Back at pony camp there were some competitions, but even when we weren't competing for anything we were still fiercely competitive with each other.

We used to just bring a sleeping bag and crash on the floor in the old weigh room for the week. It would be some craic, about 30 lads in one room and 30 girls in a room on the other side and masters in the middle trying to stop both sides mixing. But we managed it sometimes. Put it like this: the masters didn't always win. It was where we got our first taste for jumping the big fences. The organisers used to block off the big obstacles with tables and a master would stand on one of the tables to belt out instructions. One day myself and Mick Foley decided we'd had enough and ran full pelt on our ponies directly at the table. The instructor had to jump out of the way as we cleared the obstacle. He was furious and put us on work duty, peeling spuds for the next two days. Mick Foley told me later that he was advised to *'Stay away from the Carberrys. They're nothing but cowboys! Cowboys, I tell ye!'.*

When we weren't at pony camp, we would just meet up with our ponies across the fields near home. We would gallop the living daylights out of them all day, heading from Ashbourne and Ratoath across to Batterstown and Dunshaughlin, passing the Fairyhouse Racecourse on our way. One time we even broke

15

through the fence and jumped some fences on the course. For years we would say that we had schooled our horses over the Irish Grand National fences when we were still only kids.

I remember my days at primary too, but only because I got an awful hiding for acting the fool one day. When I was about nine or 10 years of age I got the blame for tripping some lad up on a Friday and I was told that I'd have to report back on the Monday morning to get the punishment. Well that was enough for me to decide that I was going to run away that following Monday. So after a weekend of planning I set off that Monday morning with two other lads. It wasn't a great plan.

We met at the school, left our bags at the bike shelters and hit the road for a day of messing. In fact, one of the lads was a few minutes late so we went off without him before we got caught. What I hadn't thought about was the fact that my brother Thomas was in the same class and of course he stood up and told the teacher that I was missing. I think he was annoyed that I hadn't asked him to go as well. He even offered to go looking for me. Anyway, Mam got to hear about it soon enough and of course I was blissfully unaware of this as we enjoyed our free day dossing around the fields and woods near home. I think Mam might have even told a teacher to give me a few slaps the next day because she wasn't a bit surprised when I came home from school on the Tuesday and told her what had happened. I think Dad was hoping I'd get suspended so he'd have someone to ride out with, but I didn't, I just got a few slaps instead. While school wasn't exactly my thing I still made some good friends during my time there, guys like John Rafferty and Ivan O'Neill. John and Ivan used to have ponies too, so we would meet up at the weekends and go and ride across the fields near our homes.

I had learned to ride at home. I always liked to ride with the leathers way up short so that I'd be sitting off the horse balancing on the irons. That's the way it always suited me. Dad had a few jumps and a steeplechase course out back but he wouldn't let us jump anything too big. So when he was out, we would jump everything we could and then we'd have to walk back through the hoof prints, levelling back the soil and sand with our feet so Dad wouldn't be able to see which way we had gone and we wouldn't be caught.

These were our special days, spent jumping and riding the ponies out the back in the paddock. But one day almost changed our lives forever when Thomas was involved in an accident at home that could have killed him. I was only eight and Thomas a year older and we were out in the paddock on our ponies. I got down off Spiddal to get a stick off the ground and my horse's head went under Thomas's pony Buckley Boy, who reared up and sent Thomas flying. But what happened next will always stay with me. Thomas's foot was caught in the stirrup and as Buckley Boy went running Thomas was trailing behind getting kicked and bounced along the ground. Just a week before a safety tack and stirrups had been stolen from the yard so Thomas had normal ones. A safety stirrup would be used for younger riders and would release the foot to save the rider from injury. But as Thomas had the other one it trapped his foot and he was dragged like a ragdoll around the yard. By the time we got Buckley Boy to stop, Thomas was unconscious and had suffered bad head injuries with severe internal bleeding. Strangely from the outside there were very little external injuries. He slipped into a coma and for days we thought we might lose him. He was just nine years old but remained in a coma for almost a week and when he finally came back to us he had to be taught how to walk and talk again. I have no idea how I would have coped had we lost him that day. I've no idea how it would have changed all our lives, and even whether I would have been where I am today. In fairness to Thomas, no sooner had he recovered and was back walking again but he wanted to get back on a horse. Unfortunately, on one of our first times back riding together, Thomas had another accident when his horse ducked him into a fence pole and he was knocked out cold again. I had to gallop home to get help but by the time we got back Thomas was back conscious with little more than a bump on the forehead.

I guess I was lucky with injuries and never really picked up any bad falls in those early days. You would get plenty of kicks off horses all right, especially when you would hang out of his tail while someone else was riding him, but that was really it. Strangely, my only time in hospital in those days was not because of horses at all. When I was 15 I walked over to the local shop and walked in front of a passing car. My leg was caught under the wheel and a large piece of skin was lifted off over the left knee. The remaining scar is a constant reminder of the five days spent in hospital.

As I said, school wasn't great and I'd count down the days and hours for it to finish. I went to Dunshaughlin Secondary school and lasted up to 16 years of age, but I never had much time for it. I never did any homework or anything like that. I remember you used to have to do a kind of entrance exam to determine your class and I managed to get into a middle one which was grand because you wouldn't have wanted to get into one of the higher ones as it was far too serious and tougher work. But I suppose I got lucky, I could have been sent to boarding school at Gormanston which is where Thomas and Mark were sent. I still don't know how I managed to dodge the bullet on that one, but it was regular school for me.

I would finish at three o'clock, head home and get on the horses all day until it was dark and was told to come in. I'd had enough of school and told Mam and Dad that I didn't even want to do the Intermediate Certificate exam, never mind the

Leaving Certificate which was two years later. It was nothing to do with the school at Dunshaughlin really. It could have been any school in the country and I would have felt the same way.

So when I was 15, in the summer after finishing my second year of secondary school Dad let me go to America to spend three months at the home of Michael Smithwick. Michael is a distant relative of Mam's, I think her third cousin, and he had his training base in Maryland. Dad had sold a horse to him called Penny Hall so I was allowed travel over with the horse and stay on for the summer. It wasn't a paid job but I rode out for him every morning and afternoon and it was a fantastic experience. It had been my first time on a plane, and what a time. We travelled from Shannon to JFK on a cargo flight. There were hardly any passengers on the flight so I sat up in the cockpit for the entire journey. Michael had a lovely set-up over there, with about 30 horses and Dad had gone over and rode a couple or winners for him over the years.

Michael was in his 60s but still rode out every morning. A superb horse man, I learned a lot about riding and jumping during my time there. Every day was just the same. Got up for about seven, rode out all day and then had dinner or most likely a barbeque with other staff before getting the head down for the night. There were some real characters there, including the Head Lad, Speedy, probably the first coloured man I ever spoke to. Speedy was a gas man and used to keep us in stitches. David Geoghegan, who worked for my uncle Arthur also came out for a while and worked nearby, so we'd tend to stick together. There wasn't that much to do in the evenings. Sometimes we would take a trip to Baltimore or Jacksonville but generally stuck to the yard. I got on with most of the guys out there but the boss's girlfriend Alex didn't like me much. She was a lot younger than he was and I think she was a bit jealous or something, always seeming to hang out of him.

America was a cracking time for me. It was my first time away from the nest and it gave me massive experience that would help me greatly in years to come. I learned to get a horse to relax and jump properly and always believed I could make a living from it. Either that, or I'd die trying. I remember Michael took me to a rodeo one day and throughout the journey there he had me going, winding me up telling me that he had entered me and that I was going to be riding the bull that day. But of course I wasn't and when we got there he told me to keep an eye on all the riders and watch their individual styles. It was good advice, I was still riding very short but watching the cowboys ride the wild horses and hold their balance stayed with me.

Back in Ireland I stuck at school begrudgingly but after America I knew my school days were numbered and I was ready to work in racing full-time. I went back to school for another year, just until the 'Mock' Intermediate Certificate exams, which were pre-tests two months prior to the actual Inter Cert exams. I scored a disaster and that was enough for me and I left school. So I guess you could say that I did the Leaving before the Intermediate. About a week before I had ridden in a point-to-point race for Dad and I knew that this was what I wanted to do full-time. Dad supported me but I don't think Mam was too happy. But she knew that there was no use trying to get me to change, as my mind was made up. I wanted to get out of school and join a racing stable as quickly as I could.

I started to ride more point-to-points during that third year in school and was fairly handy at it. Point-to-point races are for amateurs and you would generally ride horses that weren't good enough for the track. Anyone could train a horse for the points, you wouldn't need a licence or anything. That has changed a bit these days as some owners are clocking up form at point-to-points by winning races and then selling the horses on for the track. I guess this isn't a bad way to do it because at least if you're buying a point-to-point winner you know if it can stay or jump, whereas if you buy one at the sales you tend to know very little about it except its pedigree.

Having just turned 16 on the previous Friday, I had my first run two days later in a point-to-point race. Dad was trying to sell a bad horse called Golden Sea that wouldn't be right for the track. He just couldn't get him to jump so I had a go at him. And this is where my experience in the States came in handy. Using methods that Michael had showed me over there, I got him jumping brilliantly over the wooden jumps at the back of Dad's yard. So I kept the horse and started to ride him out myself with the intention of taking him point-to-pointing. It was for that reason that I got a move on and got my amateur riding licence. Thomas had his licence already and was due to ride quite a good horse for Dad in a race that weekend at Sandyford near Leopardstown. In a twist of fate, the horse Joseph Knibb would prove to be my first winner that day in what was my very first race as an amateur.

In fact Thomas was due to be in the saddle on Joseph Knibb that day, but he was stood down by a doctor who had heard about the terrible head injury he sustained in the yard years before with me. He simply pulled his licence. Thomas had suffered from some bouts of blackouts and fits since the accident so the medic withdrew his riding licence on safety grounds. I was there at the same point-to-point meeting, getting ready to saddle up for the aforementioned Golden Sea, who wasn't that fancied and I had just hoped for a clear run. Now I was on Joseph Knibb in an open race over jumps for three miles just days after I got my licence. Joseph Knibb was well fancied with serious form, having already won a few times on the track and went off at odds of 3/1. The problem was that he was to carry twelve and a half stone in the race and I was only weighing about seven stone nothing at the time. So there was a lot of dead weight to

21

be added. His owner John McGowan had said to Thomas that he could have Joseph Knibb when he was finished racing so he was quite a special horse for the family.

The race went like a dream, despite the fact that there were about 15 other runners and it was lashing rain. Dad had told me to keep a finger in the breast plate at the front of the saddle so that if he stood off and went for a big leap that he wouldn't leave me behind and knock me off the back. Anyway, at the first he stood off a mile and stretched the plate which squashed my finger. It was agony and I thought *well I'm not doing that again*. He always travelled and jumped well and I was about fourth or fifth turning into the straight with three fences left. We jumped to the front at the last and a few yards from the finish I stood up and started petting him. But it was too early, and others came back at me and almost caught us on the line. We won by a short head but Dad's nerves were shot.

It was my first real taste of big race day riding and it was an experience that set me on my way to where I wanted to go in life: to become a professional jockey. The next step would be to join a professional trainer's yard as an apprentice and make my mark at the track.

CHAPTER 3

First Steps Into Racing

By the time Spring of 1990 had ended I had decided to leave school and work in racing every hour that I could. Because of my tiny build I was always going to start on the flat, and once school was over for me I was ready to make my first steps towards my new life as a jockey. Dad was good friends with many of the local trainers and Jim Bolger had a yard near Carlow. Dad gave Jim a call and asked if he had any space in his yard for a new apprentice. Fortunately, he had. As I said, I always wanted to be a jump jockey in the end but at that time I was still incredibly small and barely tipped the scale over seven stone. So flat racing was always going to be my first port of call. I got my apprentice licence and signed for Jim Bolger's yard, earning just over sixty quid a week for a three-year contract. I was just past my sixteenth birthday but I knew leaving school was right for me. This was the first day of the rest of my life, and I was determined to enjoy each and every one. Work hard, play hard, and continue to learn as I went.

****

That first day at Jim Bolger's yard in April 1990 was daunting to say the least. Jim was one of the best known flat trainers in the business and would have had well over a hundred horses in the yard. Dad took me there and I had digs organised as I was to stay with a Mrs Murphy, where all the young jockeys were at the time. Jim Bolger's yard was at the top of the hill in Coolcullen and Mrs Murphy ran the guesthouse at the bottom of the hill. AP McCoy, Adam Lord, Pat O'Donovan, Willie Supple and Calvin McCormack all stayed there through the years. Mrs Murphy had two sons, one in the army at the Curragh who we wouldn't have seen much of, and a younger one PJ who was only about 10 years old. So it was fairly compacted but she took good care of us.

Jim's yard was strict and almost regimental. His assistant trainer at that time was a guy called Aidan O'Brien, who was only a few years older than I was. He was only about 21 years of age, but while he may have been young, you could tell straight away that he knew his stuff. He was still riding as an amateur for Jim, as well as assisting in the training, and he was point-to-pointing at the weekends. Aidan was very quiet but he was always available to chat to the young lads and give advice when required. Aidan, of course, went on to be one of Ireland's most famous trainers, winning just about everything there is to win in flat racing out of his yard at Ballydoyle in Co Tipperary. He also had quite a few decent hurdlers in his early years, not least Istabraq, who won three Champion Hurdles at the Cheltenham Festival. It was great to get to know him at that time because when he went on to run his own yard he put me up on a fair few winners.

Back then at Jim Bolger's yard, we were squared off into a routine from day one. We would go to the yard every day just after seven o'clock in the morning and split into groups. The yard consisted of two large sections and was split into four lots, two for the fillies, one for the colts and one for the geldings. About four of us would work on each side. Christy Roche was the stable jockey at the time and we all looked up to him. He had the pick of the rides and had set the mark for the rest of us to follow. Next in line would have been Willie Supple, Conor Everitt, Seamus Heffernan, myself, Stephen Kelly, AP McCoy and Calvin McCormack in that kind of order when I got there. We would ride out four or five lots in the day, breaking for an hour for lunch and then doing more for the afternoon, working the stables and cleaning up before finishing at five o'clock.

This was our life. I was still only 16 so I didn't have much to do in the evenings. We wouldn't have had the money to do much either. I was making sixty-four quid a week, with the digs costing half of that. When we got bored in the long evenings we used to hunt down this wild pony up the fields and see who could stay longest on it before being dumped off. About seven or eight of us used to amuse ourselves by jumping on the pony and riding it bareback like a rodeo, that was until he got fed up and starting kicking us on our way down so we soon gave that a miss. Other days we would grab a couple of bridles from Jim's yard and go looking for a couple of horses on a nearby farmer's field and take them out for a spin over the hedges bareback. I remember one time AP, Calvin and I took three horses but the farmer came running out after us, forcing us into a very hasty retreat. I tried to get my pony to jump a stone wall but he was having none of it and threw me off and I banged my head on the wall and I didn't know where I was. AP and Calvin had to carry me all the way back to Mrs Murphy's where they said that they left me on a bed sure I was dead. When I eventually got up I was white in the face and spitting blood, but I was grand by the next day. On hot days we'd take a dip in a nearby stream but otherwise our lives at that time, well mine anyway, was all about riding. I was treated very well by the lads, and we were all around the same age and looked out for each other. We would work all week and then head to the Bagenalstown train station on the Friday evening to catch the late train up to Dublin's Heuston station, where Mam would pick me up and bring me home to Ballybin. For most of the train journey we would hide in the toilets to avoid paying the fare and save a few quid for the weekend.

I was young but had a small bit of track experience under my belt. My first ride at a track had been just a month after my sixteenth birthday. Dad had a horse called Sallow Glen and I got to ride him at our nearby Navan track in a two mile event. I was claiming 10lbs as you do before you get your first winner. I remember I held him up at the back but was then hampered by another horse six furlongs out and while he stayed on at the closing stages, we could only finish fifth, never getting near the leaders. I rode him again at Ballinrobe later that month but again finished outside the places.

I suppose my first big taste of racing came in April of that year, just before I had joined Bolger's yard. Dad decided to take Joseph Knibb, which I had ridden to that first point-to-point win, to the big meeting at Aintree in Liverpool for the amateur race, the Seagram Foxhunters' Chase. It was just under three miles and over the big National fences and I was really looking forward to the ride. We thought we had a lively chance and went off at 14/1 in the field of twenty-five horses. He started brilliantly and we were up with the leaders for the first mile, but he tumbled and fell at the seventh fence along with four other horses and the dream was over.

At Jim's yard I was waiting on the nod for my first ride and at the end of that April he told me I'd be riding a horse called Sounds Classical at The Curragh that weekend. He had no chance of winning but that didn't matter to me, I just wanted to get to the track. The race itself was forgettable at best, as I trailed in a lowly 16th of 17 runners in a one mile maiden handicap. It may have been a no-hoper and wasn't exactly the kind of start I had dreamed of but it was racing at a big venue and later that afternoon I picked up a spare ride for Michael Cunningham on a horse called Amber Giotto after Timmy Sullivan had fallen in an earlier race. That gave me a better spin, finishing sixth and I was delighted just to get the opportunity.

In fairness, Jim Bolger would always give you a chance if he thought you were up for the job. That doesn't mean it was all plain sailing. Far from it. Jim and myself rarely saw eye to eye. He had his way of going about things and I had mine. But he was the boss and I respected that. For instance, I know he was interviewed after AP McCoy's first winner, and he was quoted as saying that AP 'was right up there with the likes of Carberry but was easier to teach'. I don't know what he meant by that, maybe that he wasn't as bold as me, but I don't really care. You work hard schooling and working the horses, and you take the instructions from the trainer before each race, but that can only get you so far. You cannot plan every furlong of a race before it happens. Things happen in the course of races that will change the plan and it comes down to the jockey to do what's best for the horse, the owner, the trainer and those who have supported the horse. I haven't always got it spot on, no jockey has, but I've always done my best for everyone involved in the race, and that especially includes the horse. I have never hit a horse if I felt it had given everything. If you hit a horse when he has nothing else to give and is not responding, it is unfair to the horse involved and only panders to others. And no one knows what the horse has left except the horse and the person on board.

In all I rode well over 20 horses before I first got into the winners' enclosure. It was slow enough to get going, although I know it has taken many jockeys a lot longer to get past the winning post. I remember Jim Bolger would tell us that even the great Pat Eddery had ridden in over 70 races before he rode a winner. Thankfully I didn't have to wait that long and my big day came on a horse called Petronelli at Leopardstown that August.

Petronelli had a bit of form and I would have had a run on him in the yard and knew he had a chance. He went off as the 6/4 favourite despite the young scrawny jockey on him. But whatever about my lack of track winning experience, my weight was a huge plus for the horse. My 10-pound claim meant the horse could run off a featherweight 7st 3lbs, which I could do easily. It was only a six-runner race over six furlongs but there was a wealth of experience on the other horses, such as top-class flat jockeys like Mick Kinane, Stephen Craine and John Reid. I know it sounds strange but I wasn't nervous. If anything I was looking forward to the run, to test myself against the best on a horse that had a decent chance.

Petronelli gave me a dream ride, came fast out of the stalls and I led from the start, winning easily by six lengths from John Reid on House Of Queen, and Mejeve back in third for Craine. It was great to get off the mark and I suppose the only downside was that it was the sixth day of August and the flat season was almost over. Just when it seemed things were going to start happening for me, it was coming to the end of the summer flat season and it would be a year before I got my next winner.

That was on a horse called Many Paws in an apprentice race at Limerick the following September for trainer John Hayden, who I had known for some time. It was over a mile and a quarter and I held him back slightly before leading into the straight and getting home at odds of 6/1. The following month I would have my next and ultimately final winner as a Jim Bolger jockey. That day at Navan I won fairly easily on Nordic Display at big odds, winning by five lengths over one-and-a-quarter miles. Mick Kinane was riding the favourite, Cloncarrig, that day but I just stuck my head down and hardly saw another horse for the entire race. While things were starting to pick up, my heart just wasn't in it. I don't mean any disrespect to Jim, but I always saw my time there as a stepping stone, as a place to gain experience.

I suppose looking back, I was just fairly bored while I was there. Don't get me wrong, Jim Bolger is a hugely respected trainer and has a great yard but I wanted to jump horses. And I must admit that I definitely improved my riding style while I was there. I was already riding quite short but I had my full foot in the irons. Jim used to encourage all his jockeys to only have their toes in the irons so it definitely helped my balance. It was just that Jim's was predominantly a flat yard with very few jump horses and plenty of jockeys ahead of me. So I didn't see much point in staying. I needed to get to a jump yard and had told Dad as much on plenty of occasions. I know Dad knew Noel Meade well and he rang him up to say that I was unhappy at Jim Bolger's, and that I desperately wanted a move to another yard.

I think Noel thought I was a bit wild having met me at a few hunts some years before. He had watched myself and Thomas tear off at the top of the hunt as young teenagers thinking we knew everything and we were never really interested in staying back and doing as we were told and closing the gates or whatever. Noel told Dad that I would be better staying at Jim's yard for as long as possible and see out my contract. Jim had a reputation as being very strict on young jockeys and I think Noel believed that it would have been a help to calm me down.

In the meantime, I was starting to attract more rides from other trainers. Patrick O'Leary owned and trained a few nice racehorses and rang Jim's yard for a spare jockey. I was lucky enough to be put on his horse Return Journey at Navan that following summer, where we won a tight finish. Patrick was very good to me in those early days. He wouldn't have been training too many at that time, but was generous enough to me, and I was able to repay him with some winners in the future.

With some extra cash coming in I started to buy a couple of old cars. Complete bangers they were, and myself and my friends had some wild nights behind the wheel. There was one particular night when about 10 of us were at the disco at the County Club in Dunshaughlin in Meath. We only had one car with us that night, my old Audi, and were going back to a house party at a pal's place a short distance away after the disco had finished. We had about eight in the car and couldn't fit anyone else inside, when my brother Mark wanted to come with us. When I told him there was no room, he said he would get in the boot. We stayed over and had an all-night session that night. The next morning was a scorching hot day and we spent the morning playing football and tennis and generally causing mayhem. Then one of the lads suggested heading off to the beach for the rest of the day, and as we went to pack up the car we found Mark still in the boot. He had woken up there and was locked inside and had been calling us all night. Apart from the obvious danger of being suffocated in the blinding heat, he had been smoking all night in the boot. I had a habit of running out of diesel so I had a big container of diesel in the boot beside his head. Needless to say, Mark wasn't one bit happy.

I was hanging out with a pretty wild bunch, and at the hunts myself and Thomas were building up a reputation of our own. We would take outrageous chances on horseback, galloping and jumping faster and longer with every hunt. I know Noel Meade kept telling Dad and Mam to keep me at Jim's to calm me down, but one weekend I came home to Dad and told him out straight that I'd had enough and was leaving with or without his help. He rang Noel Meade again and told him I was adamant I was going to leave Jim's yard and if there wasn't a place at Noel's yard that I'd look somewhere else.

I don't know if Noel felt obliged or something to give me a

full-time job but he said he would give me a chance. He has since said that he knew I had the pedigree to be a top jockey, with both my father and my grandfather on my mother's side having both been champion jockeys. I suppose it's one way of looking at it. But I know he thought very highly of Dad and later said that Dad had been a bit of a hero of his. And when Noel had started up training he always wanted Dad to ride his horses because he knew he would always get 100 per cent. So when Noel was told that I was definitely leaving Jim's yard he told Dad that he had a horse he wanted me to ride at Sligo that week called Amber King and that we'd see how we got along from there. It was a flat race over six furlongs, and the other runners went off like scalded cats. I just sat back and squeezed Amber King into the lead in the final furlong and we ended up winning very handily on the bridle. Noel seemed happy enough and told Dad that I could start with him properly at his yard the following week. I was over the moon. I made the break from Jim Bolger's yard and it was probably the best move I ever made.

Noel treated me well from the start and we just seemed to click. Over the years we have become almost family, not to mention good friends. I mightn't have been the easiest to manage during those early years but the difference is that I believed in Noel and trusted him and very much wanted to ride winners for him. Noel is incredibly loyal and patient, and God knows I tested that patience a good few times. Champion jockey Charlie Swan would have been riding a fair amount of winners for Noel at the time, and he had Stephen Craine riding for him on the flat. Clearly, there was plenty of competition for me. But Noel had plenty of class jumpers and I knew straight away that it was the perfect move for me. I suppose it was just a combination that worked from day one. I knew what Noel expected from me, and he knew what to expect from me. It turned out to be one of the longest trainer-jockey relationships in racing, with over twenty years and counting. During that time we've had our ups and downs and differences of opinion over the way to ride a horse or whatever. And at the end of each season, usually at the end of year awards, we might talk too much about the ones that got away rather than those we won on. He has always been the boss, and I will always respect his point of view, but I firmly believe that I've won on more horses that should have lost, than lost on horses that should have won.

But that is all to come. Back then, I had just become Paul Carberry the Jump Jockey and it wouldn't be long before I would turn professional and make a real living out of doing something I loved.

CHAPTER 4

Taking The Jump With Meade

Noel's yard was on the other side of Navan in Castletown, so I had to change digs as well. Charlie Swan and Harry Rogers would have been riding a fair amount of winners for Noel at the time over jumps and he had Stephen Craine riding for him on the flat. The yard would have only been about 20 or 25 miles from my family home but it was just easier all round if I got somewhere to stay close by. Damien McGillick, who worked in the yard, knew of a place going at a house just outside Kells, so I rented a small room with a family there. I would stay there for a year before moving out into a flat in Navan that I rented with Mark Cornally and Gerry Fallon, who also worked in Noel's yard.

The Head Lad at Noel's was a guy called Paul Cullen. He was well respected and generally the guys just did what Paul said. It wasn't so straightforward with me and I never really got on with him in those early days. I can see the job he has to do now but back then he was just the guy who tried to keep us on our toes and work us to the bone if he could. Noel's yard was huge. You came in through a small entrance concealed by big wooden gates and the long drive up to the house is flanked by an impressive gallops and an all-weather hurdle course down the right-hand side. Once past Noel's house and office, you drive back

33

to the stables which always had between 80 and 110 horses, depending on the time of the year. Behind the stables are the paddocks and more gallops, and fields as far as the eye can see.

I was never too late for work but never early either. Always fashionably late I suppose, 10 or 15 minutes. This used to drive the Head Lad mad. But there was a great bunch of lads there at the time like Rick and Jimmy, and we used to get our work done as quickly as we could and then have a bit of craic. But I always got the rap for keeping the others from their stable work. Finally one Friday Cullen had enough and just sacked me on the spot and told me to feck off home which I did. The next day I got a call from Noel Meade telling me to turn up at the Curragh to ride on the Sunday because he was short staffed. Naturally, I thought all was good and I had my job back. It later turned out that Noel hadn't a clue about what went on in the yard and didn't know I'd been fired. It didn't matter anyway, because I had a good run and finished in the places and turned up for work on the Monday as usual much to the annoyance of the Head Lad, who hit the roof when he found out. Noel has always had a solid stable team behind him. The Travelling Head Lad was Andy Lynch, a true gentleman. I had gone to school with Andy's son Paddy so I knew the family going back years. Both Andy and his late wife May Lynch were always so good to me through the years and her untimely death in 2007 was an incredibly sad moment for me.

The work at Meade's yard was fairly straightforward. After riding out your lots in the mornings you would stop briefly for lunch and then go back out and ride out in the afternoon. When you came back in, you would wash and brush down the horses, clean out the stables and then give them their late afternoon feed before clocking off. My problem was that I'd finish the brushing and cleaning fairly quickly and then spend an hour twiddling my thumbs while waiting to give out the feed.

And that's when I'd get into mischief. Every time the Head Lad came around he seemed to catch me winding up one of the other lads while watching them work and he thought I was just a trouble-maker. But I knew he wouldn't be able to get rid of me if I was doing the business on the race track.

I had only been with Noel about 10 days when I had my first winner as one of his stable jockeys, and that was on a horse called Beau Beauchamp at Dundalk who won nicely over the flat one mile five furlongs. From that winter of 1992 the winners started coming regularly, with horses like Random Prince winning a few nice races, including a fairly valuable race at Fairyhouse at odds of 12/1. I remember Richard Dunwoody rode the winner of the very next race that day on Flashing Steel, which I would cross swords with again fairly soon. I was starting to make inroads into my claim and while the claiming weight was dropping I was gaining valuable track experience. At the time Noel had plenty of good flat horses and only a few jumpers but was starting to see more of a future with jump horses and was beginning to make the changeover. That kind of thing happens quite slowly at yards, but I suppose it comes with success. If owners see jump winners coming from a yard, then they tend to switch their horses there. Noel had some success over the jumps before I got there, with horses such as Pinch Hitter, that won two Galway Hurdles. But he was still very much seen as running a predominantly flat yard.

In those first six months at Noel Meade's yard I started to get off the mark, and had notched up nine winners before the end of the year. But what came with the success and experience I suppose were the nights out with the lads, whether it was to celebrate or not. And of course, with the nights out was plenty of drink. From my first taste of Southern Comfort and red lemonade at a local nightclub I enjoyed the kick that it gives. There was never any shortage of people to buy you drink and when you had a good day at the races you didn't care how much you spent. Vodka and orange was soon my drink of choice and I found that no matter how many I had or how long I stayed out at night I still got up for work the next morning and did my business as usual. So as far as I was concerned, job done, I wasn't hurting anyone.

Noel was keeping me on a tight rein. So tight, in fact, that when I tried to fool him I even ended up in hot water with the stewards. I had been on my first trip down to Killarney in Kerry for the July meeting and Noel wouldn't even let me stay down in case I got into any trouble. After racing he told me to get the train back to Meath, ride out for him the next morning at his yard and come back down on the afternoon train for the following evening's racing. It was a crazy round trip but I wasn't in a position to argue. Instead, I got the train with Richard Hughes and drank all the way home and then spent the night in Kildare on the piss. Richard is now one of the biggest flat jockeys in British racing, but back then he was just starting out at John Oxx's yard. By the time the morning came around, I just made it to Noel's to ride out for a couple of hours and get back to the train station. That morning I had weighed myself and I was too light for racing, while Hughes was the opposite, and weighed too heavy. So while he sweated it out on the way back down to Killarney on the train, I drank myself silly. By the time it came around to racing time, I was now two pounds overweight. I knew I would get it in the neck from Noel. So stupidly I tried to cheat the weigh-out, by leaving behind by back protector when I got on the scales. But when I went to retrieve it I got caught, and the stewards hammered me with a three-day ban. It was my first serious brush with the stewards, but it was by no means my last.

I had started going out with a girl called Chanelle who I had met at Listowel races. She was my first real girlfriend and I was mad about her at the time. The problem was that I was mad about just about everything at that time and loved my partying too much, so we split. Chanelle later went out with my good friend AP McCoy and they are now very happily married.

*****

That December I had my first big winner at Leopardstown at the Christmas meeting. I was riding a small little horse called Bob Devani for Noel which was owned by John O'Meara, a man who would later become very close to me and would leave a lasting impression.

It was St Stephen's Day and Bob Devani was running in the two and a quarter mile hurdle and went off as the 3/1 favourite. There were a lot of top jockeys riding that day, including two that I had always looked up to, Richard Dunwoody and Graham Bradley. Brad, as he was known, was doing quite a lot of riding over here at the time as he picked up regular bans from English racing for behaviour both on and off the racetrack. And Richard Dunwoody was king of the track at the time in England and broke all sorts of records as he was crowned champion jockey year after year.

Bob Devani won well that day, beating Brendan Sheridan on Sharp Invite by a length after a good battle after the last hurdle. It was my first win over hurdles and at such a big meeting with a huge crowd I was on cloud nine. A slice of the £7,000 prize wasn't bad either. Bradley had a winner that day too and when he asked if anyone fancied drinks after racing I was well up for it. I was only eighteen at the time and Bradley was a fair bit older but in racing age doesn't seem to matter. You would regularly see older jockeys, and even retired ones, socialising with young jockeys and trainers. It's just the way it's always been.

For all the stuff that has been written about Bradley over the years, what is often missed is what a gentleman Graham was to other younger jockeys. Bradley was always on hand to offer advice when needed and years later when I made the move over to England he couldn't have been more helpful. He was always that way with jockeys who went over from Ireland and I know he helped out the likes of AP McCoy as well when he started out over there.

Now I knew I couldn't get completely hammered because I was to do a bit of work on Noel's horse Mubadir in the morning. He needed schooling over fences at Navan Racecourse. I would need to get back to Meath that night come hell or high water. Noel had been asked by trainer John Mulhern to send us over to work with Flashing Steel as Richard Dunwoody was over to ride him. Flashing Steel was gaining a bit of a profile and was much fancied for the following year's Heineken Irish Gold Cup at Punchestown and probably a future crack at the big one at Cheltenham the following year. Owned by the former Taoiseach, Charlie Haughey, Flashing Steel had won nine of his opening 12 races and was a top-class prospect.

Anyway, despite this, Bradley and I hit every pub, nightclub and wine bar we could. The trainer Barry Kelly was with us as well that night. Barry was a great man for a session, and had a ball that night. Unfortunately many years later we lost Barry, who was killed in a car crash. That night in December we hit all the late joints in Dublin, places such as Annabels which was a nightclub below the Burlington Hotel, as well as Buck Whaleys and Legs on Leeson Street. At one stage a waiter came past with a tray full of glasses of wine and I stopped him and knocked back the lot. I didn't even drink wine at that stage, but it was just the way the night was heading. Later I nearly collapsed on the stairs, and took a bit of a tumble but with drink it never seems to hurt.

I can't quite remember how I got back to Meath that night, either by taxi or someone drove. I'm not saying who did the driving because we were all hammered. Anyway the next morning I was due to be at Navan Racecourse for 10 o'clock. I got there about a quarter past after about three hours sleep and I don't think Dunwoody was too impressed. He was already on Flashing Steel and I quickly got sorted, hopped on Mubadir and headed out on to the track.

By now the cold air was making me dizzy and even when I squinted it was all a bit hazy. I didn't really know Richard Dunwoody at that stage as we wouldn't have met many times at racing but he was British Champion Jockey many times and had been a bit of a hero of mine. I guess it wasn't ideal that the first real time he met me at a racetrack I was absolutely pissed. Before racing began I stood and had a look at the first fence and just whispered to Mubadir *'Well I hope you can see the fences because I can't see them'.* I was having a bit of double vision and the instructions were to stay just in front of Flashing Steel and not go off too fast. After all, I was only on a novice that had never run over fences and I was up against the champion jockey on a seasoned chaser. I think I might have even asked Dunwoody if he wouldn't mind shouting as we came to the fences just in case I didn't see them. I don't think Dunwoody quite knew what to make of it all.

Anyway, after three or four fences I looked around and couldn't see Dunwoody or Flashing Steel at all. I was after tearing off in front and had gone clear like a drunken cowboy. Flashing Steel couldn't keep up and I was later told that Dunwoody was amazed at the speed of the horse. He actually rang Meade after that and asked for the ride on Mubadir at Fairyhouse but Noel told him that I was keeping the ride.

****

That following March I experienced my first taste of the Cheltenham Festival. I had been over in England a few weeks beforehand to ride Bitofabanter at Newbury for my uncle Arthur Moore where I finished third. But walking into the Cheltenham racetrack for the second day of the 1993 Festival was incredible. 60,000 punters pack into one area of the track surrounding the finishing line and the noise is unbelievable. Trainer Homer Scott had asked me to ride his horse Rhythm Section in the Bumper, which is the only flat race of the National Hunt's biggest race meeting. He had only run twice before, finishing second behind Noel's horse Heist at Leopardstown that January, and then winning at the same track under Tony Martin a couple of weeks later.

Cheltenham is an incredible experience for any jockey, let alone a skinny teenager having his first ride. I didn't say a word to anyone while I got ready in the weigh room. The biggest names in jump racing were all there, jockeys like Dunwoody, Graham Bradley, Peter Scudamore, Steve Smith-Eccles and Mark Dwyer. Charlie Swan was there too, riding Heist for Noel Meade, which was well fancied to give my boss his first Cheltenham winner and went off as the 9/4 favourite to do so. The parade ring outside the weigh-room behind the main stand is always packed before races, watched by hundreds of punters trying to gain an advantage in the betting ring. I went out and met the trainer Homer Scott who told me to keep Rhythm Section handy and to take him into the lead if I got the chance on the turn for home. The horse was 16/1 in the betting ring, but I remember Homer was unbelievably bullish, saying that we had a great chance of winning.

I got off to a nice start and kept my horse prominent and moved into the lead on the back straight. I hadn't really noticed, but by the time I made the turn for the last quarter mile I was out clear. But the Cheltenham hill is a lot steeper than it seems on television and the further we went, the more he was starting to tire. The crowd was going mad and I could feel that there were horses coming up behind me as I tried to will Rhythm Section all the way to the line. As it turned out, it was Charlie Swan on Noel's horse Heist and he was gaining all the time. However, my horse found a bit extra and we won by just half a length. It was an incredible feeling. My first Cheltenham winner in my first ever race at the track, never mind at the biggest festival in jump racing. Oh, and it was St Patrick's Day as well, adding to the fairytale start. Noel Meade congratulated me after the race, but he was obviously disappointed that it had been his horse that lost out. For me, I suppose it all went by in a bit of a blur. I wasn't used to the TV attention, and maybe at 19 years of age I was a bit too young to fully appreciate it. And, of course, I wouldn't have known that it would be five long years before I would get into the winners' enclosure at the Cheltenham Festival again.

I rode Bitofabanter in the County Hurdle for Arthur the following day but he was never better than mid-division and finished seventh. But still, it had been some experience for my first time at the Festival, and many more great days at the course would come in the future.

After Cheltenham I noticed I was asked to ride a lot more for other trainers. But back at home Noel's horses were firing at the racetrack. Thanks to horses like Life Saver that won four times for me that year, I was eating into my claim and would turn professional by the end of the year.

In racing, jockeys started with a 10 pound claim, which means that the 10 pounds comes off the weight that the horse was supposed to carry, to compensate for the jockey's inexperience. When you get your first winner, that claim reduced to eight pounds until your 10th winner, and then reduces to six, five, four and so on as you clock up the wins. Eventually when you reach your 64th winner, you lose all claims and can then turn professional. The weights have slightly changed through the years, but they were the rules when I was starting off.

My 63rd winner came on Life-Saver at Clonmel that November and 10 days later I got that all-important number 64 when Bob Devani won a two-and-a-half-mile chase for me at the same track. I'd had a few near misses in between, including earlier that day on Jimmy The Jackdaw when I went off as a short-priced favourite but got beaten into second. That win on Bob Devani was worth a lot more than the winner's cheque to me. When you're an apprentice starting off your career your trainer gets a cut of your winnings. Up until that 64th winner I would only have got forty per cent of my winner's prize with the other sixty per cent going to Noel, or whoever the trainer was that I was riding for. A jockey's cut is generally between eight and ten per cent of the prize money, and then you would only get 40 per cent of that eight per cent. From now on I would get the full eight per cent and that made a huge difference in the wage packet.

I finished that first full season with Noel as leading apprentice with 27 winners on the flat and had another 13 wins over jumps. At that stage I knew my future lay in jump riding but I would have to bide my time and wait for the opportunities to come. As my claim was coming down, my weight had inched up with age and I was wasting most weeks. *'Wasting'*, which keeps your weight down, is just part of a jockey's life, especially on the flat. Some days I was having just half a sandwich, and you might have only one decent meal all week. You would normally allow yourself to have that meal on a Saturday evening, after a week's racing. It sounds worse than it is, but it was just part of life, and if I wanted to be a success in racing it was part and parcel of the job.

Another part of the job was running some side errands for Noel. I remember one time he had some fairly important visitors coming over and he needed them picked up from the airport early the next morning. When he asked me to do it I was pleased. It meant I would avoid work in the yard that morning, something that was very welcome as I'd been out for a few drinks the night before. Paul Nicholls, who is now one of Britain's most famous trainers, and one of his owners, Paul Barber, were coming over to have a look at a horse in the yard and I was dispatched off to Dublin Airport because Noel was too busy to go himself. Noel was selling this horse called Ottowa, that had just won a bumper race on his first time out at Navan. Paul Barber was one of Britain's wealthiest racehorse owners and a few years later would win the famous Cheltenham Gold Cup with See More Business and Denman. Back then he wouldn't have been as well known but he had agreed a good price with Noel for Ottowa as long as he liked the look of the horse in the flesh. So while Ottowa was back in the yard getting the full treatment and wash down, I went to the airport to collect our two important guests.

At the time I was driving this old white Audi 80 Diesel, and when I met them at the airport I think I was still running on the fuel from the night before. I wouldn't have been too aware of who they were and I wouldn't have thought they were as impressed with my car as I was. I assumed they would have been anxious to get to see Noel so I put the foot down. There would have been hardly any words spoken for the entire journey. At that time the back roads from Dublin Airport were very poor, and it was a journey that should have really taken almost an hour. After just 35 minutes travelling through a series of bumpy bends and bad roads we reached Noel's yard. When we got inside the yard the two of them sort of fell out of the car white as ghosts. Paul Barber was particularly in a bad way and started walking around the yard in circles all flustered. Noel got a bit of a fright when he came out and asked his prospective buyer what was wrong with him.

'*Well Noel, I may or may not like this horse, but one thing is for bloody sure – I am NOT going back to the airport in that car!*' he said.

Paul Nicholls could at least see the funny side, and with a bit of relief turned to Noel and said: '*When I was a jockey I was told that if you didn't frighten the people in your car at least once, well then you weren't a proper jockey at all because you just didn't have it. I'll tell you Noel, if that is true, well then this lad's a fucking genius*'.

Some months later, Noel came with me to the races in Clonmel and I was driving flat out, cutting every corner. Noel was sweating in the front passenger seat and he swore that he would never get in a car with me again. Funny enough, he never asked me to pick up other trainers or owners again either.

CHAPTER 5

In The Heel Of The Hunt

Those first two years at Noel's yard were some of my happiest in racing. After my win at Cheltenham, I think Noel seemed to trust me that bit more and from then on I was rarely *jocked off*' for another rider, even one as experienced as Charlie Swan. I had just had a winner on the big stage and from then on I was getting first call on all the Meade horses. At the race track all was good but back at the yard I was having a few problems, mostly caused by myself.

Paul Cullen was the Head Lad and he was on my back about work in the yard. Paul would be a tough task master but was big into the horses and would always have their best interests at heart. He used to accuse me of not pulling my weight and in particular, of stopping others doing their work by having a bit of craic with them. I think he got on Noel's case about this and, in fairness, Noel came to a solution which suited both of us. From then on, Noel decided I didn't need to be there in the evenings at all. I don't know how this went down with the other lads but I was happy about it. Years later I was told that Noel had been talking to another trainer Pat Flynn over dinner at Cheltenham that year and they were discussing the jockeys they had working for them. Flynn had trained Montelado to win the Bumper the previous year and was running the same horse in the Supreme Novices Hurdle the next day, which they won. Seemingly the conversation went something like this:

Pat Flynn: *'Is that Carberry fella any good?'*

Noel: *'Yeah he's grand. He is going to be very good'*

PF: *'I've a great fella too named Shay Barry. But he's not much of a sweeper'.*

NM: *'What do you mean?'*

PF: *'He doesn't like to do much with a brush in the yard'.*

NM: *'So what did you do?'*

PF: *'I just kept him doing what he does best, and get him to just ride out all day'.*

So that was it. Noel decided from that day on that it would be better all round if I stayed away from stable work in the yard and just rode out lots all day, which suited me down to the ground. I was riding out all the young horses all day long, sometimes up to 12 a day. It didn't matter how young they were and when Noel, Paul or Gillian O'Brien weren't looking I'd take the horses out over fences and across the countryside for a bit of a buzz. But then Noel put ropes over the fences to stop me jumping them. There was one really good horse in the yard called Johnny Setaside that had won a few bumpers and hurdle races. When Noel switched him to the big fences he couldn't believe how *'natural'* he was and he won his first ever Chase at Galway in a big field at a nice price. I later had to come clean and tell Noel that I'd been jumping him over the hedges across the back fields for about two years before.

There was another time I took out his horse Heist and took him across the fields. Heist was a proper hurdler and had won many times at the track but hadn't run over fences. Heist was a horse with bundles of ability but used to mind himself and was a bit too apprehensive when jumping bigger obstacles. So when it came to taking on some of the wide ditches and hedges out the back of Noel's he would slow up. I went to give him a slap of the whip between the ears but he turned his head and I caught him in the eye, injuring him. When I took him back in I told Noel that we'd had an accident in the yard. But I was rumbled when the farm manager Sean McGivern noticed hoof prints leading from the yard over the hedges on to the laneway and off across the fields and realised I'd been taking Heist out jumping. I ended up getting an earful. He sent me away for a while and told me to think of an appropriate punishment. Shortly afterwards, Noel decided that it would probably be better if I just stayed away from the yard altogether and only come in to school horses when I was needed.

Meanwhile, my real kick was with hunting. I was hunting twice a week with the Ward Union and still do to this day. Back then the hunts were at their best. You could be hunting a deer for three hours, but now the rules are much more stringent and you would rarely go for more than an hour. The deer would be gone a half hour before the hounds are set off and when they are in full cry it's difficult to keep up. That's the thrill of the chase, trying to keep up with the hounds as they scurry through hedges and gaps that horses can't follow. It's almost survival of the fittest, and you test yourself against the other riders. I love the buzz of jumping a big ditch and then turning to watch the others refusing to jump behind, leaving you and your horse at the top of the hunt in isolation. Of course, you can never know where the hunt will take you and that's part of the buzz. I've had some horrendous falls through the years and have knocked myself out of many big race meetings because of hunting. But I will never give it up. For me it's my hobby, my pastime, my way of life. I was never into other sports. But hunting is special. It's a huge part of my life.

I think a lot of people have the wrong idea about hunting. There's a misconception that hunting is about trapping a terrified animal and letting the dogs rip it apart while we take a step back and enjoy the view from our horses. That is not the way it is at all. The dogs surround the deer and are kept away from the animal. The deer are reared and kept by huntsmen in humane conditions. If it wasn't that way I wouldn't be involved. I think even the people who vote in the Dail to change hunting legislation haven't the first clue about what hunting actually involves.

Hunting will always be my first love and I've said it before and I'll say it again: if hunting was a professional sport, I think I would have given up race riding many years ago. Through the years I've hunted all across the country. I started with the Ward Union, where I'm now whipping for the Huntsman Pat Coyle. The Ward Union has been a huge part of my life, and I've had many great days with Masters Gerry Reynolds, Sean Byrne and Stephen O'Connor. Sadly, we lost three of our best men, Eamon Dunphy, Larry Rohan and Pudser O'Toole, who died in 2009. I've also joined Shane Breen and Joe Taylor at the Scarteen Hunt in Tipperary and I've ridden with the North Galway Hunt, and with the Henry family who run the Meath Hunt and also with John Stafford of the Killinick Harriers in Wexford.

Noel never really minded what I was doing at the hunts so long as it didn't affect things on the racecourse. Sure how could he, as he had first met me at the hunt and he knew how passionate I was about it. So he always insisted that I take a break from hunting in the weeks leading up to big race meetings. In truth, I rarely did.

****

I was lucky that everything was going well come race days, and I actually had my first win as a fully licensed professional jockey on one of Dad's horses. While I was contracted with

Meade, I could still ride for others as long as Noel didn't have a runner. Dad had a horse running at Thurles called Sorry About That which was the probably the best named horse in training. Sorry About That was owned by Michael Mulvihill, who was an unlucky owner and I think that horse finished second more times than any other. 'Sorry About That' became a bit of a slogan after each race.

But he won that day in Thurles fairly well off top weight in a novice chase over two miles. I had held him back and took up the lead two out. I thought I might have gone too soon because Derek O'Connor came to challenge on Speaking Tour at the last but I gave my horse a slap and we probably gained two lengths in the air and I held out to win in a driving finish. I remember AP McCoy was standing at the last fence just watching the race and he later told me that he thought it was one of the best rides he had ever seen being given a horse. McCoy loved to see aggression on a horse and he liked the way I had driven him into the fence. AP still rides that way today and I suppose that's why he went on to ride as many winners as he has.

Bob Devani won for me twice that December, once at Punchestown and then at Navan. It was at Navan, also, that I had a double with Heist, Noel's horse that I had beaten into second in the Bumper at that previous Cheltenham Festival.

St Stephen's Day at Leopardstown was becoming a happy hunting ground and in 1993 I had a money-making double that could so easily have been a treble. I won the first race on Coq Hardi Affair over two and a quarter miles and then won the third race on Shirley's Delight to land a nice prize in a Grade 2 two mile hurdle. In the fourth race I was riding Mubadir in The Denny's Novice Chase for Noel but he came down at the last when we were well clear. There was no rail at the last and he tried to duck out so I gave him a slap to get him back in and there was no stride there coming into the fence which he

49

caught and turned over. I was sick. There was a massive prize on offer, but it was missing out on the treble that really hurt.

When I fell on Mubadir at the last that day at Leopardstown with the race seemingly won, Noel was unhappy to say the least. Noel said nothing after the race but I think he believed it was my fault that the horse fell. Later that day I asked Dad what he thought and he just said *'When you're on the ground, you're always wrong'.* That's the way it is in racing, if you're on the ground you're wrong. If you miss a penalty in soccer you're wrong no matter what, even if it was a good attempt. But if you hit a soft penalty and it goes in anyway, well then you're a hero. That's just the way it is, get a result and you're a legend, miss and you're the villain. Most punters don't care about how you run a race as long as you end up first past the winning line and that will always be the case.

Mubadir got back to winning ways for us in January 1994 at Fairyhouse, winning a Grade 3 Chase at long odds-on. Coq Hardi Affair and Shirley's Delight both won for Noel that month as well and he decided that all three would run at Cheltenham that March. Mubadir ran in the Arkle and was in touch but just couldn't get up the sharp hill and faded to a distant fifth. We finished fourth on Coq Hardi Affair behind the great Danoli in the Sun Alliance Hurdle, and then Shirley's Delight finished third in the Triumph Hurdle on the last day. We were disappointed not to get a winner but in fairness, Noel brought over just three horses and ended up in the place money in all three.

I was already getting excited about Aintree the following month where I was going to ride in my very first English Grand National on Dad's horse Rust Never Sleeps. The horse had very little form to speak of. I had ridden him twice before; once finishing a distant fifth in a handicap chase at Navan, and then I had to pull him up when well behind in the Irish Grand National at Fairyhouse.

Despite this, we decided to take our chances in the big race at Aintree just five days later. Although completely unfancied, we knew he could jump. At 10 years old he had 46 races under his belt and had only fallen three times, so I thought I could get around on him. As it turned out, the race was one of the most memorable in history, as just six runners completed the course. Unfortunately, we were not one of them. But I did get a fair ride, only coming down at the fourth last when there were less than 10 horses still standing. There had been a pile-up at the very first fence, and I had tracked the leading group until we hit Bechers the second time around and lost a huge amount of ground. From then on I was just trying to ease him around the fences but came down on the last circuit. Richard Dunwoody went on to win on Miinnehoma, with Just So in second and favourite Moorcroft Boy back in third. I was very disappointed after the race, but was glad of the experience and couldn't wait to have another go at it.

I was fully hyped after having my first run in the National. A good few of us were booked in to stay on in Liverpool that night and gave it an almighty lash until the early hours of the morning. The next day after just a couple of hours sleep we headed straight back to the bar and then went for a boozy meal. Myself and Frannie Woods were travelling back together that evening and by the time we caught our flight we were drunk as skunks. The problem was that I had my car parked up at Dublin Airport and would have to make the hour's drive back to Meath on the other side. At that time I had an Opel Kadett, and three Audi bangers back in the yard. And I don't think there was a sign of tax or insurance on any of them. They also went through a fair amount of crashes; I'd say the three Audis between them had more hits than The Beatles.

When we reached Dublin, Frannie was the most sober of

the two, so he drove as far as the town of Ashbourne where we stopped off for a few more vodkas and then I said I would drive the rest of the way home. We were only a short distance gone when I missed a corner and shot the car at speed into a ditch. The car was nearly on its roof but we decided to stay inside in the warmth and ring a friend to help us out. By the time my mate Mick Foley came to the rescue he could hardly find the car because it had dipped even further into the ditch. Worried, he opened the car door to find us with a bottle of vodka laughing our heads off.

On another night I crashed an Audi on a back country road and when it slid on its side I came out through the sunroof. I sliced my ear on the road and broke my collarbone. I suppose it could have been much, much worse. Apart from killing myself or someone else, there were plenty of times that I could have been caught by gardai and my life could have been a lot different. I remember some years later coming back after the horse trials at Punchestown. A friend Adam Lord was in the car with me, and after a long drinking session in Naas we got back in the car and headed home. The heating wasn't much use in the car so we wrapped ourselves up in blankets for the journey home. Next thing I remember is a garda knocking on my window. It was daylight, and we were stopped at the main junction of Kill and the Naas Road. I put down the window and the police officer told me to get out of the car. I said: *'Wait a minute and I'll just put on my shoes.'* He said: *'You won't need shoes where you're going.'* The other garda recognised me and after a bit of time agreed to let us off with a caution as long as we left the car and got someone else over to drive us and the car away. Another jockey, David Marnane, was later travelling on the same road so he picked us up and dropped us home.

I'm not proud of these moments. They were crazy days when I had more time and less sense. But I guess they were times in my life when things weren't as clear as they are now. Nevertheless, it's only fair to include them in the book.

****

I had a couple of winners at the Punchestown Festival, Be My Hope and Fane Banks, but the rest of 1994 was quiet, with a treble one day in Galway that September providing a rare highlight. It may not have seemed like anything special in the record book, but it was a treble involving a winner over the fences, the hurdles and on the flat all on one card. I started the day with Dardjini for Noel in the first race. We went off as the odds-on favourite for the two-mile maiden hurdle. There were 17 runners in the race, which made our starting price of 8/13 look a bit skinny, but he never put a foot wrong and we won doing handstands. Next up was the Connaught Tribune Novice Chase. I was aboard a horse for Dessie Hughes called Foilaclug Furry, and it was a shocking race. Ten runners started and only three remained at the end of the two-and-three-quarter miles. All the other seven, including the favourite, Very Adaptable, either fell or were brought down or pulled up. We won by a head from Fergus Flood on Golden Claw, with the only other finisher a distance behind. That was an unexpected 8/1 winner, and it was the same price for the winner in the next. In the flat race, a mile and a half a furlong maiden, I won on a horse called Jakdul for Eddie Lynam, with champion flat jockey Johnny Murtagh on the favourite Balanak three lengths away in second. Obviously I was just delighted with the 130/1 treble, but later on I was told by newspaper reporters that it hadn't been done in years. In fact, one of the few who had done it was retired jockey Martin Moloney who happened to be at the track. He came up to me afterwards and congratulated me and wished me well. Unfortunately, the stewards weren't as impressed. They gave me a two-day ban from racing for excessive use of the whip on Hughes's Foilaclug Furry.

Another win that gave me a bit of a lift at that time was on a horse called Monkey Ago at Thurles. Paddy Mullins had rang the yard the previous day and asked would I ride the horse as I had no other runners on the day. The horse had fallen or unseated his rider on his last three starts. Its battered jockey Conor O'Dwyer had decided enough was enough and opted to ride another horse in the race. I remember the race because I was following this horse called Lost Coin, and his jockey Denis Murphy kept shouting *'Don't track me, don't track me, I'm going to fall'* and he pulled him up before the next fence. Conor took up the lead on Buck's Delight but fell at the second last and I went on to win fairly handy. The race had been a bit of a carnage with only half of the 16 runners actually finishing the three-mile run.

But these were rare high points of the year. The following year didn't start much better, with just over 20 winners in the first six months and only six of them were for Noel. Meade's horses just weren't firing and I guess that put a fair bit of pressure on both of us. Who was to blame? My riding? His training? Neither of us? Maybe we were both doing nothing wrong and working to our absolute best, but just fortune was not favouring us.

That February I had a party organised for my 21st birthday but first I had to ride Cockney Lad in the Tote Gold Trophy over at Newbury for Noel. We finished fourth, and as soon as the race was over myself, Noel and my good friend Richard Hughes headed straight to the airport to catch a flight back to Dublin for the bash that night. I had booked the Jameson Stand at Fairyhouse Racecourse and there must have been about 400 people there. My sister Nina and Barry Geraghty's younger sister Sasha were on duty serving behind the bar and it's safe to say that the measures were very large that night. It was a brilliant night, with the drink flowing and the dance floor packed with dodgy hip movements. There were rafters going across the Jameson area at that time and you could reach them if you jumped from the bar. So I ended up swinging from them for a while before being carried out of my own birthday party. I didn't know back then, but it would be my last birthday in Ireland for a few years.

The following day we enjoyed a drinking session in Rory's Bar in Ratoath, playing pool and generally acting the bollix. Richard Hughes then said he had to leave that night to catch a flight back to London and, helped with a bellyful of vodka, I said I'd go back with him. Francis Woods and Timmy Sullivan agreed to go back too. Unfortunately, nobody had warned us about England's early pub closing times on a Sunday and when we got there we could hardly get a drink. We got a taxi to a disco, and were warned it was a full-on rave night. What the taxi driver didn't tell us is that it was a non-alcoholic disco so all you could buy was minerals and soft drinks. And after a while we realised it was a gay club too. Fran Woods turned to me and said: *'If anyone asks, I'm with you, you're my bloke'.*

We had enough of it at this stage so we said goodbye to Richard and the three of us headed back to the airport to catch the next flight to Dublin. Just then, the taxi was pulled over by a London police car and we were taken out and searched for drugs. Apparently, the cop car had followed us from the club and assumed we were doing drugs, which of course we were not. But it was just the finishing touch to a crazy night in London.

The next day I arrived back at my Mam's house and she said *'You look like you had a good night'.*

And I said *'Yeah, I ended up in a gay rave disco in London with the lads'.*

She replied said: *'Yeah right Paul, I know you were just down the local nightclub'.*

And to this day, she still doesn't believe what really went on that night.

****

Myself and Noel didn't have too many rows on the racetrack back then. I don't think jockeys at that age have arguments as such with their trainers. It's more the situation that if the trainer feels that you've been slacking off, or worse, not ridden a horse to the best of your ability, well then you're in for a bollicking and you tend to have to just bite your lip and just take it. I always say that no-one knows how a horse is travelling better than the jockey and if you feel that the tactics aren't working, well then it's up to the jockey to change them. But the problem with this is, if you decide to change tack halfway through a race and fuck it up, well then you're pretty much in for it.

And that's exactly what happened at the old Dundalk track towards the end of that 1994/1995 season. I was riding Mara-dyke Bridge for Noel in a two and a half mile event. It was only a three-runner race and we went off as the second favourite in the betting behind the odds-on Royal Rosy, an Aidan O'Brien horse being ridden by Charlie Swan. Noel told me to hold him back and try to take up the lead into the straight. But thinking they were going slow and my horse was going much better, I decided to kick on while on the back straight and went clear. But we emptied out on the run for home and got beaten into second when Royal Rosy whizzed past us to win by four lengths. Noel, who would usually be back in the parade ring, was on this occasion nearly out on the course. His hands and the head were going wild, and I knew when he's out that far that I was in for a bollicking.

As soon as he got to me he was all *'what the fuck were you at, what did I tell you to do?'* I told him that I did what I thought was right. But, of course, it's a lame argument after you've just been chinned on the run-in. He was fuming and had a fair old rip. He accused me of burning the candle at both ends and, basically, was questioning my commitment. It was the coolest time between us and over the next few weeks we didn't talk that much. Not like we had before.

CHAPTER 6

The Break-Up

During the summer of 1995 I started to think about making a move to England for a while. That's where the money was, with racing every day of the week. You could also get a nice retainer from an owner at that time and still fly back to Ireland on Saturday nights and ride at the big Sunday meetings.

Besides, things were getting a bit strained between me and Noel Meade. I had tried his patience a few too many times and had got a couple of warnings. The next time I stepped out of line it wasn't going to be pretty. As I said, it coincided with a time that Noel's horses weren't running very well and we both felt a little bit of pressure building.

That summer I was coming back in a car from the Friday meeting at Listowel with jockeys David Marnane and Greg Harford. We decided to break the trip with a stop-off at the Dunraven Arms in Adare, which was a popular stop-off at the time for jockeys, trainers and punters on the way back up from racing. It was only an hour and a half down the road so we said we'd drop in for two drinks – that was the agreement – and then we would head off from there, so grand, in we went. Myself and Greg had to work the next morning, schooling at Noel's. Clearly, I needed to get back up to Meath. Well, I was trying to get back but, unfortunately, I didn't get very far.

Earlier that day at the races Noel had pulled me aside at the winners' enclosure. I had just finished second on a horse called Hannies Girl from Daniel O'Connell. Noel asked me if I had seen Harford as he was missing in action. I knew well that he was still drinking from the day before, but I told Noel that he had been there earlier and that his horse was not running in the bumper and I thought he had headed home. Noel kind of looked at me strangely, and told me that if I saw him I was to tell him that he wanted him early the next morning for ride work. I shouldn't have opened my mouth but I asked him if he wanted me to work as well, because I hadn't a ride the next day, on the Saturday. He said yes, that he did want me there so I should head home and be at work for 8 o'clock. I said grand, cursing my big mouth.

Anyway, after racing we were in the owners' and trainers' bar and there was still no sign of Greg. We went to the last place we had left him late the previous night, beside the bar in the Listowel Arms down the town. And sure enough he was still there drinking away.

So we had a drink and grabbed Greg up and out of there and drove as far as Adare for our two drinks. There was a good crowd there from racing, as we anticipated. Enda Bolger and Joanna Morgan were there with a few of their mates, and the craic was good. The place was flying. So we had a few drinks and got back into the car. We were only a couple hundred yards out the road when I pulled into the side of the road and said to the lads that we may as well go back, book a room for the night and drive back up the following morning. Hearing absolutely no objection from the lads, we turned the car around and headed back to the Dunraven Arms. We organised a room with the owner Brian Murphy and told him that no matter what happened, we needed to be up and out by five o'clock in the morning to get back home for ride work. We were sorted, hit the bar and had a great old night of it, and I have no idea what time I climbed into bed. But I know it was very late.

The next thing I remember is being dragged out of the bed by the night porter, with me climbing back in and pulling up the covers. He was pulling the duvet off, me pulling it back and then he started begging me to leave, saying that he would lose his job if he didn't get us up and out to work, that Brian Murphy had warned him.

So we headed off, with me driving. We'd only gone down the road a small bit before I realized fully I was too hungover to drive. So Dave took over and I climbed into the back for a sleep while poor Greg was in the passenger seat. He couldn't talk as his voice was gone after two full days of it.

Anyway, I hadn't realised that Dave Marnane couldn't drive either and pulled in the car for a sleep shortly afterwards. He later told me that he couldn't keep his eyes open and he'd nearly hit a bank before pulling in. Unable to wake me or Harford, he decided to have a kip too. I was woken up in what seemed like minutes later by a call on the car phone from my friend Adam Lord. We were chatting away and I asked him what time it was, and he said nine o'clock and I thought 'oh shit'. With the other two still asleep I realised that we'd only travelled a few miles and I was in deep crap with Noel. I tried ringing Noel for the next hour but couldn't get him, and I couldn't get his partner Gillian on the house phone either. I was going to ask him to leave the horses and that we'd ride them out a bit later, but I couldn't get him. So we thought we would be better off just to get there as soon as possible and worry about the bollicking at that stage.

The night before, Mike Condon had been in my ear, asking me if I ever thought about moving to England to ride. Mike was an old friend and he had a couple of horses with Mike Corrigan. Condon was a good pal of Graham Bradley, a quite notorious jockey in England. Graham would later get in trouble with the authorities in Britain over race-fixing allegations as well as illegal gambling. Anyway, Mike Condon was telling me that Bradley wouldn't get out of bed unless he was being paid for it, and sure would I not want the same thing. I said of course I would if the job, the move and the money was right. He said that a lot of big English trainers were looking to retain their own jockey and were willing to pay for it. So heading back towards Noel's yard that day, my head was all over the place.

We got back to Meath and we still hadn't been in touch with Noel. So myself and Greg decided to drop off our bags and make ourselves scarce. There was a big festival happening down in Lisdoonvarna, just north of the town of Ennis in County Clare, and we had the brainwave to get back in the car and head back down to that for the craic. A good few of the lads were going there so we said what the hell. Sure you may as well be hung for a sheep as a lamb.

There was racing in Tipperary the next day, a Sunday. And in our madness we thought that Lisdoonvarna wasn't that far away from Tipperary. We'd be in the right region. There were a few mad lads from Meath heading down also, such as Ronnie Regan, Willie Fay and John Doyle. We hit Lisdoonvarna about 6 o'clock and had an almighty session. There was a Bachelor Festival on and I guess some old farmers were hoping to get lucky and find a bride. We were all a bit too young for that carry on but the craic was great.

I had a number of rides for Noel the next day at Tipperary, and I still hadn't heard from him. I thought it best to leave things as they were and worry about dealing with him at the track the next day.

That day at the Tipperary races started well. I won the Power Solicitors Hurdle on the even money favourite Persian Halo. But it wasn't for Noel, it was for Michael Kauntze. Later on that day I came face to face with Noel, and as I gave him the saddle I tried to explain what had happened and where I'd been the last couple of days. But sure at that stage my voice was gone, as I'd lost it somewhere during the last few days' drinking, laughing and singing.

Just about that time I'd developed a love for the Smokey song Living Next Door To Alice, and any chance I got I'd give it a blast at the end of the night. It became my party piece and as time went on the lads started calling me Alice in return. It got to the stage where I'd even give it a blast during races, just to let the jockeys ahead know that I was in behind and about to make my move... especially if I was on a horse that was going well. *'Oh I don't know why she's leaving, or where she's gonna go, I guess she's got her reasons but I just don't wanna know, Cos for 24 years I've been living next door to Alice... Alice? Who the fuck is Alice? ...Twenty-four years just waiting for a chance, to tell her how I feel, and maybe get a second glance'.* That 24-year wait would have much more of a significance later on when I won the Aintree Grand National. But that's another story.

Anyway, back in Tipperary I was near the parade ring trying to make my excuses to Noel Meade, my trainer, my boss, my friend. But this time he wasn't having any of it. With the hangover, the smell of drink and the lost voice, my excuses were tripping me up. The more I tried to explain, the thicker he was getting. He was getting red in the face and eventually he just turned around and walked away. I knew it was bad.

The next day, myself and Greg got to the yard early and I'd say we rode every damn horse in the yard. We were up and down all day and grabbing every horse for schooling we could, working our bollocks' off trying to make it up for the last few days' messing. He then called us back at about four o'clock and I thought he just wanted us to ride two more horses because he hadn't said anything all day. But he lit into us, giving out shite, telling us that he didn't care if we were Adrian Maguire and Richard Dunwoody, that we'd never pull this kind of stunt again and if we did we were gone.

Throughout, I'm trying to keep serious. But this Harford fella beside me is bursting his ass laughing trying to keep it in at the same time. But sure you know what it's like when you're not meant to laugh. You're standing there, trying not to laugh when you know the guy beside you is pissing himself. Anyway, Noel was furious and for me that was the last warning. So we took our bollicking and got way as quick as we could.

Anyway, later that week, Mike Condon rang me again asking whether I'd thought about the move to England as he said he had the perfect job for me. An offer was on the table from British multi-millionaire horse owner Robert Ogden, who was based in North Yorkshire. I just thought, sure what the hell. Anyway, there was no way I was going to be able to keep my promise to behave myself to Noel. Without a doubt, I would get myself into trouble again, but I didn't want to be sacked, or even put Noel in the position where he'd feel he had to sack me. So I thought I'd better get myself away for a while.

I had a huge amount of respect for Noel, and even more so now. We were like family, but I didn't like the thought of letting him down again. I was gutted for letting him down that day. I've been late plenty of times but I always made it in even if it was an hour late. I'd never gone AWOL before and I knew that it was only a matter of time before it happened again. After all, I was only 21 years of age and wanted to enjoy myself. I loved riding, I loved racing and I loved hunting. Horses were and are my life but I wanted something different. I didn't want to be treated like a bold schoolboy watching a clock. England seemed the perfect answer. I also knew that giving it a couple of years in England would improve my profile in Ireland as you would always pick up good rides on a Sunday if you were getting coverage on British TV and the English newspapers as a retained rider. Televised racing was big over there and I know that I definitely got a lot more respect from trainers over here once I made the move to England. Trainers who would never have put you up on a horse would suddenly begin to give you a call, saying that they wanted to give you rides.

And don't get me wrong, the money was a big lure too. Money talks at the end of the day, and racing prize money was on the way up over there. And now one of the biggest racehorse owners in Britain was offering me big money just to have first call on my services. I admit I was flattered.

The offer was too good to be true. A three-year contract deal worth about £50,000 in total over the years as a retainer before I even rode one of Mr Ogden's horses, and then a cut of the prize money after that, which worked out at about eight per cent. There was a further clause which meant that if I went over the £100,000 mark in prize money in a season I'd get a bigger whack of the prize money.

So I went over to his place at Sicklinghall, a town near Wetherby and he showed me all his young horses that he had bought and was waiting to put into training. He also told me about all the current horses he had with various trainers around the country including Howard Johnson, Paul Nicholls, Andy Turnell and Gordon Richards. I must admit that I really liked what I saw. I had asked Dad to come along with me and he too was hugely impressed with the set-up. The trainer Ferdy Murphy who Dad knew well had picked us up and brought us there. Ferdy is originally from County Wexford in Ireland and had made the move over to England to train years beforehand. He was training a number of Robert Ogden's horses and would have been keen to get me there. Mr Ogden didn't have a stable jockey as such at the time and was just using whoever was available. I later heard that when he decided to employ one he had asked Ferdy to get Richard Dunwoody but he was unavailable. It would have been tough to get one of the old pros to move that far up north. So Mr Ogden asked Ferdy to recommend someone else. Ferdy seemingly rang his brother Michael back home and asked who was the best young jockey in Ireland at the time. In fairness to Michael, he said that I was, and the rest is history.

So with this deal I would be No.1 in line to ride all of Robert Ogden's horses, plus I would be available to ride horses for other owners as long as they didn't clash with Ogden runners. And I still could come back to ride for Noel or any other trainer in Ireland on Sundays. I have to admit that I wouldn't have been that familiar with most of Ogden's horses because I wasn't really following British horseracing at the time. But this seemed like the perfect arrangement.

The offer was there for me to take it. Now all that was left to do was go back and discuss it with Noel. The next day I was riding out for Noel and we were sitting inside his house having a bit of breakfast and I just came right out and told him. I went through the offer and how it came about. I told him about the money and that I thought it looked very promising. I didn't say that I had agreed to go one hundred per cent, just that I was half thinking of going and taking up the offer. It was a difficult conversation because Noel had been so good to me over the previous few years. But, here again, he was hugely supportive. He thought the offer was good, but more than that, he thought that the move would do me some good. Give me time to get my head together. In fact he told me to have a proper go at it, keep my head down, work hard and don't be acting the eejit. I think looking back now, that the break was good for him too. I was running wild when I was out hunting, and was even wilder when I wasn't on the back of a horse at all.

I suppose at the time there wasn't too much racing happening as there is these days. And the winter months especially provided too much time for someone like me for messing about. Noel thought it would be better to have something to keep me occupied. The travelling and experience would make me a better jockey, and probably a better person. He said he would still use me to ride on Sundays when I was back in the country.

Critically, he also told me that if ever it didn't work out in England that there would always be a job back at his yard for me which was a relief to hear. I don't know if he knew what that meant at the time but it made the decision a lot easier and I'll always remember that for him.

So I was off to England. A new world, a new life and many challenges ahead. I was confident in my ability and was ready for the big move.

CHAPTER 7

The Years In England
1995-97

I was determined to make it as a top-class jockey in England and fully believed that I would. I was confident that I had the ability to make it there. In fact, I believed that I could ride winners anywhere. I had the advantage of five years riding winners in Ireland and I had already won around Cheltenham, at many of the main tracks, and I'd already had my first spin over the Grand National fences. I was only 21 years old but in racing terms I felt a great deal older. I never really suffered from nerves at a racetrack, or worried about the opposition. And when I talk about opposition, I mean other jockeys or horses. I was there to ride each horse to the best of my ability and that part came very easy to me. I already knew a lot of the lads in the weigh rooms, and those who wanted to chat, I'd chat to. Some others would say very little and I was ok with that too. I was there to enjoy racing. And I was getting well paid for the privilege.

When I was in England working for Robert Ogden my happiest times were on the racecourse. While riding I was always fine but off the course the travelling was tough at times. Mr Ogden had horses with trainers all over the country and often you spent more time in a car than on the back of a horse. I also struggled a bit with the television or newspaper interviews and tried my best to avoid them. It wasn't that I was being rude or unhelpful. In fact, a bit of publicity is always good. It was just that I didn't want to get into a big analysis of how my horse would or wouldn't do. Or worse, how other horses may pose a danger. I had been used to riding horses that I knew. Horses that I had schooled and ridden before. I even knew a bit about horses that my pals had ridden or won on. And that way I would always have a fair idea of how good they were and which way to ride them. Now I was riding at racecourses I had never heard of, never mind the horses I was on. So how could I realistically tell if the horse had a proper chance that day or not?

Right then and there I took a decision just to do what I did best and rely on my ability that I knew I had. Basically, I went out riding every horse believing I had a chance of winning, and I didn't care what else was in the race. If my horse ran well, then I could win. Simple as that.

There were a few teething problems off the course when I first moved over. Mr Ogden's group were meant to sort out somewhere for me to stay but this hadn't been done. So for my first couple of months I stayed in a hotel and then later I moved into a place in Middleham in North Yorkshire beside the trainer Ferdy Murphy who had been so important in my move to England in the first place. So when I was riding out for Ogden's trainers, Ferdy Murphy or Gordon Richards in Cumbria, it wasn't too bad because they were so close and I could still stay at home. But when riding for Paul Nicholls and Andy Turnell down south I would try and get somewhere to stay.

It was very strange living in the hotel for those months. There was a bar downstairs and often you would drink on your own and then roll up to bed. There were plenty of yards in Middleham, a bit like The Curragh back home. There would be plenty of lads to meet up with like Jason Callaghan, Chris Bonnar and Nick and David Bentley. Other times I would drink with this English lunatic called 'Dogman Steve' who trained greyhounds for coursing. Some nights after a skin full of drink we would get a bottle from behind the bar and go out lamping rabbits when the pub closed and we had nothing else to do. Basically this involves shining a high-powered torch around the fields until it picked up a set of rabbit eyes and then the dogs would go chase them. Steve had some very good lurcher dogs, and he would always tell you in the pub that if you bought him a drink and a cigar he would give you a pup from his favourite dog Maggie. That was his way of getting people to pay for his drink. It seems like a strange way to pass the time but it can be good craic and I sometimes still do it around Meath the odd night with my mate Ted Walsh, Ruby's brother, who has been going out with my sister Nina for years and are due to be married. Myself and Ted have had some laughs through the years, like the time I stuck a wooden cut-out of a fox at the end of my yard. Ted only lives about a mile from my house and one day I told him that I was having awful problems with foxes out the back fields. When he came up to the house later that night, he took a look out the back and spotted the 'fox'. He grabbed my rifle from the cabinet and started shooting at it like a mad-man while myself and my partner Rachel stood behind literally wetting ourselves laughing. Or the time we went lamping one night and I ended up shooting a house cat by mistake. Ted was terrified that he belonged to some poor family in the area and we had to leave in a hurry.

****

I suppose looking back Robert Ogden took a chance on hiring me. He wouldn't have known that much about me and there would have been plenty of good young riders emerging in Britain. He would have relied heavily on the word of trainer Ferdy Murphy and I knew there was a bit of pressure on me to get off the mark early for him to repay that show of faith. I know Mr Ogden had heard of my father and was an admirer of his, but that wouldn't extend my time if I wasn't doing the business for him at the track. And there would be plenty of riders waiting in the wings if it didn't work out.

Fortunately, my first day's racing for Ogden went like a film script. I was told to turn up at Newbury for the big meeting that Friday. It was a track that I knew, having ridden Cockney Lad in the Tote Gold Trophy there on the day of my 21st birthday party earlier that year. I had also had a third place finish on uncle Arthur's Bitofabanter at the course as an amateur on my second ever race in England back in February, 1993. That race had given me great experience before taking Rhythm Section to the Cheltenham Festival a few weeks later. So it was a bit of a turnaround that I was now back at Newbury Racecourse as a professional jockey just two years later and riding under the retainer of a massive British owner. I hadn't yet made the full move over to England and only arrived over that Thursday night and rode out at Andy Turnell's yard on the morning of the races.

That day at Newbury I had just three rides, Buckboard Bounce and General Command which were trained by Gordon Richards, and Squire Silk for Andy Turnell. All three, of course, were owned by Robert Ogden. The three races were one after another in the middle of the card.

Buckboard Bounce won the two and a half mile chase quite easily. He was a horse I knew quite well as he had only been bought from John Mulhern in Ireland and I had raced against him at home on many occasions. In fact, I had only beaten him on Noel's Bob Devani earlier that year at Fairyhouse. In fairness, Bob Devani was getting 20lbs from Buckboard Bounce that day and Conor O'Dwyer was less than two lengths away from us at the line. So I knew he was a decent horse. But he hadn't won in his last 11 outings and he was by no means fancied for the Newbury race for his new owners in England.

There were only six runners and we went off the 4/1 third best in the betting. Adrian Maguire was riding the favourite, Seven Of Diamonds and he went off in front but I was always confident of catching him. I squeezed Buckboard into contention and went upsides the leader Mulbank at the second last where, hitting it hard, he gave me a bit of a scare. But he was quick to recover and won easily, going further clear the more we travelled.

The next race was a two mile chase. General Command was well fancied, although he went off just behind Simply George in the betting, which was being ridden by AP McCoy. In the end, it was a great battle to the line. I got General Command up to beat AP, with everything else in the race a long way back.

I completed the dream treble on Squire Silk, who went off at generous odds of 11/2, despite winning eight of his previous 11 starts. It was a two mile hurdle and all the money in the betting ring had been for a Mary Reveley horse called Sweet Mignonette that went off odds on. But I just held Squire Silk up at the back, making my challenge at the final hurdle, and running on an easy winner.

To have one winner would have been brilliant and that is what I had hoped for that day. But to ride an 81/1 treble with only three runners was a fantastic start. Michael Condon, one of the men responsible for securing my job in England, had come over to watch the racing that day. Afterwards, we went up to the private box to meet Robert Ogden who was hosting some guests. Being a bit green, I thought Ogden would be delighted, and lavish praise on his 'new lad come good' after a magnificent treble at a televised meeting at Newbury. Well whatever chance I had of getting a big head was quickly deflated as Ogden simply said: *'I knew the three would win. I fancied all of them'.* It was

73

a bit of a kick in the nuts, but I made up for it later and enjoyed my own celebrations instead. The morning after that Newbury treble I was due to catch an early flight back to Ireland. There was a drag hunt on that morning back home and I didn't want to miss it. Unfortunately myself and Condon went on the piss instead and I missed the flight. In fact, I wasn't even awake by the time the plane took off.

Welcome to English racing, Carberry.

****

There were some strange times while out racing. Later that year I had another winner at Newbury, a horse appropriately called Act The Wag. I had been placed on the horse at Newton Abbott a couple of weeks earlier and he was well fancied on the day, winning a good three mile chase. There were only four runners in the field, something that I was getting quite used to over at English tracks. Because there were so many meetings on every day, there seemed to be a lot less runners in the races, unlike back at home. It was my only runner that day and it was nice to get on the board. I was riding at Newbury again the next day and decided to stay down at AP McCoy's house. Myself and AP go back over 20 years, having started riding at the same time at Jim Bolger's yard. Back then we knew him simply as Tony, but to all in racing he is now known as AP, and is one of the finest jockeys in racing today. After going out for a few drinks, myself and jockeys Seanie Fox and Barry Fenton and a few others ended up back at McCoy's house where the partying continued. AP is of course a non-drinker and I suppose I was doing enough for both of us. Suddenly a big storm came and it lashed rain with thunder and lightning. Now I've always been a fan of lightning and on that particular night I ended up in the back yard in my boxer shorts daring the lightning to

'Strike Me Down Now' at about 4 o'clock in the morning. Don't ask why, it was just one of those nights.

During those years we would normally be riding down south on the Saturday and if I wasn't due back in Ireland to ride on the Sunday I would stay down there with the lads for the Saturday night. That's when all the great nights out would take place.

I had set myself a target of 10 winners a month, and managed that for my first two months riding in England. I was getting on well with trainer Howard Johnson too and he was giving me first call on all his horses. During my first week over in England he had asked me to ride one of his horses called Andros Gale in a mediocre race at Catterick. Andros Gale had failed to win in any of his sixteen starts and had gone through eight different jockeys. Howard told me that if I managed to get him to win that day I would ride all his horses, and not just the ones owned by Robert Ogden. The horse was a quirky sort and didn't like being in front. So I literally left him until the shadow of the winning post before sticking his nose in front to win. I think Howard was amazed, and a small bit relieved that the horse had finally broken its duck. He just laughed and said I had sealed the deal. After six hectic weeks up and down the roads of Britain, I was then allowed a couple of weeks off to enjoy Christmas back at home. I stayed on for the New Year, and rode two winners for Noel at Fairyhouse on New Year's Day before heading back to England.

1996 started off well, with a winner in my first day back racing at Lingfield on Kingdom Of Shades for Andy Turnell and I had two more winners the next day at Newcastle. I was riding well, and was starting to really find my feet and clock up the winners. Squire Silk won a very nice race, the Tote Gold Trophy, at Newbury in February and the plan was for me to ride him in the Champion Hurdle at Cheltenham that year.

The Tote Gold Trophy race was my biggest prize yet, a £60,000 pot, and a winner on the big televised stage. It also took my winnings over the £100,000 mark that Mr Ogden had set. That meant I'd made the bonus.

Things were floating along and other highlights included two wins on Direct Route at Kelso and Musselburgh, while Morceli hacked up at Haydock to win the Black Death Vodka Chase. Morceli was one of my favourite horses ever to ride in England. A big, bold jumper, he had fallen at the last when we were clear in the lead at Haydock the previous month. So I wanted to make it up to his trainer Howard Johnson. Mam later told me that she had been watching the race on the television at home in Meath with my younger brother Peterjon who was only about five or six at the time and when the horse rolled over on me she thought I was nearly dead and let out a scream. But I was grand of course, and walked away unhurt.

After we won the Black Death Vodka Chase, the sponsors presented me with two extra large bottles of the stuff. I was riding back in Ireland at the big Sunday meeting at Fairyhouse the next day, and I took the bottles with me on the flight that night. I was staying at the Burlington in Dublin for the Saturday night and after we left the last of the nightclubs, myself and a few friends went back to my hotel room and got stuck into the vodka. I was bouncing on the bed like a lunatic and ended up falling off and cracking my head off a bedside table, ending up at Dublin's St Vincent's Hospital for six stitches on my forehead. After just a couple of hours sleep I got a lift to Fairyhouse where I fell in the first race and the stitches burst and I was teaming blood. I got it patched up and went on to ride three winners, The Latvian Lark, Persian Halo and Spankers Hill. It was a 70/1 treble, so I suppose the vodka hadn't done much harm.

****

When back in Mcath at weekends I'd try spend a bit of time helping out in the yard and with the younger brothers and of course Nina, who was well protected as the only daughter. Nina started riding as early as I did and you could tell she was so good from a very early age. She would have started riding about the age of three on our pony Jack and even then was completely fearless. I remember one time when she was only about six years old that I was on my point-to-pointer Golden Sea and she was on a little pony Mini. But she was getting on so well that I thought I'd let her have a spin on Golden Sea which was huge. Nina went off on him, tiny on his back but in full control and started jumping the fences perfectly. Mam was in the kitchen and could hardly believe her eyes when she looked out the window and saw what was happening and let out a roar: *'Get her off that feckin horse before she gets killed'.*

While I was in England Nina was about to hit her teenage years and when I was home we would take the horses out back and jump anything we could. Philip and Peterjon were also starting to ride too so one weekend I was back home Mam sent me off to buy a pony for Nina. I was to go up to Tattersalls as there was a half-bred horse and pony sale, with ponies on sale in the morning and horses in the afternoon. Problem was that I was out of racing with an injury at the time after breaking my arm and, back in Ireland, I was giving it a bit of a lash down the pub.

A week beforehand I had come home for a normal weekend and was riding at Kilbeggan when I took a fall off Donal Kinsella's horse Ballinaboola Grove. I knew the arm was shattered straight away. My head was on the ground and to me it felt that my arm was shot straight down into the dirt because I couldn't see it. In fact, it was behind me, snapped. Anyway, I had a late session the night before the Tattersalls sales so I never made it to the morning part, only getting there at lunchtime. Then I realised it was only horses in the afternoon which of course were much bigger, and not suitable for children. So I had a no-win situation. Knowing that if I went home with nothing there would be trouble I figured it would be best to get a horse. I had a look around and saw this nice grey horse and when it came through the ring it was going fairly cheap. I bought it for £1,800. It wasn't a great idea and Dad went ballistic when I got home. But sure it worked out fine in the end as I was able to use him hunting for a couple of years while Nina got used to him. We named him Jingler and he's still in Dad's yard today. So we got great value out of the deal.

****

Back in England I was enjoying a fair bit of exposure. Televised racing was on the rise, meaning trainers from all over England as well as back home were watching. I finished the 1995/96 season with 46 winners in England, which wasn't bad considering I had only moved over that November, and I had another 35 wins in Ireland. I was lucky enough that Noel Meade was still providing me with winners at home when I came back to ride at the weekends, and had four wins at the Easter Fairyhouse meeting alone. He also gave me the ride on Cockney Lad, that won at the Punchestown Festival that year, where I made it a double on one of my uncle Arthur Moore's horses, Professor Strong.

The only disappointment of that season was the fact that I picked up a two-day ban from the stewards for use of the whip that ruled me out of the first two days of the Cheltenham Festival. It meant that I missed the Champion Hurdle ride on Squire Silk. He ended up finishing fifth for Jason Titley behind

Collier Bay, but I just thought that he had a great chance of going better that year.

I got back in the saddle for the Triumph Hurdle, the first race on the Thursday of the Festival. I was riding Noel Meade's horse Embellished, and although he went off at odds of 16/1, we were quietly confident of a good run. This was a race that got away. The Triumph is always a notoriously difficult race to win, and the Irish have a terrible record in it down through the years. With 30 runners going full on for two miles it often descends into a bit of a cavalry charge to the line. Three horses had fallen at the very first hurdle, including the favourite, a horse called Debutante Days. I had kept Embellished covered up and came to make what I thought was a winning challenge at the last. But just as we approached the last hurdle in second position, the horse in front, Magical Lady, ridden by Charlie Swan sharply dipped to his left. This hampered another runner, Mistinguett, and we got clipped and brought down. It was deeply disappointing, especially for Noel, who was looking for his first winner at the Festival. Paddy's Return won for Richard Dunwoody, with Magical Lady finishing second, but Swan's horse was later disqualified by the stewards.

Later that day I had two other runners. Northern Saddler got off to a terrible start in the Grand Annual and never recovered, while Howard Johnson's Morceli went off as the favourite for the Cathcart Challenge Chase, but never figured.

I had better luck at Aintree, where Three Brownies gave me a great ride in the Grand National. I hadn't been expecting that much. Mouse Morris had asked me to ride the 100/1 shot, and told me to keep him prominent and try to get him around. I got a good start and led for much of the first half of the race. When I blundered at Bechers the second time around I thought he would drop out but he kept finding more and we actually led into the straight. In the end, we finished sixth, my first time finishing the famous course. We may have finished quite a distance behind the winning favourite Rough Quest but I was still buzzing. Mick Fitzgerald may have won the race, but I was hooked, and I knew now more than ever that this was the one race I wanted to win more than any other. It was a good week's work for me as I had also ridden two winners, Pleasure Shared for Philip Hobbs in the Grade 1 Novices Hurdle and Joe White in the John Hughes Memorial Trophy Chase for Howard Johnson. Joe White won at a whopping 33/1 and, after two-and-three-quarters miles and 18 fences, just a neck separated my horse from the next two home, Go Universal and Mugoni Beach. Joe White had been trained by my Dad in the past so he was a horse I knew well. It was also my first win over the big National fences. But I was particularly delighted for Howard, who had been a massive support during that first season in England. I had wanted Howard to let me ride Morceli over the National fences but he was afraid the horse would injure himself. I always believed that horse could have won, but Howard had a special bond with Morceli and was just not going to take the risk.

In all I had 17 winners for trainer Howard Johnson in that first season and would enjoy many great days riding for him in the future. Howard was an absolute gent to work for, and he always enjoyed a good laugh off the racetrack too. He tells a story of how he went looking for me after racing that day at Aintree and found me in full flight riding a finish on the Red Rum statue, with me shouting that *'I always wanted to ride a winner on Red Rum'.* I think he just thought I was a bit mad. Another time I had him convinced that I was looking to buy an American Buffalo. He asked what the hell I wanted a buffalo for and I told him that they were great for hunting. Anyway, it went on for so long that I actually tried to get hold of a Buffalo but I couldn't. So instead, I just told Howard that I had bought one in Ireland and had broken it and that I was now using it hunting at home. He is still convinced that I was going out riding hunts on the back of a buffalo and won't know any different until he reads this!

Many years later when I read that Howard was retiring his horse Morceli, I rang him and asked could I have him for hunting. He was such a daring jumper that I knew he would make an incredible hunter. Refusing me point blank, Howard told me that there was no chance whatsoever and that I'd end up killing him. And no matter how hard I tried, I couldn't get him to change his mind. I think he may have believed that even if I didn't kill the horse, the Buffalo probably would.

****

I enjoyed a rare win on the flat in that Summer of 1996 when I rode French Ivy to win the special Trophy Handicap for National Hunt Jockeys at Goodwood for Ferdy Murphy. But that fall at Kilbeggan on Ballinaboola Grove soon after knocked me back a bit as I was off the track for nearly four months.

I didn't get back to a racecourse until the Christmas week, and I'm sure Mr Ogden was starting to curse his luck. But fortunately I was able to reward his patience with a couple of winners on my first day back in the saddle at Haydock Park. General Command was beginning to look like my lucky charm, having won for me the year before on my first day out after going over to Ogden's yard. He obliged again, winning the Boston Pit Handicap Chase by a distance, while Alzulu won a poor novice hurdle despite hitting the last two obstacles. It was a short-priced double but it got me back to winning ways.

It was a particularly bad winter, with snow in many parts, and many race meetings went by the wayside. It meant of course that I had more time in Ireland and used the extra weeks to kick back and enjoy Christmas at home.

****

When I went back to England, the winners started to roll in nicely in 1997. I had 15 winners in the second half of January, including trebles at both Doncaster and Musselburgh. By the time it came to the first week of March I had added another 27 winners for my best ever start to a season. But disaster was about to strike.

Having won on Capt Tim Forster's horse Donjuan Collonges at Chepstow, I headed home for the weekend to ride Dad's horse Native Status in a novice chase at Naas just two days before the start of the Cheltenham Festival. We went off as a hot favourite but he came crashing down at the third fence and I snapped cruciate ligaments and a bone in my left knee. I tried to get to my feet but it went from under me, and I had to leave the track by stretcher. I was taken to Naas General Hospital, a place I was getting to know very well, and my leg was put in a cast for six months. It was bitterly disappointing and Mr Ogden wasn't too chuffed either.

Sometimes these things happen in racing. You beat yourself up about it, but you're going to have falls and miss out on big meetings. It's the nature of the game. It can get you down but you just have to get yourself back to fitness, jump back in saddle and move on. Build a fucking bridge and get over it I suppose. I know one of the greats, Adrian Maguire, missed out on about five Cheltenham meetings through injury. But it's hard to take the foot off the pedal in the run-up to a big Festival. It's when you start to move tentatively, and try to mind yourself, that you tend to take your eye off the ball. You just have to press ahead and hope for the best.

I was seriously pissed off, but determined to get back in time for the Grand National at Aintree the following month and that's exactly what I did. I knew I wasn't 100 per cent but it would take more than that to keep me away from the greatest race in the world. I was booked to ride Buckboard Bounce in the big race, a horse that was coming just right at the right time.

It was the 150th running of the Grand National, but it will be remembered for quite a different reason as it was the year that the race was postponed because of an IRA bomb scare. We had been racing as normal in front of a crowd of over 60,000 punters when the threat was posted just minutes before the big race. We were informed of the threat in the weigh-room and told that we were to leave the course as soon as possible. When I walked out to the course there were crazy scenes as thousands of punters were walking up the centre of the track, with some even deciding to jump a few fences as they went.

The Grand National was later re-scheduled for the Monday afternoon, and I suppose the extra few days helped me get back to my peak. Buckboard Bounce had ran stinkers in his last three starts but I always thought that the extra distance would help him. I believed he had a better chance than his 40/1 odds suggested, but in reality I just wanted to get a clear round. My sixth place finish the previous year had given me a taste for the fences, and I enjoyed the sense of occasion and scramble that came with it. The crowds returned in their thousands and there was a siege-type mentality among us all. We were not going to let terrorists win, and were determined to get to the starting line. We were like Gladiators going out for battle. There were seasoned pros like Jamie Osborne, Carl Llewellyn, Charlie Swan, Richard Dunwoody, Graham Bradley and Norman Williamson lining up that day as well as top young riders such as Timmy Murphy and Richard Johnson.

Another experienced pro that I greatly admired, Mick Fitzgerald, headed the betting market on Go Ballistic, but he never really figured and dropped out early on. Tony Dobbin had gone off in front from flag fall on Lord Gyllene and was chased hard by Jamie Osborne on Suny Bay in the final mile. I had been ticking along on Buckboard and was starting to stay on best the further we went. I was just hoping that the front two had gone off too fast and would run out of steam, but Lord Gyllene pushed on and drew well clear after the last, with Jamie finishing in second and my horse a close fourth behind the third-placed Camelot Knight.

It was decent prize money for the finishing position, and the each-way backers were well in as well. For me, I felt I was getting closer to the big prize and wished my day would come sooner rather than later. Or like many good jockeys before me, maybe it would not come at all.

****

It turned out to be a very successful season, with over 70 winners despite being out for months with the broken arm, and I finished it off with my first and only four-timer at the meeting in Perth. To be honest, I hadn't exactly relished going to Perth as it clashed with the big Festival at Punchestown. But they are the breaks when you are contracted to an owner in Britain. Mr Ogden didn't have any runners in Ireland so I had to be in Scotland for the Wednesday. I went home for the weekend and decided to ride at the first day of Punchestown on the Tuesday and get an early morning flight to Scotland on the Wednesday morning. I went out for drinks with jockey James Nash to a pub called Neesons on the Monday night and met a friend of his, a guy called John O'Sullivan. When I told John I was going to Perth he looked at me and said 'Sure anyone can go to Punchestown, but few can go to Perth' and he said he would come over with me for the few days. I had no sleep on the Monday night and went racing to Punchestown on the Tuesday. When I was leaving the track I spotted John carrying a bottle of champagne and I asked him if he was still coming to Perth in the morning. He said he sure was, and we ended up on a second all-night session before I got the flight to Perth. Every cloud has a silver lining I suppose, and for me it came in the shape of the 117/1 four-timer as Acajou III, Colonel In Chief and Royal York all won for Gordon Richards and Pentlands Flyer came in for Howard Johnson. I don't think poor John backed any of them because he had been out with me all night and wouldn't have thought I had an earthly chance of staying on the horses, never mind winning on them.

I then had another winner on Grouse-N-Heather at the same track the following day, so in the end it had been a very profitable week. It made up somewhat for missing out on the craic at home.

Myself with Mam, Dad, Mark and Thomas with Philp and Nina aboard our pony Minnie, **RIGHT:** while Thomas, Mark and I show off our latest designer shorts

Dad enjoys Aintree Grand National glory on L'Escargot in 1975
BELOW: While I enjoy my own piece of history after winning my first point-to-point aboard Joseph Knibb in 1990 at the tender age of 16

I've carried Nina for most of my life! **BELOW:** and I'm joined at Fairyhouse by an older Nina and brother Philip before the Irish Grand National in 2007

- Photo by CAROLINE NORRIS

With all the family to celebrate our Aintree Grand National win **RIGHT:** Striking a pose with brother Mark

Striding back with Dad after winning at Navan in 1991

- Photo by Liam Healy/P Carberry

Celebrating after wining the Cheltenham Bumper on Rhythm Section in 1993 **RIGHT:** and with John O'Meara after my win on his horse, Aitmatov, in 2007

- Photo by LIAM HEALY

Celebrating after winning at the Galway Festival on Stroll Home in 1997
BELOW: Being congratulated by Charlie Swan at the same track after
winning on Ansar

- Photo by CAROLINE NORRIS

With Dad and
brother Thomas
after winning the
Irish Grand
National at
Fairyhouse in 1998
RIGHT: Getting
the better of Ruby
Walsh on Papillon at
the final fence

- Photos by CAROLINE NORRIS

CHAPTER 8

1998 - Me & Bobbyjo

During my years in England I had been travelling back to Ireland most weekends. I guess that is where my heart really was all along. While England had the lure of making serious money and gaining new experience on the track, it was never going to be a permanent move for me. I missed my friends at home and I missed the hunting. I think going back at weekends to ride at Irish meetings for Noel and Dad and anyone else just reminded me of what I was missing and it made it tougher to leave again.

So any time I was injured, I used it as an excuse to go home, relax and recuperate in Ireland. It was during these trips back that I experienced some of my wildest days. It was a summer's Sunday evening in Cork when myself and two other jockeys, Norman Williamson and Tom Jenks, decided to set out on a crazy road trip that we would never forget. We were after being at the point-to-point end of season dance down in Cork on the Saturday night and we had only had a few hours sleep. I was out of racing injured with a broken collarbone so I had plenty of time to kill. Norman was just after winning the big double at Cheltenham, the Champion Hurdle on Alderbrook and the Gold Cup on Master Oats, and had to be up to Dublin to do a TV interview on the Monday. I had smashed the back window of my Audi, after I'd locked the keys inside. So I decided I'd drive him up and get my car window fixed while we were there. Tom Jenks was based in England at this time but had a few days off and decided to come along just for the laugh.

It was a trip of a lifetime. We ended up stopping in every town on the way up to Dublin and picking a pub for a few pints. We picked up some stragglers along the way and some girl even joined us at one stage and drove us the rest of the way to Dublin because we were all too tanked to drive. That night in Dublin we went to a disco called Major Tom's near St Stephen's Green. We were standing at the back of this huge queue when we were joined by another pal Pat Healy, who does photography at the races. Pat started to wind Norman up, saying *'If Graham Bradley was here he would walk straight up to the top of that queue and tell the bouncers who he was'.* Well, Norman fell for it and went around the outside of the queue and told the doorman who he was. It came as no surprise to us that the doorman didn't care who he was or what he had won and told him to get back to the end of the queue. We were in stitches as he walked the walk of shame all the way back to us.

We went from Major Tom's to another late bar, Bad Bob's, where Tom Jenks grabbed my shoulder and popped out my broken collarbone. The steel plate was protruding from the shoulder and it would have been agony only for the fact that I was so smashed. I decided to just leave it and get it sorted whenever we finished our road trip. Later that night we met a guy from Tralee who was saying that the best nightclub in Ireland was a place called Spirals in Tralee. *'But only on a Thursday night'* he warned. So we said we would see him there the following Thursday. Now, as Tralee is at the other end of the country we spent the next four days making our way from Dublin to Meath and then down to Kerry, stopping in almost every pub on the route. We just went from pub to pub, losing hours and days as we went.

To say it was a road trip to beat all road trips is an understatement. It was probably some of the best days of my life.

****

While all this was going on, there was one horse in Dad's yard that was beginning to look a bit special. Dad only had a few horses in training but he knew he had a real jewel in this one, a horse called Bobbyjo. The horse, a fine big bay of over sixteen hands, was owned by Bobby Burke and his wife Jo, so that's where the name came from. The Burkes were from Mullaghmore in Galway and owned the horse since he was a yearling. He had decent racing pedigree, out of Bustineto and the dam Mark Up.

He came to Dad's yard as a young five year old in the summer of 1995 and I had schooled him over poles when I was home. To be honest, nothing in his early form would suggest that he would be anything better than ordinary. In his first five starts at the racecourse he never finished better than sixth, and he had 10 runs before he won a very ordinary handicap hurdle at Down Royal at the start of 1996. In fact, to show just how ordinary he was, he had THIRTEEN different jockeys on him in his first 30 runs before the owners entered him in the 1998 Irish Grand National on the Easter Monday at Fairyhouse.

Tragedy had almost struck at Naas Racecourse in February 1997, and had things turned out differently, my career may have taken a different path. Bobbyjo was running in a Novice Chase when a five-horse pile-up resulted in Bobbyjo being brought down. But worse was to come as Bobbyjo and another loose horse broke through a fence and ran across the car park and on to the main road. As the horses ran towards the busy main town centre of Naas, Bobby Burke's brother Eugene went off in pursuit and was allowed by a passing car to sit on the bonnet to try catch up with the horses. He, with the help of a woman out walking, managed to get the horses under control and avoid possible carnage.

Thankfully, Bobbyjo was unhurt during the whole experience and actually was well enough to run at Fairyhouse just over a week later, where he won. Gareth Cotter had been on his back for the last few rides and both my brothers Philip and Thomas had ridden him before I did. I had only had a couple of spins on him before the Irish Grand National, but had won both times, at Fairyhouse and Punchestown the previous year. The time at Fairyhouse, the Tom Dreaper Handicap Chase, Noel had two runners in the race, Bob Devani and Coq Hardi Affair. I'm not sure if he wanted me to ride one of them, but the great relationship he had with my father meant that he always understood if I wanted to ride one of Dad's instead. We won well that day in a decent field, and he was clearing the fences by a big margin. I have to say, I was impressed with his progress.

But when Cotter won the Porterstown Chase on Bobbyjo at Fairyhouse in November 1997 while I was out injured, it suddenly became more serious. In fairness, Gareth did nothing wrong on him that day as he won the race with five lengths to spare over Noel's horse Heist. If you won that race, the Porterstown Chase, you stood to earn a £50,000 bonus if you went on to win the Jameson Irish Grand National. With such big stakes involved, Dad really wanted me to ride Bobbyjo in the big one. I don't know if Cotter or either of my brothers were pissed off that I was getting first call on the horse but that's just the way it is. Sometimes as a jockey these calls can go for or against you, and you don't let it bother you. Dad was the trainer and he believed that I got on better with the horse. And that was it.

Dad was pushing me to commit to ride Bobbyjo and asked me to determine whether I was available on the Easter Monday in April. As it was a Bank Holiday in England as well that year there was plenty of racing happening over there that day. So it was touch and go whether I would be allowed back to ride in Ireland. Luckily, as it turned out, Robert Ogden didn't have many horses riding on the day so I got the green light to come over and ride Bobbyjo. In fact I didn't know for sure until the Saturday, just two days before the race, and only worked on him for one session on the Sunday.

Noel also had two fancied runners in the race, Eton Gale and Heist, horses I had won on several times in the past. But the agreement I always had with Noel was that while I would always ride his horses when I was at home and available, all bets were off when the Irish and English Grand Nationals came around and I could pick the horses that I wanted to ride. And while I really wanted to ride Bobbyjo for Dad, I knew Heist would have a serious chance if everything went his way. It was just another thing to consider for the race that day. In fact, the last time I had run in a race against Heist was the time I won on Rhythm Section in the Cheltenham Bumper five years previously.

This was a hugely important race for the Carberry family. Obviously, it would have been nice to repay the faith and loyalty that the Burke family had shown through the years, but there was a very personal touch to the race as well. Dad had won the Irish Grand National twice on Brown Lad in 1975 and 1976 and was now bidding to join an elite group that had both ridden and trained an Irish Grand National winner. For me, it was like coming full circle and emerging from the sizable shadow cast by Dad, despite his small stature.

There were 22 runners in the race over three miles and five furlongs. We knew we had a serious chance but you never really allow yourself to get too worked up about it when you're going into these big handicaps. Literally, anything can happen or go wrong. You just have to get down to the start and take your chance, try to stay out of trouble and don't let yourself get left too far behind.

I knew from watching some of his previous races that I wanted to try and set off in the middle, or just a bit handier, and keep him covered for the first half of the race. Me and Dad had talked about some of his other races when he had gone off too quick and ran out of steam by the end. This was the Irish Grand National over a tough three miles and five furlongs and you would need all your stamina to see out the trip. This time I would keep him midway, try keep up with the first 10 runners and hopefully be there to make a move coming to the last fence. They were the instructions and thankfully on the day, it just seemed to happen that way.

Jason Titley was aboard Noel's Eton Gale, while Kieran Gaule got the ride on Heist instead. Both were up with the leaders for most of the race. The favourite Bob Treacy was up with the leaders for most of the race too, but both he and Heist fell together at the fifth last fence. Bobbyjo jumped super the whole way around and coming to the second last it seemed that Ruby Walsh had Papillon going by far the best of the others so I decided to follow him. Papillon was fortunate to be still on his feet after almost being brought down by a few fallers at the fourth fence. Given that Ruby's horse was trained by his father Ted, it was incredible that the finish in an Irish Grand National would be fought out by the two father and son teams. Ruby did not have the profile that he enjoys in racing now, but I knew him well and he was a very accomplished rider.

In the Irish National that day, Ruby was going extremely well on Papillon, but he was carrying top weight with 12 stone and we were 11 pounds lighter. Thankfully, that made the difference in the drive for the winning post. I took up the lead at the last fence and while Ruby came back at me on the run-in in a super finish, I was able to push Bobbyjo out to the line to win by half a length. We had drawn away from the rest of the field, headed by Charlie Swan on Call It A Day, with another English runner Full Of Oats back in fourth. Just as I crossed the line I stood up in the irons and waved the whip in my right hand to the stands. The distinctive red and yellow colours of Bobbyjo were coming home victorious and the occasion definitely got to me.

All hell broke loose. There was mayhem at Fairyhouse as the Carberrys and Burkes led the celebrations in the crowd of over 25,000 punters. For my family, the reality of the occasion was only beginning to sink in. Dad had won the race twice as a jockey on Brown Lad, but suddenly we were making our own piece of racing history together. It was the first time in 123 years that the Irish Grand National had been won by a jockey that was riding a horse trained by his father. He had been one of the best backed horses in the race, having been backed from 18/1 that morning down to 8/1 on the afternoon of the race. Clearly, there were plenty of happy punters. And I suppose the fifty grand bonus for the owners from winning the Porterstown helped with the celebrations too. The entire night went by in a daze. I was quite a while conducting interviews after racing finished and was gagging to meet up with all the lads who had already got the celebrations in full swing. By the time we got to the annual end-of-year Hunt dance late that night, we were absolutely flying. The hit film at the movies that year was *The Full Monty*, about a group of unemployed steel workers in northern England who turned to stripping to make a few quid. And that night after my Irish National win myself and the brothers ended up on the stage recreating the final scene of the film, doing the Full Monty to the sound of Tom Jones' *You Can Leave Your Hat On*. Unbelievable stuff altogether.

It was a day I'll never forget, not just for me, but particularly for Mam and Dad. They had put so much into the training and upkeep of the horse that I felt it was everything they deserved.

Incredibly, eight years later my younger brother Philip went on to win the Irish Grand National on Point Barrow in 2006, a horse trained by Pat Hughes and then our younger sister Nina won it in 2011. Nina went one better when winning on Organisedconfusion, because it was trained by Mam's brother Arthur Moore, another piece of family history. When Dad won the Irish Grand Nationals in 1975 and 1976, few would have predicted that even one of his children would go on to win the famous race, never mind three of his kids. It's a proud piece of history for the Carberrys and it is very unlikely ever to be matched.

****

The race had been like a triumphant return from my time riding across the water in England. The Cheltenham Festival that year had been fairly quiet, although I did manage a winner on the first day aboard Unguided Missile for Gordon Richards, winning the William Hill nicely with seven lengths in hand over Glitter Isle and the favourite Even Flow. The rest of the week was fairly quiet, although I came close in the County Hurdle, finishing second on Advocat for Noel at odds of 12/1, and I was fourth in the Arkle on Edelweis Du Moulin for Gordon Richards. I didn't get a ride in the Gold Cup and watched from the stands as Andrew Thornton pulled off a surprise win on Cool Dawn.

I had a nice win on Marlborough at Newbury in a maiden hurdle two weeks later and went on to Aintree with a full hand. I had a decent win on Direct Route and managed to get him home in the Novices Chase, after a great battle with Richard Dunwoody on Ashwell Boy and AP McCoy on the favourite

Champleve. In the Grand National I rode my highest ever priced horse, a Martin Pipe horse called Decyborg who went off at odds of 200/1. He ran just like his price, and I pulled him up just after halfway, about a mile behind the winner Earth Summit.

But that summer I was coming to the end of my three year contract in England and I had my mind made up that I was going to go back to Ireland to ride full-time. It wasn't that I was unhappy there, not at all. Robert Ogden was a gentleman and always treated me very well. In those three seasons I had ridden over 170 winners in Britain but many of Robert's horses weren't firing as well as we thought they would have. Ferdy Murphy had also split from him and at times I was travelling all the way down south for one ride on a Monday, then back up north for one ride on the Tuesday and so on. His racing manager Barry Simpson was making things difficult too, expecting me to ride out every morning at a different trainer's yard which was completely impossible. I just seemed to be spending more and more time in the car and less racing time in the saddle.

I also missed the hunting. I know I've said it before, but hunting really is my passion. It's the sheer unpredictable nature of it that has me hooked. You just never know where it's going to take you, it's the thrill of the chase. I get to spend hours doing what I love best; jumping long and high, chasing, competing with people who get a kick out of the same thing.

There was no solid offer from Mr Ogden for me to remain in England even though I knew I could stay on with the same terms. But I had done my time and I was ready to switch course and go home. I was still riding Sundays for Noel Meade and he was building up a solid string of horses at the time. The decision was made quite easy for me in that I knew there was a job for me back there. At the end of that season I met up with Noel at The Lesters, the British Racing Awards in London. I was there with my old friend Richard Hughes who was very funny when he had a few drinks in him. The whole night he was doing impressions of Noel, saying he walked like the character Mr Softmint from the TV adverts. I spoke to Noel and he said if my mind was made up, then there was a stable jockey job waiting for me. Noel looked at me straight in the eyes and said that if I came back to Ireland full-time he would make sure I made a lot of money and that I would be champion jockey within a year. Barry Geraghty was a young jockey at his yard at the time and was riding much of Noel's horses during the week. He said I would take over at the weekend when I was home.

Barry was a few years younger than me, but I would have known him for years, and had known his brother Ross and father 'Tucker' Geraghty before him. We became firm friends over the following few years and have remained close ever since. Barry is a sound man who comes from just over the road in Drumree and we would often share a car on the way to race tracks all over the country. We've shared some great times in racing, some awful times in various Accident & Emergency rooms after falls, and some amount of laughs along the way.

One day I caught out Barry lovely. Around 2004 a good few of us had been out racing and we went down to the *Blue Jean Country Festival* in Athboy. That particular night there was a pig-roasting. There always seemed to be something going on in the summer nights, and there would be all kinds of craic. Anyway, at the end of the night we were all going back to Gavin Cromwell's house in Trim to continue the party. Gavin has been involved in the industry all his life, working in training and also as a farrier. There was myself, Gavin, Gordon Elliott and Barry as well as a few others. Anyway, Gordon was staying at Cromwell's at the time and one of them took the pig's head from the Festival back to the house with us to give to the dogs out back. Later that night, with plenty of drink on board, I got the pig's head after the dogs were finished with it and stuck it into Gordon's gear bag. There was feck all left of it and the smell was awful. We were racing the next day and Gordon opened his bag to find the pig's head with me bursting with laughter. Later that day we found Barry Geraghty's bag in the weigh room and stuck the pig's head in there instead. Barry took the bag home after racing and stuck it in his kitchen. Since there was no racing on for a few days Barry never went near the bag until the smell started to stink out his house almost a week later. He got some shock when he opened it, and the slagging was unreal.

But that was just some of the madness that was going on. Anything went for a laugh. I was burning the candle at both ends and when I was out at the weekends with friends all kinds of madness would happen. I had also developed a love of 'car surfing' at this time. It had started a couple of years before when I had an old Audi 80 that had a sun-roof and I would get someone to grab the steering while I'd stick my head out the top. Plenty of nights, when one of the other lads was driving back home after a night on the lash, I would give them a scare by climbing out the passenger door car window as we were driving at speed down some country lane.

It would generally involve getting up on to the car roof and trying to stand up or just lying on top for a while before getting back in one of the back windows. Other times I'd roll the window down full and bend my back out to see how near I could get my head to the road without killing myself. In fact, one time I actually fell out of the speeding car on to the road and it was a fair distance before the lads knew I was gone. It was about four o'clock in the morning and we were on our way back from a night on Dublin's Leeson Street, a late night haunt after the nightclubs had ended, and the handle over the door snapped off as I was hanging out. I nearly ripped my ear off, and grazed the elbows. But at the time I was fully souped up on vodka and

97

hardly felt the pain at all. I just got up, dusted off and waited for the lads to come back and pick me up.

Another time we were coming home from a nightclub in Portmarnock in Dublin called Tamango's and as we were coming through Dunshaughlin we spotted a badger on the road. The lad that was driving that night had a shotgun in the boot of his car so we pulled over and got it out. I had the gun and stuck my head out the window in pursuit but the badger got away and I ended up shooting a big tom cat instead. When we pulled over to inspect the kill I lifted the cat by the tail only to see his body came away from it and fall to the ground because it was that heavy. Some other nights we would go back to my friend Adam Lord's house after being drinking and take out a pony and a lamp. It would be pitch dark at all hours of the morning and we would take turns of getting on the pony with the torch lighting up the fence and then when you were just about to jump the fence the other lad would turn off the torch so you would be jumping it completely blind. More often than not, when the torch was switched back on the rider would be stretched out on the ground, with everyone else pissing themselves laughing.

There were very few serious injuries though. However, one night at the end of the Galway Festival week we were staying in the Corrib Village, which was like a student campus of apartments that were rented out during the summer months. There were some ponies there in the paddock and one occasion we were coming back about four or five in the morning and we decided to take them out. There was myself, Leo Temple, and Warren Ewing. It wasn't good enough just to ride the ponies, we also had to find something to jump. Well the two lads both had falls. Warren was saying that his nose was broken but sure you wouldn't take notice of him because he's a bit of a moaner and would always say he'd broken his nose if he even saw a trickle of blood. But Leo broke his wrist and it put him out of racing for a while.

When we were on a good session, anything went. One day a group of us were in McCarthy's pub in Fethard in County Tipperary. We were after being at a friend Amber O'Grady's 21st birthday party the night before and were there for a 'morning after session'. It was a summer's afternoon and plenty of people with kids were sitting outside enjoying the weather with a few drinks. We were in the pub when one of the lads came in and said that there was a horse tacked up on a trailer outside. Immediately, one of our group, Michael Foley, dared me to take out the horse and ride him into the pub. I had a broken arm in a cast at the time but I still didn't need to be asked a second time and after the lads helped me take the horse out of his box I got up on him. We hadn't a clue who owned the horse and the lads opened the pub doors and I walked in and shouted for a drink. The pub was packed and I don't think some of the drinkers knew what to think. There was a scatter of kids and tables being moved and just general mayhem. In particular there was this punter going crazy at the side in a snug and it later turned out that it was his horse! He was saying *'That looks like my horse...hey, that IS my feckin' horse, get him the hell out of here!'* The owner of the pub was going mad too, and it was all under control until the horse's head went near a fan that was whizzing around the ceiling with a pair of women's kickers that had been thrown up on it. The horse started to rear up a bit and my friend Paddy Lyons, who wouldn't know one end of a horse from the other, grabbed hold of the horse and helped me get him back out. The owner was completely freaked at this stage but calmed down a bit later after I apologised to him and put the horse back in his box. I think he was ready to swing for me. Strangely, we didn't even get barred because we knew a guy Stan Murphy who worked in the place and we were allowed back in to finish our drinks. It was some laugh and the rest of the drinkers took it well.

****

I finished that season with five winners at the Fairyhouse meeting and a winner at the Punchestown Festival, where Howard Johnson's Direct Route won the Grade One Triple-print Novices' Chase. But I had enough and after all the thrills and craic after the Irish Grand National, I knew I was ready to come back to ride full-time in Ireland. There was no bad break-up with Mr Ogden, just a hand-shake and a promise to ride for him any time I was needed when I was available and over in England.

I was about to move on to some of my best seasons in racing.

CHAPTER 9

My Big Mistake

It felt good to be back at Noel's yard. Once I reconciled myself that I could enjoy a full career in Ireland, while still being available to go over and race at the big meetings in Britain, I was happy to just take my chances back home. I hadn't burned my bridges in England and I could still enjoy a great relationship with Mr Ogden and all the trainers I worked for over there. After I had moved back over, I was still getting regular calls for rides in England and managed quite a few winners. By that time I had taken on an agent, Ciaran O'Toole, to handle all my bookings. There weren't too many jockeys using agents at the time and I know Noel Meade didn't think I had the need for one. But it seemed a logical step for me. The declarations would usually come out while you were working down the yard, and by evening time, all the best spare rides would have been taken. As I've said before, I wouldn't be great on the phone and I certainly wouldn't be one for trawling through the declarations and ringing around trainers for runners. Noel's yard had over a hundred horses at the time, but there still would be times when you might travel 200 miles for two rides. So Ciaran was able to handle my schedule a bit better. I've stayed with him for most of my career, and he has plenty of lads under his wing now.

****

The end of 1998 was complicated, but worked well. I had told Noel that I would be back available full-time, but I had a few pre-booked rides to complete at tracks like Newcastle and Musselburgh for Howard Johnson. Suddenly the travelling was really starting to get to me and I knew I had made the right choice to come back home. But no sooner had I come back than disaster struck and I was sidelined for three months with a broken leg.

I had gone over to Wetherby in England to ride a horse called Flat Top for Michael Easterby in a Class C Handicap Chase. A couple of other rides had been booked for Howard Johnson, but Flat Top was well fancied. The favourite in the race, Corston Joker, had refused to even jump off for Robbie Supple and we were the next best in the betting. We went off fairly quickly in the two-and-a-half-mile race but I was always struggling to keep in touch. I was starting to ease down coming to the fourth last fence when Brendan Powell fell on Ballyline and brought my horse down. It was a shocking fall as my horse crumbled under me with my foot in the stirrup and my entire leg snapped. It was a nasty break, and as I lay on the ground I could see the bone coming out of my leg. Even 13 years on, I still remember what it looked like and it sends a shiver down my spine.

I was out of racing for months and while I was recovering I decided to take a holiday to Spain for some rest and recuperation. It was while I was there that I had my only real flirtation with playing another sport when I ended up playing golf. But it wasn't a very nice experience and I nearly got beaten to a pulp by a group of angry golfers in shorts and shades.

I had booked flights and accommodation from the Sunday with a friend James Nash, while another jockey Conor O'Dwyer and his wife Audrey were coming down for the week as well. As

Conor's apartment wasn't going to be ready until the Monday, I told him that he could have a bed at our place for the Sunday night. So while Conor and Audrey settled in, myself and James Nash went off on an almighty bender around every pub and club in the strip and it was 7am when I got back to our apartment. As I got there Conor was leaving with a set of golf clubs for a round of golf that he had arranged. I said I'd go and join him for the day. I had no sleep, never mind golf clubs or balls or anything so I had to hire everything I needed at the golf course. The first few holes went along fine, I was terrible, but at least I was able to hit the ball. But when we got to about the eighth hole I hit my ball way out left near another fairway. When I got to where I thought my ball had dropped, there were two balls on the ground beside each other. Ignoring all the rules of golf, I just picked one and hit it. My shot was awful. So I just went over and hit the other ball as well, and that's when all the trouble started. These three burly golfers waving golf clubs surrounded me and one was shouting:

'What the fuck do you think you're doin? You hit two balls and one of them was mine!'

And I said: *'Sure I didn't know which was mine so I just hit the two of them to make sure'*

I just thought it was hilarious, and couldn't understand why he wouldn't just take out another ball and hit it. I think he was more intent on wrapping his golf club around my neck. After lots of roaring and shouting, Conor managed to calm the lads down and explain to them that I was a jockey and it was my first time playing golf. Luckily, the guys had heard of me, and knew I had the reputation of being a bit... well, eccentric. They soon chilled out and let us go on our way, but my appetite for golf had faded somewhat and I packed it in shortly afterwards.

I learned three valuable lessons that day: that I'm terrible at golf, that it's not too bad to have the reputation of being a headcase now and then and finally, that those golf lads take their sport very seriously.

****

I had a dream return to action. I was definitely happier back racing full-time in Ireland, and as a result, I was riding better than ever. I got back fit in time for the Galway Festival and had one of the most satisfying wins of my career aboard a John Queally horse called Ratoath Gale in the GPT Sligo Maiden Hurdle. He wasn't fancied to win and went off at odds of 14/1. But I was feeling all energetic after my rest and my exploits on the golf course and I was pushing the horse from around a mile out and just kept hammering away and eventually got up to win on the line, beating David Casey on the well-backed favourite Its Time For A Win. It was my most potent time on the back of a horse and my strike rate was unreal. I had almost 60 winners after I came back from that August to December, including trebles at Thurles, Fairyhouse, Punchestown and Tralee.

I always enjoyed riding at Tralee. It was way off the beaten track and, while you were racing there, all the jockeys, trainers, owners and punters would have to stay around town, meaning the nights would be good craic too. I tended to room with Norman Williamson quite a lot at the time. We had both been riding in England, although he was mostly down south at Kim Bailey's yard. Norman was one of the best riders in racing, but there was no shit about him either. He enjoyed his racing, and he enjoyed a laugh too. I used to enjoy winding him up before races. Jockeys would often chat before a race about tactics, such as who was going to make the running and so on. When he'd ask at the starting line which way I was going to ride my horse, I'd just tell him the exact opposite. One time at Haydock Park he was on a well-fancied Kim Bailey horse in a handicap with around 25 runners. I was on a no-hoper, and when he asked what my plan was for the race, I told him I was going to go straight off and make the pace. He said *'Lovely stuff. I'll go in behind you and follow you out'.* He had been instructed to keep his horse handy and track the leader so he tucked in behind me and waited for the starter. When the line went up I didn't move a muscle and everyone else got a huge start on us. We were the last two runners at the first hurdle and he was shouting, *'What the fuck are you at, I thought you were going to make the running?',* and I just said, *'Ah, sorry, I was only messing'.* It wrecked his head.

My treble at Tralee that June was priceless. I had gone down to ride in the three-day meeting in the Kerry town but had nowhere to stay as usual. I often just drove down to these meetings with no fixed abode, nowhere to stay. James Nash was staying about 15 miles away in Listowel for the week, so I basically knocked on his door and asked for a bed. James had been an amateur rider at Dermot Weld's yard but had taken a couple of years out of racing before going back to ride for Willie Mullins. Nash was staying in the Listowel Arms and had a room with a double bed and a single one and I ended up in the single bed. Now James was a great man for a good drinking session at night but he would be dying the next morning and would always get up with his head in his hands saying that he needed a drink to recover. So that particular time we ordered a tray of lager to our room and finished them off before I headed off to the races, where I had three winners from four rides.

At Tralee, I got off to the worst possible start when I took a nasty fall in the first race on a horse called Arty Grey. I was up with the leaders but three of us took a fall at the fifth-last hurdle down the back straight. But as I tumbled, I somehow managed to land back on my feet, only now I was facing the opposite direction, with all the other runners in the race coming directly at me at full speed. I started to run in between the horses, dodging each at the last second like a crazy game of chicken. When I got back to the weigh room, all the lads were talking about it and as we watched the replay, still half-cut with alcohol I shouted: *'Now, that's what you call a deadly fall',* much to the amusement of the lads.

Later that afternoon I rode three winners for a 90/1 treble. In the second race on the card I was riding the 5/2 favourite Sarah Supreme off top weight in the maiden hurdle. I had been told to set her off in front and I hardly seen another horse for the two and a half miles. The horse won well, beating The Sceardeen by four lengths, with most of the 18 runners well strung out behind.

Merry People won the two-and-a-half mile Kirbys Steakhouse Handicap Chase. Merry People was an eight-year old trained by John Queally and was enjoying his 50th run on the track. He would go on to give me a fright in the English Grand National at a huge price the following year. But that day at Tralee he just stayed all day. I was pushing him from the halfway point and it looked like we would get swamped by the fast-finishing David Casey on Inniscein, but Merry People just pulled out that bit extra on the run-in and we won by a neck at odds of 8/1.

I completed the treble on Legitman for Enda Bolger in the Ring Of Kerry Handicap Hurdle over two miles. It was a rare treble in that none of the three were for Noel Meade and it was even stranger considering the crazy tumble I had in the first race. Maybe the first fall just woke me up a bit. But then again, strange things seemed to happen to me at Tralee Racecourse and a lot of the time I enjoyed just winding the other jockeys up.

On another occasion at Tralee Racecourse, Norman Williamson was sitting in the weigh room and I arrived in with a full formal suit on backwards. Complete with shirt and tie and everything, even the boxer shorts were back to front. I sat down beside him and got undressed and his face was just priceless. I think he just thought there were a few screws loose. We were sharing a hotel room in the centre of Tralee town at the time and I had taken a trip to the hairdressers across from our hotel that morning. Norman had woken up and found I had already left. He rang me and asked where I had gone and I told him to take a look out his window. I was sitting under one of the big hair-driers that women use in the hairdressers directly across from our hotel room and I was waving up to him. I had decided to get my hair dyed white. The problem was that I left early and the hair didn't quite turn out as I had hoped. So instead of Eminem-style white hair, my head turned out more like an orange colour. It was more ginger-shady than Slim Shady.

Later that day we were called in front of the stewards. Norman was after winning the feature race, the Denny Gold Medal Handicap Chase, on Merry People, while I was second on Heist for Noel. I had won on the same track with Merry People just a few months before but was claimed by Noel for this one. The ground was bottomless and after two and a half miles we were all fairly flat out. Norman had cut across me and squeezed my horse on the turn, and they eventually won by just over a length. Afterwards, the stewards were out to get him. We were called in together.

They were asking me all kinds of questions.

Did I think the interference from Norman's horse cost you the race?

I just kept saying *'No, not really'.*

Do you have anything to say to Mr Williamson about his riding?

'No, not really'.

Do you not think you should have won the race?

'No, not really'.

They were basically trying to get me to give them any reason to disqualify Norman's horse but I was having none of it. I've had my problems with stewards through the years, but I'd never deliberately attempt to get another rider disqualified and banned. We were told to leave the room and the stewards deliberated for what seemed an eternity. As it was taking so long, we were convinced they were going to throw out Norman's horse and he was in a sweat. It was easily 10 minutes later when we were called back in to be told that the placings would remain unaltered and that no action was required. Later that day Norman met one of the stewards and asked why it had taken so long for them to reach their conclusion.

'We all needed time to stop laughing at Carberry's hair,' he swears he was told.

****

1998 had finished well . The move back to Ireland suited me and Noel's horses were firing. But the New Year started with a racing disaster that would haunt me. I had just ridden a nice winner on New Year's Day for Noel, a horse called Sun Strand, in the appropriately named Hangover Maiden Hurdle at Fairyhouse. Two days later I was riding at Naas in a two-and-a-half mile novice hurdle on another one of Noel's horses, Sallie's Girl. It was a Sunday meeting and there was a decent crowd.

Sallie's Girl had come into the race with good form, having won her last four races, the last of which I'd won handy enough off top weight at Navan just two weeks earlier.

But there was a hotpot in the race, To Your Honour, that started at 4/7 favourite, which meant Sallie's Girl went off at a generous price of 5/1 joint second favourite alongside Glazeaway ridden by Conor O'Dwyer.

Sallie's Girl was owned by JJ Shaughnessy and her previous

runs were all in three mile events on heavy ground. When I put on his colours I had in my head that it was a three-mile race. But there was another reason for confusion that day. Because of bad ground at the track that week, the start had been moved. At Naas they usually started at the seven furlong mark but because the ground was unsafe they moved it to a different point, and again, all the time I assumed it was a three-mile race.

I never checked the feckin card and, unfortunately for me, the owners, Noel and everyone who backed Sallie's Girl that day, it was only a two and a half mile contest. I still thought we had three miles ahead and would pass the finishing line three times. What happened next would end in quite a lot of embarrassment, harassment and abuse, not to mention the wrath of the stewards.

I was going incredibly well throughout the race. I led for most of it and was virtually clear when I decided to ease the pace. Sallie's Girl had lots in the tank but the big danger was the favourite To Your Honour that was going well in behind and saving steam. But entering the straight, the favourite slipped up and went down, taking one of the other runners, Rossmill Native, down with him.

Suddenly we were in the clear, just me on Sallie's Girl and Conor on Glazeaway, but my horse was going much better and there's no doubt he would have won.

As we came into the straight I was cruising, still thinking that we had another circuit to go. I was latched onto the inside back of Glazeaway, who had Conor beating the shite out of it. It was all out and I couldn't understand why Conor was going so hard with another lap of the Naas racetrack still to go. So I shouted at him *'what are you doin?, There's another circuit to go, there's another lap to go,'* but he just looked at me like I was some gobshite and pushed his horse out to the line. As we crossed I suddenly felt sick, I thought *'it couldn't be, could it?'*. Usually, if there was any doubt at all in my mind, I would stick my horse's head in front before the line just in case. But this time I was so sure that I just played the waiting game, sure I was pulling double.

O'Dwyer at this stage had slowed down after the winning post and standing up on his saddle, he turned to me and asked what had I been shouting at him. When I told him that I thought we still had another lap to go he said he hadn't been able to make out what I was going on about and that he knew well the race was over. Just then I thought ... *'oh Christ, I'm going to be killed'.*

As I led the horse in, there was plenty of abuse from the crowd but you just have to shut it out. I remember some of the roars were nasty, but most people were just talking through their pockets and wanted to get it off their chest. It wasn't like I tried to stop a horse; it was a mistake, end of story. Obviously the punters are important but my first thought is to the trainer and the owners. As I came back in and took Sallie's Girl to the 2nd place pole, Noel Meade and the owner, JJ Shaughnessy were there to greet me. They were angry to say the least, but all I could do was hold my hands up and say sorry, that I'd made a mistake. I just said: *'look I'm terribly sorry, I got mixed up'.* Thankfully, Noel was decent as always and JJ just said that everyone makes mistakes that there was nothing we could do about it now, which was a bit of a relief because JJ is a quite a big man from Galway and I wouldn't fancy getting a belt off him.

As I walked back into the weighing room, I expected to get the call from the stewards and sure enough I was marched in. A 10 day ban. I just held my hands up and explained my mistake. Sure what else could I do? They were fair enough but there was nothing they could throw at me that would make me feel any worse than I already did. In fact, many years later my youngest brother Peterjon would get a 40-day racing ban for doing something similar. On that day at Uttoxeter in April 2011, Peterjon slowed down Monty's Moon after the line, only to later realise that the 'winning post' was in fact the 150 yard marker and allowed two horses to sweep by him. In fairness I, of all people, know that these things can happen in racing.

After the Naas nightmare I decided I needed to keep the head down for a while. I used those 10 days to go on my first skiing holiday and nearly killed myself! Knowing that Noel wouldn't have been too happy, I kept quiet about my plan for a ski holiday. I think I'd caused him enough grief. Thankfully, I was able to amend my mistake somewhat with the owner when winning on Sallie's Girl in a Grade Two race at Navan a month later when the outsider in a four-runner contest, beating AP McCoy on Derrymoyle by a length with the joint favourites Birkdale and Commanche Court ridden by Ruby Walsh beaten by a distance.

It was a simple mistake, but one that I still get the odd slagging about over 10 years later.

****

Cheltenham was now just around the corner and Noel had a decent string going over. We had really high hopes for Cardinal Hill in the Supreme Novices. He was unbeaten in his first three races and was then just beaten into second when I rode him at Fairyhouse on his last time out. Even though we had gone off as the odds on favourite, I was happy with the run and believed he would improve for it. We were only beaten a head by a Willie Mullins-trained class horse called Alexander Banquet, that was unbeaten in six races and fancied to win the Sun Alliance Hurdle. The Grand National was getting ever closer as well and even though I had been unsure about Bobbyjo's chances, he just seemed to be improving at the right time. Either way, I was sure of a good spin around the National fences. And if everything was to go our way on the day, who's to say we couldn't go on and win it?

CHAPTER 10

Winning The Aintree Grand National

Cheltenham 1999 started fairly miserably for me. I had been unseated by Cardinal Hill in the Supreme Novices Hurdle, while Nocksky and Cockney Lad both ran below par in the Handicap Hurdle and The Arkle. Nomadic had run into fifth in the Champion Hurdle behind Istabraq, but the Tuesday had finished with me pulling up on Tamarindo in the William Hill. The real disappointment of the day had been the run on Cardinal Hill. He was a JP McManus owned horse at Noel's yard and had gone off favourite for the opening race of the Festival. Cardinal Hill had won three of his first four races and was a real classy hurdler. I had let the eventual winner Hors La Loi III get a bit away from us and when I squeezed Cardinal Hill to make up the ground at the bottom of the hill he dipped at the second last hurdle and popped me out of the saddle. We were just four lengths down in second position at the time and I was on the deck, sick as a parrot.

The next day, St Patrick's Day, I had an easy winner which made my week. Looks Like Trouble was a horse trained by Noel Chance, who had won his last two starts with Mick Fitzgerald in the saddle. Because Mick was claimed by Nicky Henderson to ride King's Banker I was happy to take up the ride. The Sun Alliance Chase is run over three miles, with 19 fences, so it's always a fair test of stamina and jumping. An Edward O'Grady horse, Nick Dundee, was a hot favourite for the race, and was many an Irishman's banker for the Festival. He had been unbeaten all year, winning six of his last seven races. Looks Like Trouble was very much an outsider, but had his supporters on the day, and was backed from 20/1 into 16/1 just before the off.

AP McCoy had gone off in front on Lord Of The River, but Norman Williamson was always pulling double on the favourite and took Nick Dundee into the lead at the fourth last fence. I had to push my horse just to get upsides him, but it seemed to be just a case of how far Nick Dundee would win by. But as often happens in racing, things didn't go exactly to script as Norman came crashing down at the third last fence and I was left way out clear and trotted up to win by a distance. The 5/4 Irish banker may just have been beaten but the crowd still gave us a rousing reception back in the parade ring.

The remainder of the Festival was quiet in comparison. Sallie's Girl, who got me into so much trouble at Naas earlier that year, was placed in the World Hurdle. But, apart from that run, there was very little else to cheer about, as Dorans Pride completely emptied out when coming up the hill in the Gold Cup and finished unplaced.

****

However, while I was otherwise engaged at Cheltenham, a very special horse was ticking along rather nicely across the Irish Sea. On the very day of my Sun Alliance Chase win on Looks Like Trouble, Bobbyjo was busy winning a low profile hurdle race at Down Royal in Northern Ireland. Now a hurdle race for two and a half grand over just two miles could hardly be seen as an ideal preparation race for an Aintree Grand National over four and half miles and 30 massive obstacles. The big race was just over three weeks away, but Down Royal is where he had been sent.

Bobbyjo had been completely covered up since his win in the previous year's Irish Grand National. He had been given a starting price of 50/1 to follow up the Irish Grand National with the English Grand National at Aintree a year later, but had been drifting in and out in the betting as his form took a dive in the intervening 12 months.

The Burkes, who owned Bobbyjo, had decided to give the horse a break after the exertions of the Irish National. No doubt he enjoyed being paraded around his home town of Mount-bellew, but Bobbyjo didn't see a race track until five months after his big win at Fairyhouse. When he did appear at the end of that October 1998 at Galway he was completely unfancied and he ran that way too. He had been put out to grass and was fairly flat when he came back. Gareth Cotter was back on board as Bobbyjo went off at 9/1 in a field of just six runners in the AIB Bank Handicap Chase over two miles and six furlongs in desperately heavy ground. A Michael Hourigan horse, Tell The Nipper, was all the rage in the betting ring that day, having just finished second behind 1996 Cheltenham Gold Cup winner Imperial Call in the Munster National and went off the even-money favourite for jockey Adrian Maguire. In the end he was beaten into second by JJ Walsh's Waterloo King, with Bobbyjo finishing a distance behind, fifth of the six runners. Bizarrely, I was riding in the same race that day on Noel's amazing horse, Heist, who incredibly was enjoying his 61st track run. Heist may not have been the horse he had once been, but he was still good enough to finish 15 lengths ahead of Bobbyjo that day.

The next time Bobbyjo ran was at Fairyhouse the following month, where he finished 66 lengths behind the winner in a three mile contest. It was hardly convincing form and by the time he lined up for Barry Geraghty in the Paddy Power Handicap Chase at Leopardstown at Christmas that year he was a 33/1 outsider for the three mile race. Again, he finished a distance back in the field, well outside the placings as Calling Wild won for Paul Nicholls and Joe Tizzard. The only thing that you could say in Bobbyjo's favour was that he was still clearing the fences well and never looked like falling. In all of these races he was carrying almost 12 stone and the ground was terrible. He was never a speed sort. The longer the race went on, the better he was staying.

I was back on Bobbyjo when he ran at Leopardstown in January for the Pierse Handicap Chase, carrying top weight in bottomless ground over three miles. It was a big ask and he was completely unfancied at odds of 25/1. Again, he jumped well and stayed on at the end, making up several places to finish fifth. It was a bit of a family occasion that day, as Philip rode another one of Dad's horses in the race, Native Status, who finished back in the field, while Uncle Arthur had three runners in the same race, which was won by Tony Martin's Hollybank Buck.

It was the first time that Bobbyjo showed a bit of proper form since the Irish Grand National, but he was still unheard of in the betting for that year's Grand National at Aintree. However, when he improved a place by finishing fourth in the Tom Dreaper Handicap Chase at Fairyhouse later that month, we started to feel like he was slowly coming back to his best. Meanwhile, back home, word was starting to get around Meath that Bobbyjo was going to have a crack at the big race in Liverpool that April. Dad wanted to have another crack at the Irish Grand National at Fairyhouse but the owner Bobby Burke was adamant that he was ready to make the big step up to the Aintree event instead. For many punters, Bobbyjo's recent form was irrelevant, as his victory in the Irish National was still fresh in many backers' minds. Over in Galway, the Burkes were starting to talk up their chances as well and Bobbyjo was starting to get clipped in the betting.

That race at Down Royal on St Patrick's Day was an unusual place to be for a final prep race for the Aintree Grand National, but it was a master class in keeping a horse hidden to protect his price. When he bolted up with my brother Philip in the saddle, it showed that his fitness was good, but told very little about how he would perform over the jumps. We knew, however, that jumping would never pose a problem. At home he was working very well for Dad and the nearer we got to the big race, the more positive we became.

The prize on offer was just too big to dare dream about. Apart from the obvious financial gain with a first prize of almost £250,000, there were much bigger matters at stake for us. The Grand National hadn't been won by an Irish jockey on an Irish horse for 24 years. I was not old enough to have ever seen an Irish horse win it. None of my friends or peers had seen it either. We had been starved of success for far too long. And of course, the last time the Irish had won it was back in 1975 when Dad won it on L'Escargot. He had tried to bring over a horse to win it as a trainer before, but never with a horse that had a lively chance of making the frame. Surely, it would be too much to dream that I could come back to his place of triumph and win the world's greatest race on a horse trained by Dad... could it?

'...Twenty-four years just waiting for a chance, to tell her how I feel, and maybe get a second glance.'

****

The week before our trip to Aintree, it was the turn of the Irish Grand National on the Easter Monday at Fairyhouse. Obviously Bobbyjo was bypassing this for a crack at the Aintree version, and wasn't there to defend his crown. Instead, I was offered the pick of Arthur Moore's three runners and I chose a horse called The Quads, that was later sold on to Ferdy Murphy in England. The Quads was well fancied in the betting although I think it was more a case of the punters couldn't decide which one to make favourite and it turned out that there were five horses put in as 8/1 co-favourites by the time the race went off. One of these was Papillon that had come so close the previous year when second to Bobbyjo. In the end, Glebe Lad won it for Tom Rudd, with another of Arthur's runners, Feathered Leader, coming in second for Conor O'Dwyer. They say that weight will stop a train and it did that day as Papillon finished well back while again trying to give two stone to most of the other fancied runners. Ruby and Ted Walsh would have to wait another year before their dream would be realised. As for The Quads, we finished a distance back in sixth place after hitting the fourth last fence hard.

It was not all bad though as Cardinal Hill got back to winning ways when we won the Jameson Gold Cup Novice Hurdle at short odds. I had followed Conor O'Dwyer on Native Upmanship for most of the two miles and when I let Cardinal Hill go after the second last hurdle he careered away to win easily for Noel Meade and JP McManus. The week then got even better when I managed three more winners, as Irish Light won a chase on the Tuesday and I had a double over the hurdles on Wednesday with Winter Garden and Strong Run. It finished the week on a high, but there was no time for celebrations as we headed for the airport and on to Liverpool to take on the best of British horses over their finest fences.

****

We went to Aintree with one clear goal, to win the Grand

National. For years I had dreamed of winning at Aintree and I had believed that my best chances would come if I was riding in England full-time. But three fruitless years, as far as the National was concerned, had passed over there and now I was back riding in Ireland. But something special was on the cards. Bobbyjo's price had started to tumble and was hovering around 20/1 as the day approached. I still joke that I think most of that money was down to my brother Thomas who had been backing Bobbyjo almost on a weekly basis since Christmas. He first had him backed at odds of 50/1 and was forever giving everyone updates on what price he was in the betting. He was completely obsessed with the fact that Bobbyjo would win the English Grand National and, in fairness to him, he had more belief in the horse than anyone.

Dad had warned me to take it easy on the night before the big race so I decided to go on the lash on the Thursday night instead. Racing had been quiet that day, with just one run on Sharpaten in the Novices Hurdle, where we finished a long way back, last of the six runners. I only had one runner on the Friday card, a horse called Native Status for Dad in the John Hughes Handicap Chase. This was the horse that fell on me at Kilbeggan that day, snapping my arm, and to be honest, I wasn't very hopeful of a good run. That Thursday night I went out on a right session in Liverpool city centre and didn't get back to my hotel until the morning. I was only in my room a few minutes when I heard a familiar voice out in the hallway. I looked out to see an old friend 'Shango' from back home swinging a bottle of champagne so I called him in and we drank the bottle that morning. Then we got another bottle of champagne. And then another. Soon the morning had passed in a daze and race time was fast approaching.

I was well jarred and headed to the Aintree racecourse well after racing had started. In fact, I almost missed my race and, by the time I arrived, Dad had already given up on me and asked David Casey to ride Native Status instead. As I walked in the weigh room I met Casey walking out with Dad's colours and I just grabbed them off him and got changed. Dad looked at me and said *'Where the hell were you?'* and I just said *'In the sauna'* before weighing out. The horse ran a stinker. It was a struggle to get him home for the last mile, and we finished tailed off.

After racing, I was in bits, with a mixture of the hangover and lack of sleep seriously taking its toll. Dad knew well that I had acted the maggot the night before, but he had no idea that I hadn't even got to my bed. The Burkes had brought over a big crowd from Galway and had arranged a meal for that night in the hotel. But I was in no fit state to stay up for the night. So I made my excuses and left for bed about 9.30pm and didn't wake until the morning. It was probably the best thing that could have happened, because I felt extremely fresh when Dad got me up for breakfast before heading to the racecourse for an early morning prep run. Bobbyjo was in great form and I was sure of a good run later that day. At this point I was just counting down the hours to the big race.

****

The start of the Grand National can always be a bit mental. All the jockeys stop for a group photograph as you leave the weigh room and head towards the parade ring. After a quick chat with the trainer and owner, you head out towards the track for the pre-race parade, which basically involves being led in order of your racecard number by horsemen in front of the stands, before peeling off and making your way towards the start. My instructions from Dad that day were hardly spoken at all. I knew the horse well, and Dad certainly knew the jockey on board. I think it was more just a case of, *'good luck, and enjoy it. Try get him into a rhythm and keep him handy early on'.* That kind of thing. Dad stayed back in the ring with Bobby Burke and his brother Sean, where they watched the race on the big screen as Dad nervously sucked on a cigar.

With all the formalities over, I was much more comfortable once I got down near the starting line. I don't know if any jockey enjoys all the commotion involved with the lead-up to the big race. I know I don't. You certainly realise that this is no ordinary race, but you still just want to get on with it, get away from the roaring crowd and get yourself and your horse out on the track. Once down there, it can suddenly seem very quiet, as you mix with other horses and riders going through the exact same roller-coaster of emotions. Once down near the start, we always have a few minutes to prepare and generally you would take your horse down to have a look at the first fence. For anyone riding in the Aintree Grand National, the biggest fear is to fall at the first. End up on the deck at the very first obstacle and you spend the rest of the race as a spectator, leaving it as long as possible before making the embarrassing walk back towards the stands.

That year there were only 32 runners. This is still a daunting number, but not as bad as when the maximum 40 go to the start. With four and a half miles and 30 fences ahead of us, you never want to go off in front too early. But you need to avoid running behind bad jumpers as well. In the National, all bets are off, as far as past form is concerned. There are just too many runners to try to track the horses who are favourites in the betting. Likewise, you don't think to yourself: *'I better keep clear of the 200/1 shots'* either. You just try and settle into the race, watch who are going well around you, and most of all: Stay in the saddle. You are completely aware of all around you. You have to remain sharp and watch the horses that are going well and, in particular, the ones that are going badly. The last thing you want is to jump into the back of a faller and knock your horse out of the race. You get one shot a year at this race and you want to give your horse every opportunity to win. Don't get left too far off the pace, stay out of trouble and stay on your feet. It's not rocket science. You just need everything to go right for you on the day.

Once the starter let us go, there was a huge roar from the stands as I went across the road and passed the stands in about eighth or 10th position. I got over the dreaded first, but not everyone made it. Joe Tizzard was on board the morning favourite Double Thriller for trainer Paul Nicholls and there was a huge groan from the punters as he exited at the first fence. A few more went at the fourth, while Mick Fitzgerald took a nasty tumble midway on Fiddling The Facts, which had been all the rage in the betting that morning. Meanwhile, I was ticking along nicely on Bobbyjo. We had been the subject of a fairly significant gamble ourselves. That morning we had opened up at 20/1 in the betting but had been backed right down to 10/1, about fourth or fifth shortest in the betting ring. I was delighted at how well we were travelling and jumping. I always knew he would jump well and stay out the trip, but the worry would be that he may not be able to keep up with the pace. But I was never outside the first 10 runners and, bar a slightly slow jump at the Canal Turn on the first circuit, we were clearing the fences with plenty to spare. Blue Charm had cut out most of the running and was still travelling well for Lorcan Wyer. Brave Highlander and General Wolfe were also up with the pace, as had been Fiddling The Facts and Feels Like Gold, running well for Brian Harding.

As we went out on the final circuit, I just tried to keep Bobbyjo clear of trouble and get him around. I knew I was in with a real chance of a high finish, or even better, the biggest prize in National Hunt racing.

By the time we reached the final four fences we were lying in fourth position when Adrian Maguire cut across me on Addington Boy and I had to switch Bobbyjo around him. If anything this may have helped me because I was able to give my horse a bit of a breather. Merry People was going extremely well too, but he fell at the second last fence and Bobbyjo had to change course in mid-air to avoid being brought down. By this stage the front two, Blue Charm and Call It A Day, went for home and we got a little outpaced and for a few strides I thought our chance had gone. But the further we went the better Bobbyjo was staying and when the leading two went to jump the last I switched out right, pinged the last fence, and landed in the lead.

I was now on the right side and knew I had to make it to the elbow first to avoid any horse getting up on my inside. The elbow is the part of the course where you have to veer way out right after the last fence and then almost turn left into the run-in past the stands. But as I got to the turn it all seemed very quiet: we had driven clear and the race was at our mercy. It was at this point that I genuinely thought for the first time that I could win it. Lorcan Wyer, the jockey on Blue Charm had been involved in a right battle with Richard Dunwoody on Call It A Day and I think they ran each other into the ground. Richard's horse had been one that I had feared. Not only was Woody one of racing's greatest ever jockeys, but he had also won the Grand National twice before. He knew exactly what it took. It wouldn't have mattered what he was riding that day, he would have been a threat regardless.

As the massive crowd cheered me on the run-in I stole a quick glance at the big screen and saw that I was 10 lengths clear coming to the line. The feeling was incredible. I stood up and punched the air. I had done it. We had done it. The Aintree Grand National. Just like Dad. Just for Dad.

All of my life I had dreamed of this moment. From an early age, myself and my brothers had watched reruns of Dad winning the Grand National and heard all the stories. In fact, we watched reruns of every Grand National that we could. It got to the point that after you watched the videos so many times you would know what would happen next, who would jump and who would fall. You would just know before it happened on the screen. It was the ultimate achievement in racing. Even when we were kids, myself and Nina used to bring our hunting ponies out across the fields jumping the big hedges and wild bushes dreaming that we were riding in the Aintree Grand National. We even called the various hedges names such as Becher's and The Chair and would carry out our own commentaries where it was us winning the National. But this time it was no kids' game. This was real. The fairytale had become a reality.

****

After the winning line I took off my goggles and tried to take in the moment. I was being congratulated by the other jockeys but it was all going by in a daze. My brothers Thomas and Philip and a few friends came running out on the track screaming, completely oblivious to the other horses coming in. One even ran in front of Call It A Day, who had finished third. The horse swerved and threw Richard Dunwoody to the ground. He was furious, and Dad was later called before the stewards for not keeping the lads in check. But I was just lost in the moment as Philip led us back to the parade ring. The crowd was going wild as we passed in front of the stands and I was milking the moment, swinging my whip and waving my fist to the crowd. Back at the old Aintree parade ring, the winners' enclosure was inside a covered area with old rafters stretching across about 10 feet in the air. As I was led in, I stood up on Bobbyjo, grabbed the rafter and started swinging from it like a monkey before jumping to the ground. It wasn't planned or anything, I guess no one could plan for a day like this. As I got down and hugged Dad it started to sink in what we had achieved. Des Lynam was doing the post-race interview for the BBC but I could hardly string any words together. Bobby Burke, who was now based in London and had brought a bus load of supporters up for the day, was beside himself with joy. I was delighted for him, as he had horses training with Dad for years and he deserved the success.

I had to leave the celebrations to them and head into the weigh room. As interviews had been scheduled for the next couple of hours in the Press Room, I had a little time to enjoy the moment with the lads in the weigh room and watch the replay of the race. If this was a dream, I never wanted to wake up.

After the interviews were over, I had a quick stop-off at the Moate House Hotel to drop in my stuff and grab a bite to eat. I had a quick drink in the bar and then headed over to the Adelphi where Mam and Dad had been staying. The Burkes had organised a meal for 20 which turned out to be more like 90 as the celebrations got into full swing. Back in Ireland, there was racing at Wexford but they were able to watch the Grand National during a break in races. It had been 24 years since an Irish horse won and I was told that the lads were cheering like they were on the horse themselves. A good few of them, including Barry and Ross Geraghty, James Nash and Shane Lyons all got straight on to their phones and booked the evening flight over to Liverpool. I believe the Ryanair flight was just crammed with lads from Meath all piling over to join in the celebrations. By the time I got to the Adelphi about 10.30 that night, the place was hopping. My friends Mick Foley and the two Lords, Niall and Adam, carried me in on their shoulders into the main function room and the place went wild. It was a hell of a night, and I still can't even remember what time I finally hit the sack, if I did at all.

****

One of the biggest regrets of my life is not going back to Ireland the following day. There were parties in almost every pub in the county back in Meath. There are various tales of queues of happy punters lining up outside bookmakers in Meath and Galway waiting to collect their winnings after the big race. But before Aintree week I had arranged to go to North Yorkshire to collect the last of my things after moving out of my lodgings there a few months previously. Regrettably, I stuck to the plans, despite winning the National. I had a car arranged and ended up staying there until the Tuesday, three days after the race.

In the meantime, all my friends had gone back on the Seacat boat sailing on the Sunday. They had been partying non-stop all night and they still talk about that boat trip to this day. Seemingly, all the lads had lined up their bags around the circular bar in the middle of the ship and were running their own version of the Grand National like lunatics for the first hour or two. But then the ship got caught in terrible waves and was thrown from side to side. Having travelled too far to turn back, the ship continued on, with the lads still attempting to 'ride Bobbyjo to the finish' around the bar while tables and drinks crashed down around them. By the end, a fair few of them ended up getting violently sick, and my brother Thomas slipped up and smashed open his nose on the foot rest of the bar.

But this only added to their day, and they all ended up back in Meath toasting the success. For the next few days the lads hung around the local pub waiting for me to come back and give them a proper excuse for a celebration session. Meanwhile, I was AWOL somewhere in a pub in the heart of the Yorkshire

Dales enjoying a quiet celebration of my own.

CHAPTER 11

Crashing Back
Down To Earth

I was on a high after Aintree. Everyone wanted to meet up when I got back to Meath in Ireland. It wasn't that surprising since it seemed the entire country had backed Bobbyjo to win the National. It's hard to believe that just a week after all this joy and excitement I would be having a life-saving operation and a doctor would tell me I had been 15 minutes from death.

In the week after the National I did a small bit of riding, going to Gowran Park on the Wednesday and coming back down to earth by finishing 16th of 17 finishers in a two mile hurdle on one of Noel's horses. But the real action was the nights after the races. I was on a high and it was almost like everyone in the county wanted to have a drink with me and wanted to go through the Aintree race, fence by fence. It had been 24 years coming and seemed to have given the country a lift. The Celtic Tiger was roaring and I was the best man to ride it. I mean, there was a whole year's celebrating to be done. I remember it might be months later and you would forget about Bobbyjo for a while and then someone would stop you on the street and talk about where they were for the race and you'd feel your whole body rising.

But Noel Meade wasn't too happy and the following week I think he'd had enough of my celebrating. He wanted me back

129

working so he called and said I'd to be at the yard the next day to ride out some horses. I think he thought I was going out too much and maybe that was true. But that night I still went out as I'd arranged to meet some of my hunter friends and was staying with a friend Francis Lyons that night. I'd been staying with him since coming back from England, until I got myself sorted. Anyway, we had a right few drinks and went home but I remember the next morning getting up for work, walking outside and wanting to go back to bed. The weather was poor, and as I walked in the dark through pissing rain I felt like turning back. Anyone will tell you that I hate riding out in the rain. I'm not too fond of the cold either and like to pack up, but the rain is worse.

It was just after 7am and I felt like going back inside but I decided *'feck it'* and headed off to Noel's. At the yard we were doing a four furlong round gallop. There were three of us that morning, Barry Geraghty, Peter Kavanagh and myself. I was on Atha Beithe and we had already done a circuit. As you came around you go down a bit of a hill and although it was flat enough my horse stumbled and fell. I flew off but landed on my hunkers and leaned forward to rest on my hands while trying to get my bearings. But disaster struck. Barry was off in front but Peter's horse was right behind and hit me full on into the back with such force that the horse went down and threw Peter Kavanagh over his head. It seemed the horse's front leg had gone in behind my ribs and the pain was killing me. I was in bits but when Noel ran over I think they were more worried about Peter because there was blood trickling down his forehead from inside his helmet.

I was lying on the gallop and I knew something was wrong but I suppose after being out the night before and then having a fall I was a bit all over the place. All I could taste was a mouthful of sand and I was gasping to catch my breath. I needed water and desperately tried to get the mouth moving. I must have been some sight as I crawled across to the side of the gallop and started licking some rainwater off some leaves and grass at the side. I was just trying to get some taste back in mouth, get some saliva moving to try and get the damn sand out. I felt I was choking. So there I was trying to clear my throat while young Peter Kavanagh was panicking because blood was now flowing over his race goggles and I think the poor lad thought he was dying!

So I think Noel was more worried about Peter and tried to calm him down while I tried to gather myself. It was just a week before the big festival at Punchestown and this was the last thing I needed, I remember thinking.

Noel put Peter in the front of the jeep and bundled me in the back and brought us back up to the house. He asked me if I wanted to go to hospital to get checked out but I said that all I wanted was to sleep. Apparently with spleen injuries that is quite common and all you want to do is sleep. Anyway I climbed into one of the beds and tried to get some sleep for an hour. At this stage the pain was throbbing at the back of my stomach and tightening the whole way round. Noel said he'd get a doctor to the house but I said no, that I just wanted to get my head down and sleep it off. I did nod off but woke a few minutes later as it was uncomfortable so I moved a bit, slept for another while and then woke up with the same thing, moved a bit more to get comfortable and slept for another few minutes. I was told later that this is what happens with burst spleens and it's just the blood spilling out.

Noel kept coming in to check on me and could see I was in a bad way. He asked what I thought and I said there must be something burst in my stomach. He rang Fred Kenny, our local doctor who looked after the jockeys at the time, and he came out and took me with him to Navan Hospital. I remember the traffic wasn't great that day and I had a couple of blackouts on the way. We jockeys tend to have a fair tolerance for pain, it's just the way we are, but that day it different. The pain was simply unbearable.

At Navan Hospital, I got checked out and pissed a little blood but they couldn't find anything wrong with me. They asked me to hang around for a while to do a second urine test a little later to be sure. By that stage Barry Geraghty came out to check on me and he was going to drive me home as soon as I was finished. But they wanted another sample. I was struggling to pass urine and I asked Barry to piss into a bottle for me. Sensibly, he was having none of it. Eventually I managed a small amount and they said it came back clear and that I could go home with nothing more than a cracked rib and some bruising. It was more of an orthopaedic hospital and wouldn't have done any internal scans. I think they kind of said something like: *'go on ye soft lad and piss off home'*. So I did.

Barry drove me home and I hit the couch. But any time I'd eat or drink my stomach would swell up and the pain would start again.

That was the Tuesday and the doctor had stood me down from racing for the week. By the Friday I was getting worried about the following week's Punchestown Festival and went back to the hospital doctor to get clearance for the next week. I was checked over and told that I should be grand to ride. I went home feeling a little relieved. Later that day a friend of mine Paddy Lyons, whose brother Francis I was staying with, was heading to Fethard in Tipperary for a couple of days so I decided to take a lift with him and I was going to stay with my then girlfriend Carol Hyde at her brother Timmy's place in Cashel.

The journey down to Cashel was as rough as I have ever known. I could feel every bump on the road. Every bang hurt and my stomach was getting more bloated all the time. We went for a bite to eat and a drink but I knew something wasn't right and I went back to the house to lie down. We were meant to go out that night but the pain was getting worse. I just lay there for the night.

The next morning I had a bath but the pain wasn't easing and feeling very weak I went back and lay on the bed. When Carol told me to get up I couldn't move, I just couldn't lift my body off the bed. I was fainting a lot too so she said that she was going to take me to hospital but I said sure I wouldn't be able to move. I said *if I move I'm gone*, that's just the way I felt at the time. She rang a doctor and he came out to the house. He walked into the bedroom and said straight away that I'd a burst spleen.

Carol's father Timmy then came into the room and said he'd get a helicopter to take me straight to the Blackrock Clinic in Dublin. At this stage I was really worried and told them not to try and move me. I wouldn't have got to the door. I didn't think I'd get that far. I believe that decision saved my life.

They rang an ambulance and they carried me down from the upstairs bedroom and out to the ambulance. Right then I started taking a fit because I couldn't get any air into my lungs. I was panicking and feared the worst. They attached the gas and I came back around. If they hadn't had the gas I was a goner, there's no doubt about that. I was later told that I had been just 15 minutes from certain death due to internal bleeding.

So I was taken into the general hospital in Cashel and was examined by Dr Merchant who said he would have to operate straight away. He asked if I was ok with that I just said yeah grand, and off we went. I drifted out of consciousness and the next time I woke up I was stitched up and spleenless.

It was funny because I was told later that when I was in theatre, the doctor rang Mam. She was in England at Sandown because our horse Bobbyjo was running in the Whitbread Gold Cup. The doctor told her that her son was in hospital having an operation but with the crowd and the bad line she could hardly hear and wasn't sure which son he was talking about. The more Dr Merchant tried to explain the procedure the more mum was shouting, *'which son do you have, which son is it? I've got five and it could be any of them!'*

I was kept in hospital for a week, and over the next few days it gave me plenty of time to think of what might have been had I not made it to hospital on time. It helped that for a lot of the time I was sedated.

Another bit of gas that kept my spirits up was when Jon Kenny, an Irish comedian from the show D'Unbelieveables came in to visit. Jon was massive then with his hugely successful stage show alongside Pat Shortt and he lived near Cashel. I would have known him from before, but that day I could hear him outside roaring, *'Sure what the feck do you get a man who has everything?...a bale of briquettes',* and in he marched with this bale of Irish turf under his arm and put them down on the bed along with a bottle of champagne and a pair of childrens' sunglasses, the big plastic type. He's a real character and I was glad of the visit. It certainly brought some spirit back to me and I was sad to see Jon ended up in hospital himself some years later. Thankfully he recovered well. Carol and Timmy were there at the hospital all the time, but like most Irish lads I just wanted my Mammy. Unfortunately all the family was in England and they couldn't get there until the next day. Paul Shanahan and Tammy Twomey also came in to visit. Tammy, who is now with Charles O'Brien, had also burst her spleen back when she was with David Wachman and she told me that she had a similar experience. All she wanted to do was sleep before they knew what the problem was. Ruby Walsh also had his spleen removed some years later.

It hasn't really affected me. In previous years they used to keep you on medication. Now, however, things are different and even though you only have about one 10th of your actual spleen left, they say you just have to mind yourself and watch what you eat and drink. One of the nurses told me that you had to give up the drink but I waited to see what the doctor said and hoped to get away with it. Anyway, I went back for a check-up with Dr Merchant about two months later and I was after drinking the shite out of it since the fall. He just said that he didn't know what I'd been doing for the last few weeks but I was absolutely flying and I *'should keep up the good work'* as he hadn't seen anyone recover so quickly. I just said grand and assured him I would stick with what I was doing.

But seriously, I do have a lot to thank Dr Merchant for and Mum wanted to show our appreciation by naming a horse after him. So some time later we had one of Denis Mulvihill's horses and we named him Mr Merchant. Unfortunately, while Denis was a great owner for us, he just never seemed to have any luck with horses and Mr Merchant wouldn't win a raffle.

****

Looking back now I know how fortunate I was. Others haven't been so lucky. Falls and injuries are the toughest part of racing. In many ways racing is a very tight family and we all look out for each other. We may race as rivals and always want to get the better of each other, do all we can to get a winner. But off the track we are a very close group. We hate to see jockeys get hurt and thankfully in recent years there have been very few very serious falls.

Unfortunately, one of these was my good friend Shane Broderick, who I've known for years. We were about the same age and I knew him coming up through the ranks when he was at

Michael Hourigan's yard. He was and still is a close friend of mine and I was riding the day he had his horrible accident.

We were at Fairyhouse on the day of the 1997 Irish Grand National. Jason Titley had ridden the winner of the National on Mudahim for trainer Jenny Pitman and like every year there was champagne in the weighing room after racing had finished and the craic was good. The race had been a real cracker and Fran Woods had been desperately unlucky not to have won on Arthur Moore's horse Amble Speedy. They had been severely hampered by a loose horse before being beaten by a short head. So there was an extra edge to the race. We knew Shane had fallen like a few others earlier in the day but we had hoped he was ok. Shane had runners in most of the races that day but had come off his horse Another Deadly in the second last and had been taken to hospital. Shane was a young star on the rise. I've no doubt he would have made champion jockey and just two years earlier he had steered Dorans Pride to victory in the Stayers' Hurdle at the Cheltenham Festival when he was only 20. In fact, Shane had been in flying form that day at Fairyhouse after having a fair ride in the National on Flashy Lad and then winning the 4.35pm race on Royal Oasis for Paddy Heffernan at odds of 14/1. It's hard to believe that just 35 minutes later his life would change forever.

Anyway, the celebrations were in full swing at Fairyhouse with us all oblivious to the full extent of Shane's injury. Just then the course doctor, Walter Halley walked in, took a glass and skulled it in one go. He wouldn't normally drink but he had just taken Shane back and he looked shattered and needed something to calm him. He said Shane was in a bad way and he was on his way to the Mater Hospital in Dublin.

A couple of us went in to visit two days later and there wasn't a whole lot of movement. There were all these tubes coming out of him. It was very scary stuff. About a month later I went to see him at the Rehab centre in Dun Laoghaire. By that stage we knew he was recovering slowly but that there was not much anyone could do. He was paralysed from the neck down. We had known the awful truth a few days after the fall. Seeing him at the rehabilitation centre made it all very real.

Every day you go to the races, you can ride up to 500 runners a year, and each time you realise that it could be you coming home injured, or worse not coming home at all. But you just have to try and not think about that kind of thing or give up riding altogether. I've had falls and broken bones and it could just have easily have been my spine. Sometimes it's the simplest of falls that do the most damage.

There have been others that had brushes with death. Peter Toole from just down the road in Dunshaughlin had moved over to Berkshire where he was riding for Charlie Mann when he fell at the first fence on a 100-1 shot at the 2011 English Grand National day. Peter fell into a coma for days after he suffered bleeding on the right side of his brain. I went in to see Peter a few weeks later and thankfully he was sitting up and although he hadn't got his speech back at that stage, he was well on the road to a full recovery. Matt 'Strawberry' O'Connor had the same injury two years earlier after falling in a Beginners Chase at Thurles just days after celebrating his 21st birthday. Thankfully Strawberry recovered and made it back riding.

These are the risks. But you somehow just have to keep going. It's terribly sad to see these things happening, but unfortunately they happen in racing. You have to try and take care of yourself and make sure that you are still walking at the end of it. I knew what I was getting into when I took the job and I know I'll break more bones before I finish in racing.

CHAPTER 12

I Bet You Couldn't Give Up The Drink

JP McManus is one of the true gentlemen of racing. I'm always asked about JP and the famous *'Bet that I couldn't give up the drink'* story. There's been so much rubbish said about this that I guess I'll set the record straight once and for all.

First of all, you don't call him JP, it is Mr McManus. He doesn't ask that, it is just that way and always has been. I've too much respect for him and many of the lads have that too for it to be otherwise. He's such a big figure in national hunt racing now, but honestly I don't really remember when I first met him. I know I rode a couple of horses for him in England. There was one in particular, a horse called Slideofhill, trained by Jonjo O'Neill. He was well thought of by JP but he'd lost his way a bit and had been beaten out of sight in his previous three races. He was very difficult to get into a jumping rhythm and I was asked to have a go steering him in a chase at Sedgefield. We were tailed off after a circuit in the three and a quarter mile race but I didn't panic and just started to cajole him into the race and get him interested. By the time we passed the stands a second time we were still last but a lot closer last. Then on the back straight I started picking up and I got Slideofhill up to win on the line. It still sticks with me because Timmy Hyde told me later that Jonjo had said that he thought it was the best ride he ever saw a horse getting and that's always nice to hear. I managed to win on the horse again on his next time out at Ludlow, and without sounding a bit big-headed, I believe eight other jockeys rode him without success since then. I had also won on JP's horse, All The Aces, at Naas in the early days when he was trained by my uncle Arthur. So I knew him and he knew me.

At the time I was going out with Carol Hyde, Timmy Hyde's daughter, and because of the spleen injury I was out of racing for almost five months. We were going to Paul Shanahan's wedding and later on in the night I was out smoking with Ciaran McManus, JP's son, when he bet me £50 that I couldn't give up the cigars. I took the bet and I was in flying form. I was enjoying the craic and the drink that night and spent most of the night on the dance floor. Later that night I was talking to JP and I was laughing about my bet with Ciaran. But then he said he was worried about me. He said that he'd never seen a talent like mine but he thought I'd be doing a lot better if I wasn't drinking. He just didn't want to see my talent wasted. He then said that he'd increase the stakes to £50,000 if I could give up the drink for two years, with no loss if I failed.

I thought he was joking at first, but Mr McManus doesn't joke. So I said fair enough but told him that the two years couldn't start until I was back riding. After all, I was only two months into my five months recovery for my spleen injury and I was enjoying myself too much. So we agreed to it there and then and I swear to God that I was off the booze for two years until the autumn of 2001. I suppose it was a case of mind over matter. I had to do it and there were plenty of people who thought I couldn't. But I did and I got the money at the end. JP dedicates a huge amount of time to his charity work and it was only right that I donated a chunk of the money to a charitable cause. Carol used to say to me that JP had been so generous to me because I was going out with her and he was trying to look after me. I don't know if that was true as JP has always been good to me, including long after my relationship with Carol ended.

But looking back, I don't think I ever had a problem with drink as such back then. After those nights on the lash Noel used to say to me that *'you must feel ill,'* but honestly I didn't. I never got sick from drinking. I always got up and went riding, did the work and felt fine. There was never a bother. These days I know what he meant because after a night's drinking in the later years I could hardly function. It can make me feel rubbish because I'm getting old. But back then it never bothered me. I could drink all night, wake the next morning, just get up and get on with it. I suppose that was part of the problem.

****

I went off the drink on September 12, 1999, and signed off with an almighty session that lasted a couple of days starting earlier in the week. I was back in the saddle two days later as a sober gent at Tramore Racecourse where I was due to ride for trainer Pat Hughes in the first race, on a horse ironically called Very Tempting. The two mile hurdle race went like a dream and I made all the running to win by five lengths. It was great to get back racing, and to have a winner on the first day back topped it all off. But the day was not without drama as I took a crashing fall later that afternoon off one of Noel's horses Anker Ring in my first race back over fences. I had been off the track for five long months and I feared the worst as I hit the deck in the two-mile beginners chase at Tramore that afternoon. I was annoyed at myself afterwards for putting myself in the firing line as Anker Ring's race had been run by the time he fell at the second last fence and I probably should have pulled him up. My back was sore afterwards and I decided not to ride for another week, to return in time for the Listowel meeting.

When I went back my form was better than ever and I was fortunate to ride almost 40 winners in the last few months of the year including a big price treble at Navan, and doubles at Thurles, Fairyhouse and Leopardstown. I had five winners in all at that Leopardstown Christmas meeting, but it was the double on Oa Baldixe and Sausalito Bay that really impressed.

Both were starting to stand out as outstanding chances for the upcoming Cheltenham Festival. Oa Baldixe had just hacked up in the Grade Three Monksfield Novice Hurdle at Navan and went into the Leopardstown race as the odds on favourite. He was expected to win, but the manner in which he cruised through the race was extremely impressive. Likewise, Sausalito Bay turned in a superb performance to land the Riverside Park Hotel Maiden Hurdle. Noel had just got Sausalito Bay into the yard as he had been running on the flat over in England for the past few years with trainer Ian Balding. I had been schooling him over the hurdles at home and knew he was quick and fluent but was delighted to notch up a win at the track. Sausalito Bay travelled very well throughout the race and, although he came off the bridle on the run-in, he stayed on readily to win by a few lengths. There and then it was decided that both Sausalito and Oa Baldixe would take their chances at Cheltenham, with Sausalito Bay running in the opening race of the Festival, the Supreme Novices Hurdle, and Oa Baldixe running in the Sun Alliance Hurdle the following day.

I also went into that Cheltenham with a real live chance of landing the Gold Cup for the first time. Willie Mullins had given me the ride on Florida Pearl after its jockey Richard Dunwoody retired and I thought he was the most impressive jumper in training. He had already won twice at the Cheltenham Festival, winning the Champion Bumper in 1997 and the Sun Alliance Chase in 1998. And the previous year he had finished third in the Gold Cup behind Mick Fitzgerald on See

More Business. Not surprisingly we were quietly confident that I could go better in the 2000 running of the big race.

Willie decided to give Florida Pearl two runs before having a crack at the Gold Cup and I rode him in a handicap chase at Leopardstown in January and then again at the same track in the Hennessy Cognac Gold Cup the following month. We won both races nicely, beating the future Grand National winner Amberleigh House ridden by my younger brother Philip by a short head in the first race when giving him over three stone. But his win in the Hennessy was particularly impressive. He simply ran the field into the ground over the three miles and I was able to win easing down by six lengths in the end from Dorans Pride with everything else in the field beaten by a distance.

Meanwhile, I was due to ride Sausalito Bay at Naas on the last Sunday of January for his final run before heading to the Cotswolds. But I went to a nightclub the night before tanked up on Red Bull and danced all night. I couldn't sleep and, instead, got dressed for racing and just sat down on the couch at home to kill time about 10 o'clock that morning. Next thing I remember was getting a phone call from Noel asking where I was. It was 20 minutes before race time and even though I jumped straight in the car, I was never going to make the first race. Jason Titley took the ride instead and thankfully won the novice hurdle easily at odds of 15/8. It wasn't an ideal start to my day and Noel was going mad as it was his only runner of that day's card. The stewards weren't too pleased either and I got reprimanded for failing to fulfil my riding engagement. There was no way I was going to tell them the real story, insisting that my car had broken down. It had been the third time I was done for failing to turn up for the first race after missing one at the Christmas meeting at Leopardstown in 1997 and then arriving too late at Listowel in September the following year. At least there was a bit of a silver lining that day at Naas as I went on to win on Fandango De Chassy for Tony Martin in the handicap chase in the afternoon.

****

As can always happen with me, the lead-up to Cheltenham was not without incident. I had gone out hunting and suffered a bad fall that should have ruled me out of that year's Festival. The fall was so bad that both myself and the horse suffered broken backs, yet we both continued on until the end of the hunt. I had gone for a big jump at a ditch but the horse, a hunter of mine called Carol's Choice, had caught his hind legs behind and shot me over the top landing me on my back, on a rock. I was in severe pain, but I just put it down to an old injury. A few weeks previously I had taken a rough fall at Naas and my back had been sore since, so I thought I had just inflamed that injury. I remember the Master of the hunt standing over me, giving out shite that I had taken a different course than I was meant to and I just told him to get away from me as I was in pain. When I got to my feet I put on a back brace to be safe and then I remounted and both myself and the horse continued on until the end of the hunt that evening.

That night I knew there was something more serious going on because the back pain wasn't letting up Wisely, I went down to the hospital. I went for tests, including a back scan and x-ray and when the doctor came to see me I was pacing up and down the room hoping that he wasn't going to rule me out of racing. He then asked me if I could bend down and touch my toes, which I did. It was painful, but I didn't let him know that and just leaned over and grabbed my feet.

The doctor left the room and a short time later he returned with a few of these trainee doctors in white coats and clip-

144

boards. He asked me to touch the toes again and as I did it he turned to his team and said:

'Now, he should not be able to do that'.

I was later told that the x-ray had shown that a wing on one of the bones on the base of my spine had snapped off in the fall. My back was effectively broken. According to the doctor, I shouldn't have been able to move off the bed, never mind bend over. Now he may have been exaggerating for dramatic effect, but it's true that jockeys have a much higher pain threshold than other people. It just comes with the territory, built up over time through wear and tear.

Anyway, since that injury I had suffered badly from haematomas. These were basically a collection of blood in pockets in the body, and they would sometimes show like dark reddish lumps through the skin. I had them for years and still do get them occasionally, but they rarely cause me any bother. This is all quite relevant when looking back at Cheltenham that year.

I had gone into that Cheltenham Festival with a good book of rides. On the first day I had Sausalito Bay which we thought had an outside squeeze in the first, the Supreme Novices. Another of Noel's horses, Frozen Groom, had an outstanding chance in the Arkle, having won the Baileys Irish Arkle at Leopardstown quite easily in January, and two other Meade-trained runners, Native Estates and Coq Hardi Diamond had outside chances of making the frame in the William Hill and the Ladbrokes Final Hurdle.

All the pre-race talk before the Supreme Novices was for the Irish 'Banker' of the week, a JP McManus horse called Youlneverwalkalone. The Christy Roche trained horse was unbeaten in four starts and was backed in to odds of just 5/4 to win the race for jockey Conor O'Dwyer. Other well-backed horses in the race included AP McCoy's mount, Rodock, and future three-time Gold Cup winner Best Mate.

I had gone out in Cheltenham town the night before racing and although I was off the drink, I was well up for a bit of craic. And after listening to endless chants and versions of the song Youlneverwalkalone in pubs like O'Neills in the town centre, I finished off the night in the early hours at the town's tiny but lively 21 Club. The next morning I was at the track early to ride out a couple of Noel's horses where I met a lot of the other jockeys and trainers. The empty stands are deathly quiet as you give your horses a spin and chat with the other lads about your chances that afternoon. It's the only real time you get to have those quiet chats because by race time the Cheltenham Racecourse can turn into a manic circus, where it's a case of survival of the meanest and fittest. As you walk the parade ring, punters and media encroach and hang on every word, trying to get an edge for the upcoming race.

The loudest cheer of the week is always the one that greets the start of the Supreme Novices' Hurdle. It marks the commencement of battle: Jockey versus jockey; trainer versus trainer; punter against bookmaker. My plan was to set Sausalito Bay off in front and hope that he stays as the others came at me up the hill. There was over two miles and eight hurdles ahead for the 15 runners, and I set a very fast pace. Conor O'Dwyer tracked me for most of the race on Youlneverwalkalone, but it was a complete outsider called Phardante Flyer who was causing most problems and passed me briefly on the back turn. Coming to the third last, a group of five had gone away from the rest and, while I used the chance to give Sausalito Bay a small breather, I got a big jump at the last hurdle to land in the lead.

But just then, disaster almost occurred. I suddenly got this piercing pain like a knife had just sliced my back. I was sure another jockey had caught me square across the back with the whip and the pain was unbearable. I could literally feel the wet blood on my silks, but I kept the head down and drove Sausalito Bay to the winning line. I gritted my teeth and battled though the pain, beating Jim Culloty on Best Mate by just under a length, with the favourite Youlneverwalkalone back in third. Just three lengths separated the first five horses home that day, but as I crossed the line I was wincing with pain. The haematoma on my back had burst and I couldn't let anyone touch me.

Back in the parade ring, the TV cameras were on Noel as he kissed the ground to welcome back his very first Cheltenham winner. I was delighted for him as I knew exactly what it had meant to him. Back in 1993 I had beaten Noel's horse Heist into second when I won the Bumper on Rhythm Section and he had been trying to get off the mark every year since. This was the very least Noel deserved for all his hard work over the years, but it was just a shame that I couldn't enjoy the moment with him. When I got back to the weigh room I knew I wouldn't be able to ride again that day. So I was stood down. It was a bitter-sweet moment. I had just won the first race of the 2000 Cheltenham Festival on a 14/1 shot for my boss but it was possibly my last race of the week. I had gone from ecstasy to agony in minutes.

I got changed and watched the rest of the day's racing on the TV screens, with particular attention to the horses I'd been booked to ride. Barry Geraghty took the ride on Frozen Groom in the Arkle, and was going very well and probably would have won only for falling at the third last when leading the race. Later that afternoon Coq Hardi Diamond was unlucky in the Ladbrokes Final. He was badly hampered when making his run and finished down the field, while Native Estates fell for Norman Williamson when well behind in the William Hill.

The pain was still pretty unbearable that night and on medical advice I opted out of racing on the Wednesday and decided to try and rest to get back in time for the Gold Cup on Thursday. I still thought Oa Baldixe had a great chance that day in the

Sun Alliance but it never figured for Barry Geraghty, finishing well back in the race won easily by Norman Williamson on the favourite Monsignor.

By Thursday, the swelling on my back had gone down and I was raring to go. I only had two rides booked for the day, with my hopes pinned on Florida Pearl in the big one. First up though I had a ride in the Triumph Hurdle for Noel on his horse Fable, who had won four times over hurdles and, despite a poor run on his last time out at Leopardstown, his owner Des Sharkey decided to let him take his chance. I felt comfortable enough in the saddle knowing that he was a long solid jumper that would get me around and give the back a fair workout before the Gold Cup. But unfortunately Fable had a nightmare in the Triumph Hurdle. They went off very quick as they often do in that race and we were outpaced from the start, trailing home nearer the rear than the winner, a French horse called Snow Drop for the Doumen team.

This is the Gold Cup that I still feel got away from me. On another day, in another running and with slightly different circumstances, Florida Pearl could have, and probably should have, won the race. The reigning champion See More Business would go off favourite for Mick Fitzgerald and trainer Paul Nicholls, but I was sure that we had the beating of them. Florida Pearl had been beaten into third behind the horse the previous year, but I just thought that 'The Pearl' had improved and shown his real class in the year since then. We went off as 9/2 joint second favourites alongside Looks Like Trouble, that I had won the Sun Alliance on in 1999, with McCoy's horse Gloria Victis next best in the betting, having drifted from 4/1 to 7/1 just before the off.

The Gold Cup was run over three and a quarter miles and 22 fences but I can't remember much of it. It all seemed to go by in a blur. I got Florida Pearl into a nice jumping rhythm at the rear of the field and, bar a slight mistake at the sixth fence, he was travelling well. Coming to the turn, I knew I had the favourite See More Business beaten as I passed him and Gloria Victis to lead from the third last, and I genuinely thought I had the race. But just as we climbed the hill, Florida started to send out distress signals and we were passed at the last by Richard Johnson riding Looks Like Trouble. I suppose in hindsight, Florida Pearl was at his very best over three miles and just didn't have it in the tank to stay that extra quarter mile. And, while you may get away with it at other tracks, you would never get away without the extra staying power up the Cheltenham hill. In the end, we were beaten by five lengths and just held off the fast-finishing Strong Promise for second. There is no shame finishing second in a Cheltenham Gold Cup, but I was desperately disappointed afterwards. I remember on the final drive for the line watching the arse of Looks Like Trouble and thinking *I could have been on him* but in truth I would never have gotten off Florida Pearl. He had the best form going into the race, was one of the biggest earners of my career, and I was glad Willie Mullins gave me the chance to ride him. I just wish it could have been a different result that day. But my disappointment was quickly put into perspective when I realised that Tony's horse Gloria Victis never made it back, after breaking his leg in a fall at the second last fence.

****

A few weeks later I had a nice winner at Aintree called Ross Moff for trainer Tony Martin, when we won the Barton and Guestier Handicap Hurdle. Charlie Swan had been riding Ross Moff and had finished third at the Coral Cup in Cheltenham, but Charlie was claimed to ride Darapour for his boss Aidan O'Brien in the race at Aintree and I got the leg up. After being squeezed on the turn, I hardly moved muscle on Ross Moff, who eased into the lead and won well despite coming under pressure from the favourite Frantic Tan in the final strides to the line. It was a nice winner to pick up and I won on him again next time out at Fairyhouse in the Power Gold Label Novice Hurdle. That was over £30,000 in prize money between the two runs.

But the real focus of that week was the return of Bobbyjo to the Grand National stage. Incredibly, it was my first time on him since our glorious day twelve months before. While I was out injured my brother Philip had ridden him three times and Adrian Maguire once, but he had never even made the frame. So his form was nothing like that of the previous year, but he still went off as third or fourth favourite to repeat the feat. But unfortunately, this time it just wasn't happening for him. He made a few mistakes which was very unlike him in the past and soon got outpaced. Bobbyjo did complete the race though, finishing back in 11th of the 40 runners. But the real story of that year's race was the success of Ruby Walsh on Papillon, trained by his father Ted. The Irish hadn't won the Aintree Grand National for 24 years until myself and Dad managed it, and then just a year later another Irish father and son team would repeat the act. It really was quite remarkable, but I wasn't a bit surprised. I had ridden Papillon at Fairyhouse that January and even though he was well beaten, you could tell he would love Aintree. He was slow and quirky and if he couldn't see a fence he had no interest in running at all. But then when he would see a fence he just sprung into action and suddenly got lively again. I just knew that Aintree would be right up his street and told Ruby that I thought he had a huge chance before the race.

I was delighted for the Walshs as they are a great Irish racing family.

Surviving a bad
mistake to cling on
to Michael Mor at
the final fence at
Tipperary in 2003

- Photos by CAROLINE NORRIS

Punching the air after winning the Supreme Novices' at Cheltenham on Sausalito Bay in 2000
INSET: Enjoying the moment with my boss and good friend Noel Meade

- Photos by TOM HONAN/INPHO

On Florida Pearl, finishing second in the 2000 Cheltenham Gold Cup behind Richard Johnson on Looks Like Trouble

BELOW: With the other four Irish jockeys to have won the Aintree Grand National since my win in 1999, Robbie Power (Silver Birch), Ruby Walsh (Papillon, Hedgehunter), Barry Geraghty (Montys Pass) and Niall Madden (Numbersixvalverde)

Saluting the crowd after winning the Grand National at Aintree in 1999
BELOW: Dad makes a triumphant return to Ratoath aboard Bobbyjo –
unfortunately I missed all the celebrations at home

Looking all over a winner aboard Harchibald (centre) when runner-up to Hardy Eustace in the 2005 Champion Hurdle at Cheltenham
BELOW: Finishing second again, this time to Brave Inca, at Punchestown the following month

Giving sister Nina a
well-deserved kiss
after she won the
2005 Fred Winter at
Cheltenham aboard
Dabiroun
RIGHT: Waving
the Tricolour at
Cheltenham after
winning the
Supreme
Novices' Hurdle on
Go Native in 2009

Taking off on Morceli, perhaps the best jumper I ever rode – pity Howard Johnson wouldn't let me keep him!

BELOW: Enjoying my Lexus win on Beef Or Salmon at Leopardstown in 2004

- Photo by MATT BROWNE/SPORTSFILE

The devastating moment Best Mate collapsed and died at Exeter. I could only watch helplessly as Henrietta Knight arrived at the scene
BELOW: Discussing tactics with Noel Meade before racing at Leopardstown

CHAPTER 13

My Time In The Sun

Two weeks later, the Walshs did it again to win the Irish Grand National at Fairyhouse, but this time with Commanche Court. Dad had two horses in the race that year. I rode Bobbyjo again, and my brother Philip was on Native Status. But the best days were behind both horses and we had to pull them up a long way before the finish. It was the last time I rode Bobbyjo at a racetrack. Philip had a few more rides on him without success and he was retired shortly afterwards.

****

A few weeks later I ended up in Lillies Bordello, one of Dublin's most exclusive nightclubs, with my friends Mick Foley and Niall Lord and his brother Adam. I went out for a smoke and Mick was talking to this big fella sucking on a cigar. After a bit of chit-chat, this guy was asking me all about racing and asking what it was like to win the Grand National and all. He was a nice fella and eventually I asked him, *'So what do you do for a living'.* He looked at me and said quietly, *'I play golf'.*

The other lads all had their heads in their hands. It turned out it was Darren Clarke but sure I hadn't a bull's notion who he was. I never watch other sports outside racing or hunting, and I don't read books or newspapers either. The lads were all embarrassed. Clarke may have been the best golfer in Europe at the time, but unless they started playing golf on horseback I had no interest. Now don't get me wrong. I have huge respect for everyone that excels in the sport or career they have chosen, but I simply didn't recognise him at all. I watched him win the British Open many years later and I thought to myself: *'He must think I'm some gobshite'.*

It wasn't the only memorable thing that happened that night. A few minutes later, Niall dragged me to one side and told me that someone famous was dying to meet me. He brought me over to the side of the club where former Irish soccer star and TV pundit Eamon Dunphy was sitting. As I got there Dunphy roared at the top of his voice:

'Paul Carberry, you are a fucking legend'.

And as if this wasn't loud enough, he turned to this stunning young girl beside him and shouted:

'You should get down on your knees and give this man a blow-job. Don't you realise you are in the presence of a real Irish legend.'

I had to get out of there... and no, I didn't avail of his kind offer.

****

I had three winners at the Fairyhouse Easter Festival in 2000, and finished the season with almost 90 winners, including late doubles at Downpatrick, Roscommon, Wexford and Navan.

After the brief summer break my career was suddenly out on ice through a nasty break of my own. The new season was to be cut short, with a combination of injury and then an outbreak of Foot And Mouth Disease taking out the best six months of the season.

That September 2000 I went to the festival in Listowel and started positively enough with a winner on Fearsome Factor for Michael Halford on the first day. But the next day disaster struck when I fell at the second last on Super Franky for Charles Byrnes in the Kerry National. I had come to that fence alongside David Casey on Scallybuck. We were both beaten horses, but Scallybuck jumped across me and forced me down. As I fell, my left leg cracked, and even though the scan later missed the hairline fracture, I knew it was broken.

My injury was just put down to ligament damage and while that would rule me out for a while, it meant that I could get passed fit a few weeks later when I was due to ride at Fairyhouse in a Maiden Hurdle on board Noel's classy Harbour Pilot. I had taken a few weeks off since the fall at Listowel and, even though I knew my leg still wasn't right, I didn't want to miss the ride. But the day before the race I made the mistake of going hunting and I could have ended up riding in a hearse rather than on the back of a racehorse. During the hunt I jumped a ditch too close to a tree and while I tried to protect my injured leg I hit the other one, leaving me with a dead leg in my 'good' one. With both legs now strapped up I decided it would be best if I just followed the afternoon hunt by car. Unfortunately, that proved to be even more dangerous. I was driving a hire car that day as my one was in the garage and when I overtook a truck on a country road a loose horse from the hunt came around the bend and tried to jump over my vehicle, smashing its hind legs through my windscreen and then somersaulting into the path of the oncoming truck. It was a devastating scene and I am still unsure how I came out of it without a scratch.

Despite the previous day's dramatic smash I went as planned to Fairyhouse, but shortly after I got there my luck was about to run out. Harbour Pilot had won twice on the flat and went off the short odds-on favourite to win the 30-runner hurdle race.

The horse had opened at 5/4 in the betting and was backed into 8/11 before the off, but our race was over almost as soon as it started when he slipped up on the flat. We were just about to come to the first hurdle where Harbour Pilot clipped the heels of the horses in front and hit the deck and rolled over my left side. This time there was no need for a scan to diagnose the problem because by the time the ambulance crew arrived the bone was sticking out of my leg. It had just snapped clean through and I was out of racing for four months.

I missed some of the best months in Irish racing and unfortunately by the time I was back ready to ride again Foot And Mouth had hit. The risks of disease meant the restriction of travel for livestock and humans. Racing was cancelled for two months from the start of February 2001, and resulted in the cancellation of that year's Cheltenham and Punchestown Festivals.

We were back racing in mid-April at Cork but it was a slow restart and after the Fairyhouse meeting the following week we had time to kick back and enjoy ourselves at a good friend Warren Ewing's Stag party over in Amsterdam. It was a wild weekend, but I was relatively fresh because I was still off the booze. Myself and Barry Geraghty flew back to Belfast Airport as we riding later that day at Sligo over in the west of the country.

It was an evening meeting and I managed to win the first race on a well-backed favourite called Class Society. But Barry was fairly bullish about his chances in the second race aboard the favourite, Beebeep, a horse trained by Francis Ennis. All weekend Barry had been using this catchphrase 'Not today Buddy...not today' in this fake American movie accent that he had picked up while riding over in the US a few weeks beforehand. The race was a two mile slog over hurdles in desperately heavy ground, with 16 horses in the race. I was aboard a Tony Martin horse called Finians Ivy. An outsider, Carnmore Cross, made most of the running before fading away as Barry took up the lead and went for home from the second last. As he passed tired horses, he thought he had the race wrapped up. I know he took a quick look over his right shoulder for any danger but couldn't see me coming on the other side. Another pal Greg Harford was standing at the last fence, and as Barry jumped it, he shouted *'Beebeep'* to Greg, almost saluting his impending win. But at that point I drew upsides and shouted, *'Not today Buddy...not today'* and raced to the line. His face was priceless. My horse won by six lengths and we had a good laugh about it after the race.

We often socialise with other jockeys. It's like any walk of life. They are the guys that I spend most time with when I'm not at home. You sometimes spend hours in a car with them, all day in and out of the weigh room, and then wind down with a drink at times when racing's finished. There would be plenty of overnight stays involved as well. They are also the guys you compete with on a daily basis, risking life and limb almost every half hour.

So when there is a gap in racing, we often go abroad together too. Over the past few years a good few of us would head off at least a couple of times a year. We have gone skiing a handful of times, although few will admit it to their trainer. We have had plenty of holidays in the sun in Spain as well but, of course, that's another story. There has been bungee-jumping into the sea in Ayia Napa in Cyprus and there have been trips to the U.S where we enjoyed some of our best times.

I've been lucky enough to go over to America quite a few times for racing, most recently on a couple of trips to ride Gordon Elliott horses at Saratoga. We have run Salford City over there twice, a horse owned by my friend Adam Lord, among others. But it was another trip to New York that I will never forget, as I almost ended up the city's slammer.

The trip was superb, even if it was a bit of a trek to get there. 'Freak', otherwise known as Seamus Durack had booked the trip and we went from Dublin to Gatwick in London, then on to Philadelphia and on down to JFK in New York. There was myself, Freak, Barry Geraghty, Ruby Walsh and James Nash. We were staying at the Hilton on Time Square and we went on a helicopter ride and ate at the famous restaurant Pier 17 with some of Dad's friends who were living over there. One night we were out on the town and as we arrived back there were three mounted police on horseback outside our hotel. Nash and Geraghty had arrived a couple of hours before us and Barry had ran under one of the horses, which pissed off the policeman on board. So when we arrived a couple of hours later they were in no mood for messing from some boozy Paddies. While Durack was chatting to them, I went behind and tied two of the horses' tails together. One of the cops spotted it and gave me a fair old slap across the face and told me to move quickly on or they'd take me downtown.

****

I was coming to the end of my two years off the drink and I still hadn't made my mind up whether I would go back on it or not. It hadn't really affected me that much at all. I missed it, but not as much as I thought I would. During the winter months I hardly thought about it at all to tell the truth. When the racing is full on, you just get your head down and keep your mind on the job. When it comes to the big meetings at Leopardstown, Fairyhouse or Punchestown it helps that you're not starting the day hungover and the same applies when you're away for the big festivals at Cheltenham or Aintree. But during the summer months I struggled with it at times. There just always seemed to be something on and most of the times it revolved around a few drinks. The racing would be poor with not much at stake and there was plenty of action around in social circles, whether it would be music or dance festivals or end-of-season award nights.

I had gone off the drink in September 1999 and the two years ended the day after the 9/11 attacks on the Twin Towers in New York in 2001. I remember I was riding at Galway and I won the Smirnoff Vodka Handicap Chase on a Michael Hourigan-trained horse called Rockholm Boy. Later on in the weighing room everyone was talking non-stop about the attacks in America the previous day. I can recall looking down and realising that I had been wearing a pair of Guinness-branded socks during the race. It was one of those lightbulb moments when I thought *'I've just won the Vodka Chase wearing Guinness socks... I think I better go back on the drink!'* And that was that. I went out that night and got absolutely thrashed.

I hit the drink hard that night and decided there and then to get out of the country and enjoy a few drinks without anyone passing judgement. I had earned the holiday after two years on the dry and decided that this was the best way to cope with it. I would go away, ease back on the drink, and make a decision later about whether to go off it for good or not. Apart from the money from Mr McManus, I had saved quite a bit in the meantime and was riding the best I had ever done. I rang my friend Paddy Lyons and we went to Spain, where I enjoyed the break and plenty of boozy nights on a week-long blow-out. We had only booked one-way flights out there and said that we would take each day at a time. Seven days later, with both of us ready to get back, we got a cab to the airport and booked seats on the next available flight home. But I still hadn't made up my mind whether I wanted to go teetotal again and when I came back to Ireland I stayed off the drink for a few weeks before hitting it even harder the following month. So it wasn't as if I just went straight back on the drink and was drinking for years afterwards. In reality, I'd drink when I felt like it and then go off it for a while. But gradually I got sucked into the regular sessions.

****

Later that year I took a couple of heavy falls and while I was out injured I got an interesting offer to open a new Sports Bar in Torrevieja in Spain. A guy called Fergus Kilcoyne , who was boss of the bars at Limerick Racecourse was opening his Pharaohs bar on the Cabo Roig strip and had invited myself, Barry Geraghty and his brother Ross over for the launch. For us, it was a nice little break for two nights with the bill for flights and hotel sorted. We were picked up at Alicante airport and treated very well for our time there. At the opening, I met a guy called Johnny Glennon who was a friend of a trainer I knew. I was out of racing with a broken arm and had plenty of time on my hands. So when Johnny asked if I wanted to stay an extra couple of days at his house, I jumped at the offer. I thought I had convinced Barry and Ross to stay over as well, but by the next morning they had both changed their minds and decided to head home. Johnny picked me up at the hotel and I went to his house nearby that he shared with his lovely wife Louise and two kids. It was only meant to be for a night or two, but I ended up staying 10 days. Those days went by in a complete blur and, in fairness, it was probably tough on them too. I was completely ripping it on the alcohol and Johnny still laughs that he was fit for a hospital bed by the time I got a flight back home.

I've gone back to Louise and Johnny's place many times since and have always had a ball. They've been very good to me through the years and I really appreciate their hospitality. Sometimes when I just needed to get away, or needed a break while I was sidelined through injury, they have always made me welcome and we've had some great laughs along the way. About five years ago they opened up a great boozer called The Portobello at Pinar De Campoverde in Alicante and it's been a huge success for them, attracting a mix of locals and tourists.

One week over there my phone got busted. But it wasn't just a case of losing use of the phone. Gone too were all my numbers for work and it left me in a bit of a hole. I needed a new SIM card from Ireland and, as I knew my mate Adam Lord was heading over to Marbella that week, I rang him and asked him to bring a SIM card over with him. Adam's parents had a beautiful house over there in a very exclusive gated community on a golf course. Now Marbella was over six hours' drive from Torrevieja but Johnny drove myself and his son Niall down for a couple of days and we stayed at Adam's place. Johnny still claims that he received three different speeding fines from Spanish cops on the journey down.

The Lords' villa was incredible. A very quiet community set on an expensive golf course. One of those nights on the sauce I decided that I wanted to have a spin on one of the golf buggies. There was one outside a nearby house and I used a teaspoon to start it up. Johnny's son Niall was my wingman and we drove across the open plan gardens and flowerbeds, causing complete mayhem. Next thing we could hear was a big coloured security guard shouting at us to stop the cart. He was over six foot and was waving a golf club so I just put the foot down. Golf buggies can't go very fast and it's even harder to steer when you have an angry security guard banging the roof with a golf club threatening to beat three shades of shite out of you. After crashing into two cars I eventually smashed into the side of a house and the security man had us cornered so I just held my hands up and agreed to walk back to the gates of the golf course with him. As we were marched to the gates I half expected a smack at the back of the head with the golf club he was waving. I don't know what he was planning to do with me, but once I reached the gate myself and Niall legged it and got away. The next day a complaint was made to Adam's parents, so I got out of Dodge and went back to Torrevieja. The parents were great about it, all things considered, but Adam was going mad at me for months.

Then again, Adam was no saint himself. When we were in Marbella we were standing outside a pub drinking and watching all the expensive cars going by. There was one annoying prick who kept passing by every 15 minutes in an open-top red Ferrari with white leather seats. He was about 60 years of age and kept smiling as he slowed down to pass the main strip. Adam says to us, *'I swear, if that eejit passes one more time, God help me, he won't be smiling'.* Just as he said it, the prick passed again and Adam lost it and threw a full pint over him and his car. There was murder. Cops were called and it took ages to sort it out.

Myself and Adam and his brother Niall Lord got into some crazy scrapes through the years. I've known the family for most of my life and the three of us were involved in the pony club and camps and then with the hunts together. Adam went on to work at Jim Bolger's yard when I was there, but I guess his six foot body was never going to cut it as a flat jockey.

A couple of years after causing the mayhem at the Lord house in Marbella, I was on the road again with the two boys. Niall was getting married and we'd arranged a stag party over to Ascot races. I sorted tickets to the course for all the lads and after racing we ended up back in London and headed straight for a strip club. The place was fairly dead and all the lads were just sitting around watching the girls dancing on stage. It was boring as shit on a stick, so I thought I'd liven it up a bit and get up and dance with the girls. But this big asshole doing DJ in the place pushed me off the stage and I fell against the corner of the speaker and sliced a four-inch gash into my back. As I lay there, with my back covered in blood, one of the lads Warren Ewing started telling the bouncers that he was a lawyer and that I was going to sue the place if they didn't ring an ambulance. The ambulance arrived straight away. Meanwhile, two of my friends started fighting and one hit the other and busted open his eye. So it ended up with two of us in the back of the ambulance and getting stitched in the local A&E ward.

****

I finished the year 2001 with some of my best months in racing, bagging 30 winners during November and December alone, including two doubles and a treble at Punchestown. The December treble was particularly memorable as Florida Pearl won the John Durkan Grade One when going off as the outsider in a four-runner field, and then I won on two Tony Martin horses, Linden's Lotto and Falcon Du Coteau for a 80/1 three-timer. There were other highlights, including a nice double at the Leopardstown Christmas meeting and winning a valuable hurdle race by a distance at Navan on Limestone Lad. But for now, most of my thoughts were towards the upcoming Cheltenham Festival. After the injuries of the previous year, as well as the cancellations through foot-and-mouth disease, this was one festival that I didn't want to miss.

CHAPTER 14

From Champ To Chump In The Saddle

All jockeys want to make the Cheltenham Festival and it had been two long years since I had been there. After the forced cancellation of the 2001 meeting I was determined not to rule myself out on this occasion. So I took a break from hunting in the weeks leading up to the 2002 festival. Noel had a decent string going over and we thought we had real chances of landing the Sun Alliance Chase with Harbour Pilot and the Cathcart Cup with Arctic Copper. Harbour Pilot had been a fairly useful hurdler but had taken to chasing like a dream the previous year. As he was a fine big jumper making very few mistakes, we were confident of a clear round. I had also been asked to ride Marlborough in the Gold Cup for Nicky Henderson and thought it had a live chance of making the frame.

The Tuesday at Cheltenham started with a dream result for Irish punters. The well-backed favourite Like-A-Butterfly had won the Supreme Novices for Charlie Swan and the bookies were in a sweat. I finished seventh on Scottish Memories, not a bad effort on a huge outsider considering I was squeezed into the bend on the turn for home. I didn't have a ride in the next race, the Arkle, but watched in the weigh room as Barry Geraghty won on Jessica Harrington's future star Moscow Flyer. It was a dream start for Irish punters and the Cheltenham roar was rocking the stands.

I was riding a Dermot Weld horse Ansar in the big race of the day, the Smurfit Champion Hurdle, but all the pre-race talk had been about the favourite Istabraq. The three-time Champion Hurdle winner had over 20 hurdle wins under his belt and I've no doubt that he would have won a fourth Champion Hurdle for JP McManus the previous year had the festival gone ahead. But a year older, his best was behind him and many believed that it would be his last race. He went off as favourite but pulled up after the second hurdle, and was retired straight afterwards. I led for most of the race but faded badly up the hill, finishing back in sixth.

But I had my first winner of the meeting in the next, the William Hill Chase over three miles. I was riding Frenchman's Creek off a low weight for trainer Hughie Morrison and was told to keep him fairly handy. But, with 23 runners all heading down to the first, I decided to stick him out the back and have a proper look at how the race was being run. On the final circuit I starting picking off the tired horses and was still on the bridle when I challenged the leader Carbury Cross on the run-in. We hit the third last fence and also hit the last one, but managed to win with ease. It was a cheeky ride, and there were plenty of happy punters in the parade ring that had taken the 8/1 odds.

It's funny because I remember coming back in on Frenchman's Creek past the vast stands and waving punters and thinking that it would be nice to just be at Cheltenham as a spectator. I wished I could be there as a punter, enjoying the racing and having the craic. I remember looking into the crowd and wishing I could be in among them, off duty and, for once, simply enjoying a few drinks while lapping up the atmosphere. They say beware what you wish for. Little did I know that by the end of the next day's racing, injury would force me to the sidelines and I would end up watching Gold Cup day from the stands.

The following day had started quietly enough. I finished well back in the Sun Alliance Hurdle and in the Queen Mother on Thari and Knife Edge, while another Noel Meade horse, Fnan, was never in contention in the Coral. But I was looking forward to the ride in the Sun Alliance Chase on Harbour Pilot, winner of three of his last four races over the big jumps. His win at Leopardstown that February had been particularly impressive. He had easily won the Grade One Dr PJ Moriarty Novice Chase, destroying a decent line-up including Truckers Tavern and Christy Roche's highly-rated Youlneverwalkalone. But the big race at Cheltenham just never went to plan, with only six horses finishing out of the 19 starters and I wasn't one of them. But even worse from my point of view was that I picked up an injury that ruled me out of the rest of the week. Harbour Pilot had been travelling quite well in the race but unseated me at the 12th and as I put my hands out to break my fall, Norman Williamson's horse Colonel Braxton stood on my right hand, breaking a bone. I had hoped that it would be ok, but by the next morning it had swollen up and when I stood in the hotel bathroom unable to lift my toothbrush to my mouth I knew I wouldn't be able to ride. I rang Noel and then Nicky Henderson to give the news, but Nicky was more upbeat than I was. *'Why don't you ride anyway, even with one hand you would still be better than most of the other lot'* he had said. But my hand was in agony and I knew my festival was over. So after a trip to the hospital I went to the racecourse as a spectator. Now, there in the vast crowd, it didn't seem as enjoyable as I had expected it to be. I guess that no matter how much craic there was to enjoy, no matter how much atmosphere there was to soak in, nothing, absolutely nothing beats being in the saddle.

While I stood in the stands watching Best Mate win his first Gold Cup, with Ruby Walsh on Commanche Court in second and Marlborough back in fourth, and then watched Arctic

165

Copper dump Barry off his back at the first fence in the Cathcart, I thought that it may be best to get away for a while for a few days in the sun. The next day, as I got off the plane to lashing rain at Dublin Airport on the Friday afternoon, my mind was made up. I rang jockey Seamus Durack and Ronan O' Dwyer and we got flights out to Marbella to stay at my friend Adam Lord's apartment. Ronan, who is now training horses, was riding at the time and had just broken his shoulder, while Seamus had smashed his leg. So the three of us were well suited. We were some sight going around Marbella, with my arm in a sling, Seamus on crutches and Ronan's arm in a cast. After a few stiff drinks we would hobble along the beachfront and any time someone stared at us we would take turns shouting, *'Whatever you do, don't fly Air France!'*

I came back from Spain the following Saturday and Bobbyjo's owner Bobby Burke had arranged a helicopter to pick me up and take me directly to Mountbellew where they were unveiling a life-size sculpture in the centre of the town to honour their hero horse. Bobby had commissioned and paid for the statue and I guess the helicopter was their way of making sure I made it over for the event, where myself and Dad stood side by side to mark the unique occasion. I still had my arm in a sling but we were treated like royalty. I have to say the Burkes have always been good to my family. The statue still stands in the centre of Mountbellew for everyone to see. I think most of the town had backed the horse during its two National wins and many felt that it had given the entire area a genuine lift.

****

I got back racing the week before Aintree but had very few real chances for a winner, although Lord York came close when second to Dark 'n' Sharp in the Martell Red Rum Handicap

Chase. That year I was riding Ad Hoc in the Grand National for Paul Nicholls but we were brought down at the fourth last when still in with a good shout. We had gone off as the joint second favourites behind AP's horse, Blowing Wind. Despite a couple of mistakes, Ad Hoc was back travelling well for me before turning in and I thought we were going well enough on the heels of the leaders. But there was carnage at the 27th fence as Timmy Murphy fell on Davids Lad and, failing to avoid him, we were taken out. A loose horse had been causing problems and two others, Spot Thedifference and Djeddah, went at that fence too. Jim Culloty went on to win the race on Bindaree, with What's Up Boys in second and Blowing Wind third. It was another near miss for me but you never know what may or may not have happened had we stayed on our feet.

While Aintree proved to be a week to forget, it was that year's Punchestown Festival that provided my highlight of the year, with five winners and almost €120,000 in prize money. I had four winners for Noel that week, and we opened up with two Grade One wins on the Tuesday with Strong Run winning the BMW Chase, and we made it a big-race double with Scottish Memories in the Evening Herald Novices Hurdle later. Old Opry won the novice hurdle at big odds the following day and then I had another double on the Thursday, winning the handicap hurdle on Moratorium before landing the Stayers' Hurdle on Limestone Lad for James Bowe. I had four winners at Fairyhouse as well, but I had chosen the wrong Noel Meade horse in the Irish Grand National when Ross Geraghty won on Noel's other horse The Bunny Boiler. I had decided to stay on Arctic Copper, owned by a syndicate of Irish politicians, but he could only manage fourth. However, it was a great training performance by Noel and I was delighted for him.

****

They say that a pat on the back is only inches away from a kick in the arse and I know exactly how that feels after a very profitable April, in which I had 13 winners. But that May meeting at Kilbeggan turned into a real nightmare as I completely fucked up a race for Noel, and ended up getting hammered by the stewards and banned from riding for seven days.

I hadn't been riding for over a week after taking a rough fall off a Paul Nolan horse called Quality First at Navan eight days beforehand. I was looking forward to getting back in the saddle, but Kilbeggan hadn't exactly been too kind to me through the years. I often joke that I seem to leave that track in the back of an ambulance more times than in my own car. And that day, I could have left in the back of an ambulance all right. But it wouldn't have been after a fall off one of my rides. More likely, it would have been after being lynched by a crowd of punters baying for my blood.

It was a Monday evening meeting and I had a poor start, after pulling up on Killargue Star, a horse trained by Gerard Stack in the three mile novice hurdle. I was third on another Gerard Stack horse, Plettenburg Bay, in the next hurdle race and had high hopes of bagging a winner in the following race. I had gone that night to Kilbeggan to ride a nice big grey horse called Heart Midoltian for Noel in a novice hurdle over two miles and three furlongs. He was a nice quick jumper and was well fancied after winning for me at Navan the previous week and was backed in to odds of 8/13 for the Kilbeggan race.

There were 15 runners in the race and two outsiders, Better Than You and Little Miss Rosie had cut out the pace. I just sat in behind in about fifth or sixth for most of the race and was absolutely cruising when I took up the lead at the second last hurdle. Without pushing my horse at all, we soon went clear and I was able to ease down the favourite after the last. I trotted up to the winning post but just as I crossed the line, another horse came past me. I hadn't a clue who it was or where he came from. To be honest, I wasn't even too sure if he had actually crossed the line before I did and a photo finish was called. But I knew one thing for sure; I had made an absolute bollocks of it.

Usually in those situations where you've gone clear in a race, it is all very quiet and muted. Sometimes, you have a quick look at a big screen if there is one, just to make sure there is no one coming back at you on the run-in. If there isn't a prominent big screen, you would tend to listen to the race commentary by Des Scahill or whoever is there on the day. But either way, the crowd would generally react and there would be an almighty roar that would let you know that something was coming behind. Yes, I should have looked over my shoulder or between my legs. The truth is, everything combined to make an absolute shocker that day. It was, as they say, the perfect storm.

First of all, I hold my hands up and say that I made a stupid mistake. I got caught napping and got chinned on the line. I hadn't stopped the horse, but I had stopped pushing the horse to the line, and for that there is no escape. The rules of racing say that you must continue to ride your horse to the finishing line regardless of how far you are in front. But to this day, I am still a bit pissed off with the jockey on the other horse. During a race, if I see someone dropping their hands and easing down when I'm coming up behind I will always shout at them to 'keep riding, keep driving, I'm coming behind you'. That's just the way it is, because you don't want to see a jockey getting grief from the crowd and then hammered by the stewards. I've done it loads of times during finishes of races. Admittedly though, it's usually when you're in fourth or fifth and the lads in front ease down. It rarely happens to the horse in front.

But on that occasion, a young claiming jockey was riding High Tower, a 5/1 shot for trainer Michael O'Brien. He saw his chance of a winner and he took it. Of course, there is another way of looking at it: that he was an absolute genius to snatch a winner from the jaws of defeat. He took a winner that was toasted by his backers at the track and in the betting shops. But it wasn't toasted inside the weigh room. A couple of the other lads later asked the young jockey why he hadn't given me a shout and I was told that he said *'Because he wouldn't have done it for me'*. But that's just bullshit. Anyone who knows me knows exactly what I would have done, but this young lad clearly didn't know me. I would always shout to other boys to keep riding if they drop their hands too early. If you do someone a favour in racing, they will always do one back for you. That's just the way it has always been. It's a tight group and you would be riding against the same guys hundreds of times each season. But he chose not to do me a favour, and while I don't hold it against him, I don't think he's riding too many winners these days.

Meanwhile, things were getting nasty outside on the track and I was subjected to a fair amount of abuse as I led the Heart Midoltian back in. Opinions are like arseholes: everybody's got one. And, unfortunately that day, the punters chose to share them with me.

You see this is the crunch of the matter. The race went to a photograph and if my horse's nose had been down at the right time and I won the race, I probably wouldn't even be discussing it here in the book. But that's racing; it can all come down to a short head in a photo. You are either a hero or a bollocks. That short head is the difference between cocky lunacy and gross stupidity.

As I entered the parade ring I saw my trainer Noel Meade and I knew he wouldn't be happy, but I couldn't help being distracted by the large group of angry punters surrounding the area marked for '2nd Place'. A couple of other jockeys who hadn't been riding in the race came out to escort me back. Ruby Walsh and Barry Cash had been watching the race on the TV screen in the weigh room and knew that things could turn nasty. In fairness to them, they came out and stood each side as I dismounted and made my way back inside. It was a small gesture but I really appreciated it. I don't think people realise how close jockeys are as a group. Some of us ride out together, and travel together to race meetings. Others you would only see in the weigh room or down at the starting line. When the tapes go up, you will do all you can to beat them and come out on top. You travel at full speed over fences and hurdles, hoping that they will have a nightmare, and that you will have a dream run. You risk life and limb together, while all the time doing anything you can to have your head in front at the finishing line. But once back inside the weigh room, you laugh and joke and just move on to the next race. They are my friends and colleagues, and we will always stand up for each other.

It had been a bad day at the office. You just have to pick yourself up and get on with it. Fortunately, those type of incidents are rare but they do get under your skin. It's not just dealing with the owners and trainers, it's the punters that really affect you. I have never stopped a horse, but when horrible things happen like that time at Kilbeggan, you almost feel like you have to clear your name. You feel like you have to over-compensate and ride a different style, in fear that a similar mistake would prove unbearable. Thankfully, there were no repercussions from the owners. I kept the ride on Heart Midoltian, and was able to get him home in front at Cork a couple of months later. But it wasn't the proudest chapter in my riding career.

****

I finished the season as champion jockey for the first time, with 109 winners, my best result in racing. It's funny though, because winning the title was never my number one priority. Yes, of course, it was nice to receive the award. And I suppose it means that you can't be too bad at your job. But, in all honesty, if I had the choice I would always take 150 winners a season and finish third or fourth or even 10th in the jockeys' table. I wouldn't be one to keep an eye on the championship table and stress myself over where I was placed. For me, it has always been about racing and jumping and finishing the best that you possibly can. It was about being good at what I do and racking up winners. Riding winners, that is all it has ever been about, and I believe that is what it should be for every young jockey. I never had too much time for jockeys that hammer a horse just to try and improve their finishing position from sixth to fifth, or to get past the fourth placed horse either. I will rarely slap a horse just to try and make a place when the race has already been lost. Punters may not like to hear that, but I will put it another way; when I am on a horse I will do 100 per cent of everything in my power to get that horse to win, whether it is odds on or a 50/1 outsider. There is no such thing as a no-hoper. But I don't agree with lashing a horse out of it just to make a place. I don't care about coming fourth, third or second. I never did. It's always about winning and always will be. And if a race has already been lost, what is the point in over-stretching a horse when he may well come out and win for you the next day? There is always the next day.

I never set out to be champion jockey as such. I just saw it as a consequence of riding a lot of winners. Steering 109 horses to victory and bagging over €2 million in prize money was not a bad season's work. Charlie Swan was champion jockey nine times in the '90s, and had the pick of the rides. I was never going to get near to him in my first few years as a pro. Going to England meant figuring in the race for the jockeys' championship was not an option. When I came back from my time in England, Charlie had retired and Ruby Walsh was champion. So it was nice to finally pass the winning post in front in what was my first full season injury-free. Noel was champion trainer that year as well, regaining his title after Willie Mullins had finished as top trainer the previous season. Willie had won the title with Ruby Walsh as top jockey. But now Noel was back top, and would hold that spot for many seasons to come. So I was happy for Noel, as it meant that we were working well as a partnership. When I came back from England I told him I was going to give everything to racing. He told me that if I came back I would be champion jockey the following year. That didn't happen because of my list of injuries, but just one year later, here I was as Ireland's champion jockey. Dad had been champion jockey four times, so it was nice to emulate him as well. I guess it was coming full circle. Growing up, my only ambition in racing was to win the Grand National at Aintree. I had done that. And now I had become champion jockey in Ireland.

It was also a big help with the bills. My cut of the prize money meant that I was comfortable with my finances too. I had invested some money in a few houses and had bought an old farm with 40 acres which I hoped to rebuild. At the time I was keeping a couple of hunter horses there on the land while I got myself sorted. There was 10 grand coming out of my account in mortgage payments every month. When you got broke up and were out of racing for three months, you had to find that money from somewhere. At the time The Turf Club contributed over €440 a week to tide you over while you were out injured. That has been doubled since, but it was tough to get by on it back then. I don't think people outside racing understand that unless you are on a massive retainer with a big trainer, you get nothing if you are unable to race. Your earnings come out of prize money; if you are not racing, you are not earning. I think some people think that top jockeys earn millions, but in truth, we earn in a year what some professional soccer players earn each week. And of course, their wages don't stop when they pick up an injury. That's why I was forever asking Noel about securing a financial retainer from his main owners because when you get broke up, you end up broke. And there's no such thing as insurance either. Because of the high risks involved, no insurance company will touch us. I've had bad breaks through the years, and sometimes your main concern as you are being taken away by ambulance is not the pain, but the lost wages. How long will I be out for this time? How am I going to manage to pay the bills?

CHAPTER 15

Riding Harchibald
Takes Real Dedication

It was around this time that Noel got Harchibald into the yard. Sometimes a jockey is good enough to be linked to a great horse. Barry Geraghty had Moscow Flyer and Ruby had Kauto Star, Jim Culloty had Best Mate, and my dad had L'Escargot. Now I'm not saying Harchibald is like any of these, he didn't achieve the same success at Cheltenham and he wouldn't have won the type of races they did, but for me Harchibald will always be different. You see, that's just the point. Harchibald *wasn't* like any other horse.

It was a golden time for hurdlers and the Champion Hurdle at Cheltenham was *the* race of the year. The quality of fields in the years 2004 and 2005 were exceptional, mostly led in the betting market by Irish runners. This made for great races and the racing fans responded to them.

Harchibald deserved to be a champion hurdler and never in my riding career have I been asked more about the way I rode a horse or asked by punters to speculate what would have happened had I ridden him differently. And unfortunately, bar the time when I mistook the finishing line on Sallie's Girl, never have I had to put up with so much abuse after a race. But that's racing, you take the rough with the smooth. Of course Bobbyjo will always be my number one moment in racing because of the connection with Dad and all, but outside that, Harchibald probably gave me the most thrills.

He had been bought by Des Sharkey near the end of 2002 from France where he had some nice enough form. He had won three races over there on the flat over a mile two furlongs, and a mile four furlongs.

I schooled him in Noel's yard straight away and we knew that we had a good horse. He jumped really well, took off like an airplane and did everything right. We were very positive about his future prospects.

We ran him first at Fairyhouse on a Saturday meeting that December 2002 and word had obviously got out that we thought he was a good thing because he started at odds of 3/1 and was backed at the track so we went off as 9/4 favourite. It was a valuable enough 30-runner maiden hurdle for three year olds over two miles on soft ground, a surface which wouldn't show him at his best. He was always best on firmer good ground so this would provide a stiff enough first test.

That morning as I arrived at the track Noel met me as I was going in. After a quick chat he said to me: *'There's an awful smell of drink off you. If you have any chewing gums you should take them'.* He knew I'd been on the lash the night before as it was the lads' night out for a few Christmas drinks and I'd had a late one. He wasn't exactly delighted, but I got the gum and got on with it.

The race was hot enough. Ulysees had started off joint favourite that morning in the betting shops but drifted from 3/1 to 6/1 by the time the race started. Obviously the horse wasn't right and he never really figured in the race. Other fancied runners included the decent Mutineer for Dessie Hughes and Hidden Genius, who had Shay Barry on board.

I hid Harchibald in at the back at the start and I almost never made it past the second, where the horse made a bad mistake as you go away from the stands. He stepped at it and nearly threw me off. My whole body was on one side but I managed to get back in and stay on. It was nearly a disaster but from then on he travelled very well and I moved to about 10th place when we reached four hurdles from the finish. There was plenty of horse under me and he was still on the bridle passing tired horses. I closed up and went to join the leaders at the last and he stayed on nicely to win comfortably enough in the end.

Anybody who has ever seen Harchibald run knows that he's a quirky character to say the least. He doesn't like being in front too long which can make it tough to win big races at times. But you just have to keep him in there and get his head in front at the right time, which is usually just a few yards from the line. And this can lead to all kinds of sweating from punters and bookies too.

This was his first time to have been ridden on a track over here and we knew there was plenty more to come from him.

Later that day in Fairyhouse I completed a double for Noel on Rosaker at odds on, and nearly slipped up as an outsider came at me on the run-in. I lost my whip as I went for the line but just about held on by a head.

I also had two good second placed horses for Noel, first on 8/1 shot Saddlers' Mark and then on Nomadic at odds of 9/1, but was a fair distance on both occasions behind the hot favourites Be My Belle and Bust Out, both ridden by Barry Geraghty. I then finished off with a second on dad's horse Merulana in the last. All in all, it was a good day at the office, with two winners, three second places and a third, but the real star of the day was Harchibald. And it meant that Noel was happy enough, despite my ragged appearance earlier in the day. Who knows what he'd have been like if things had gone wrong that day.

For Harchibald it was an impressive start but it would be a

number of months until he again showed the kind of class that would make him a Champion Hurdle contender in the future.

****

I had plenty to look forward to riding in the 2003 Cheltenham Festival. And although I came away from that week without a winner, I was involved in the shake-up in plenty of the big races. Close but no cigar I suppose. I thought I had a real chance in the Arkle on Adamant Approach for Willie Mullins. I had finished a distance behind him at Punchestown on his last race when Ruby Walsh was in the saddle and I was on Nomadic. For Cheltenham, Ruby had been claimed by Paul Nicholls to ride his future Queen Mother champion Azertyuiop that had won nine of his 13 starts. So I got the nod for Adamant Approach but the race was over almost before it began, as he dived and took a tumble at the second fence.

Having had three cracks at the Gold Cup, Florida Pearl was given a chance in the Queen Mother Champion Chase over the shorter two mile trip the following day. But he always struggled and finished well back in the race won by Moscow Flyer. On the Thursday, I got a much better tune from Harbour Pilot in the Gold Cup. Best Mate was the short-priced favourite to retain his crown, with all the Irish piling on Beef Or Salmon, which went off next best in the betting. We were complete outsiders that day at odds of 40/1 but Harbour Pilot jumped well and we managed to snatch third on the line without ever getting near the winner Best Mate and the second-placed Truckers Tavern. Beef Or Salmon fell heavily with Timmy Murphy at the third fence that day and I truly believe that fall stopped the horse ever winning at the Cheltenham track in the future.

Limestone Lad was well fancied in the Stayers Hurdle.

Limestone Lad was trained by James Bowe and was a great horse for the big stage. We won four races with him that season, including three Group Twos and the Christmas Hurdle at Leopardstown. So the form was rock solid going into Cheltenham. We went off as the joint favourite alongside reigning champion Baracouda for the father and son Doumen team. As usual, the instructions were to set off on the three miles out in front on Limestone. As his best form had been on heavy and soft ground, the good ground that day wouldn't have been the best for such a dour stayer. We led for almost the entire race until just before the last hurdle and eventually finished third, five lengths off winner Baracouda with Iris's Gift in second. Limestone Lad never ran again because of tendon trouble.

****

Harchibald had endured a few poor runs on bad ground through that previous winter, including a hammering by Mutineer when coming home second last in a two mile hurdle at Punchestown in January, and I suppose some were starting to doubt his ability. But we were still only getting used to him and perhaps he was being ridden too handy in those races. It took us a while to get the key to him, that he had to be dropped in behind, and we also knew that he'd improve on faster ground. I just don't think he really stayed a stiff two miles. So after a while I realised that if you could just sit on him and take it easy over a slow first two furlongs, then he has a chance to stay on and see out the trip. When the ground improved he ran a good race in a novice event at Aintree in April. That race was won by an outsider, Le Duc for Paul Nicholls with Ruby Walsh on board, but Harchibald was just a few lengths off the winner, with the future Arkle Chase winner and Champion Chase runner-up Well Chief just ahead.

That year again in the Grand National I had the ride on Ad Hoc for trainer Paul Nicholls. Ad Hoc had been travelling so well when he was brought down in the previous year's National that I thought he had a real chance. I hadn't ridden him since as Ruby Walsh was now going full-time with Nicholls and had the pick of his horses. Nicholls had five runners in the 40-strong field and Ruby opted for the favourite Shotgun Willy, but neither of us had any luck in the race as I was unseated at the halfway point and Ruby pulled up shortly afterwards. My good mate Barry Geraghty had his moment of National glory that year when he rode Monty's Pass to victory for Cork trainer Jimmy Mangan. That horse had been backed in from 40/1 to 16/1 on the day of the race so there were plenty of happy punters at the track, and it was nice to see another Irish horse manage to win it. It was the third Irish trained horse in five years to manage it.

By the time it came around to the Punchestown Festival four weeks later, we were quietly confident of getting a nice run from Harchibald. Unfortunately, I was off the track through injury and it would be with Barry Geraghty on board. Harchibald won easily enough, beating Master Papa by one and a half lengths in a juvenile hurdle.

Meanwhile, things were going very well for me and Noel at pretty much every track. Our partnership was rock solid and his yard was on fire. We had doubles at Naas, Kilbeggan and Limerick, and doubles two days running at the April Fairyhouse meeting. I was also getting offers of good rides from other top trainers and had six winners for Michael Hourigan in that April alone. James Bowe was also very good to me and I enjoyed several wins on his top two horses, Limestone Lad and Solerina. I won four times that season on both Limestone Lad and on Solerina, with the highlight for the latter being the Grade One win in the Deloitte Novice Hurdle at Leopardstown, where we beat future Champion Hurdler Hardy Eustace. But both horses accumulated huge prize money that year. So I managed to retain the jockeys championship, finishing the 2002/2003 season with 106 winners, while Noel Meade was once again champion trainer. It proved that the previous year was no flash in the pan. I was now two-times Irish Champion Jockey and I was letting my racing do my talking.

****

Harchibald only ran three times in the 2003/04 season, finishing unplaced at Tipperary before winning well at Leopardstown when favourite at the end of February. Going off at 100/30, he gave King Carew a five length beating. Tuppenny Cody had gone off second favourite and had tried to make all, but I was always going to catch him and I landed in the lead when Tuppenny Cody came down at the last to leave us clear and I passed the post easing down. We knew we had a proper horse on our hands now.

People were starting to talk about Harchibald as a future champion hurdler the following year but, for now, we were looking at the Vincent O'Brien County Hurdle and we went into that Cheltenham Festival the day after St Patrick's Day in 2004 full of hope.

With two miles and a furlong ahead of us and almost £40,000 at stake, the County Hurdle is a fair prize and that year we went off as 7/1 joint favourites, with another 22 horses in the race. Ruby Walsh was riding the other joint favourite, Sporazene, for Paul Nicholls and a Willie Mullins horse Adamant Approach was well fancied too. Everything seemed to be going to plan and I was tucked in behind on Harchibald as outsiders Benbyas and Copeland set the pace.

During the week's racing I'd dropped a few of Noel's horses in behind and they never improved from where they were. So the instructions from Noel before the race were very firm: *'I was not to leave him too far back and I was to ride him more positively from the start'*. So I did that, and he travelled and jumped well.

Harchibald hit the fourth last but I wasn't too worried. I thought there was plenty left in the tank and a lot more racing to be done. He continued to travel well down the hill and turned with loads in hand. I was going well and sent him into the lead after the second last but now I believe it was too early. Being in front with the Cheltenham hill ahead didn't suit Harchibald and instead of hacking up I was suddenly pushing him. When we hit the last hurdle we were at one pace and beaten and ended up back in fifth place, although less than three lengths off the winner Sporazene. But I still got some grief off punters coming back in, as we had looked like we were going a lot better than we were.

I came away from that race knowing for sure that Harchibald would have to be held longer and that the extra furlong was just too far at any kind of pace. I knew I had got there too soon and I thought, *'well I won't be doing that again'.*

That was the year that Hardy Eustace won his first Champion Hurdle for Conor O'Dwyer and Dessie Hughes. Hardy Eustace had not been fancied despite winning the Sun Alliance Novices' Hurdle at Cheltenham the previous year. He went off at a massive 33/1 that day and won well, beating favourite Rooster Booster and Dickie Johnson by five lengths, with Intersky Falcon back in third. A year later it would be champion Hardy that broke our hearts in the 2005 Champion Hurdle.

****

Harchibald would get his first taste of competing against the very best hurdlers a month later when he would take on both Hardy Eustace and Rooster Booster, the Champion Hurdle first and second, at the Emo Oil Irish Champion Hurdle at the Punchestown Festival. Despite winning at Cheltenham six weeks earlier, Hardy did not go off favourite as it was still seen by many as somewhat of a fluke result. The English raider Rooster Booster went off the 13/8 favourite, with Hardy second best in the betting and Harchibald a 12/1 outsider. Hardy Eustace won the race, gamely keeping his head in front of Rooster Booster just like he had at Cheltenham. I ended up fourth on Harchibald close up and thought it was a good result in a class field. It was a fair end to the season and we held high hopes for the year ahead.

That new 2004/2005 season began at Tipperary in October, where we finished way behind odds-on shot Solerina, but we weren't too bothered as the ground was awful that day and we just wanted to give him a spin because he wasn't fully fit after the summer break. But the following month, Harchibald went on to win two valuable hurdles, stamping his credentials as a real competitor for the Champion Hurdle crown the following year.

First he saw off title contenders Back In Front and Macs Joy to take the €21,000 prize at Punchestown in mid November. It had been seen as a straight match between the top two in the market, as Hardy Eustace was still off the track since the summer break and may have had a slight injury. Harchibald went off that day as a 10/1 outsider. But before we left the parade ring Noel said to me that I wasn't to mind the other two and that we would win that day if we just ran our race. True enough, when I switched him inside after the last, he took the lead on the run-in and, as the other two boys were fighting it out, we just whizzed past them and won handily at the post.

Next up was a crack at the Fighting Fifth Hurdle at Newcastle in England two weeks later. It was good ground that day and we believed he had a really good chance of landing the £43,500 prize because he was absolutely flying at home. Anyway, as always, things didn't exactly start off to plan.

Noel had me booked on the 7.20am flight from Dublin. But I went out the night before and had a right few drinks. I ended up back at a friend's house and stayed up all night. I remember looking at my watch at six o'clock and thinking I'd have to leave and go straight to the airport. But somehow I fell asleep instead and was woken up by a phone call from Noel. He said *'where are you?'*. I said I was still in bed, obviously not saying anything about the night (and morning) before. He said his partner Gillian had rang saying she was about to board the plane and had been looking for *'Dedication'* but there was no sign.

'Dedication' was a nickname Noel had given me some years beforehand. We had been at the National Hunt Awards night for the 2002/2003 season and I was leading Irish jockey for the second year. Noel was up on stage receiving his award for being top trainer for the third year in a row. Brian Gleeson from RTÉ was interviewing him for the audience and when he asked Noel what he thought had made me such a good jockey I jumped to my feet and roared *'Dedication!'* at the top of my voice. It was a good laugh and so the name has stuck for a good while since. Some of the older jockeys, especially in England, still call me Alice but at home now it was Dedication.

Anyway, I was in bits and had to think quickly about getting over to Newcastle for the big race or Noel would kill me. I rang Emer Hannon, a travel agent from Navan who was looking after my flights at the time, and still does. I'd have been lost without her at times. She got me a flight to Leeds about two hours later and Neil Mulholland, who now trains in England, picked me up at the airport. I remember the flight was bang on time and on the other side my bag was the very first off the conveyor belt. For once everything just went to plan and I made it to the Newcastle track in time for racing. I think Noel was stunned to hear that I had turned it around so quickly.

At this stage we had the measure of how to ride Harchibald, popping him in behind and keeping him covered up until the last strides. Don't touch him and ask him to win on the bridle. I had three other rides at Newcastle that day but couldn't finish in the frame so I was relying on a good run from Harchibald.

We went off as the 9/4 joint favourite alongside Inglis Drever, a decent horse ridden by Graham Lee, and a horse that would go on to become a three-time World Hurdle champion in the future. But Harchibald ran all over him, never came off the bridle and won easily, seeing off Inglis Drever in second, with Royal Shakespeare and Intersky Falcon lagging behind. Harchibald was showing champion pedigree and was gaining a reputation of an exciting prospect to watch.

After that race we decided to have a crack at the Grade One Stan James Christmas Hurdle at Kempton on St Stephen's Day. Despite the prize money of almost £60,000, I didn't think the field was great. Rooster Booster, the champion hurdler from 2003, was the main opposition. We had finished behind Rooster Booster that April at Punchestown, but whereas Harchibald had gone on and improved, it was felt that Rooster's best days were behind him. That said, he was still a class horse and with his ability to go off in front and run a quality field ragged, we didn't really know what to expect. Despite the ground being slightly softer than we would have liked, Harchibald went off odds on, with Rooster Booster and Richard Johnson second favourites with another smart sort, Arcalis, next in the betting.

Sure enough, Dickie Johnson sent Rooster Booster off like a scalded cat and went flat to the boards from the off. With just a couple hundred yards of the two mile race gone, he was already well in front and wasn't stopping, while I had Harchibald stone last. By the fifth of the eight hurdles Rooster Booster was 25 lengths clear when I started to ease Harchibald closer and make my move.

It can be a strange thing to judge when a horse goes off way in front like that, especially if it's a fancied one. Some jockeys talk about counting between furlong poles to make sure you are at the proper pace but I never did that. I just use my own judgement and I knew that day that Rooster had to stop some time because no horse can go flat out for two miles. You can also get it horribly wrong, and I have plenty of times, but you just have to trust your ability to judge the pace. Sometimes you can get caught out in the summer months when the ground is harder, but it's very rare in the winter time, when the ground is soft, for horses to stay at the strong pace for the entire race. Other times you could be on a horse that wouldn't be able to go with the pace, so there's not a whole lot you can do except sit him back in and hope for the best.

Anyway, I'd halved that distance by the time we got to the second last hurdle. But there was still a fair gap to make up and I had to start gently pushing Harchibald a bit. For the first time I thought maybe it was too much, but right then Harchibald came back fully on the bridle and ate up the ground without breaking a sweat. The horse up front was starting to tire. I knew we had him, and I think so did the crowd, who were roaring on the run-in. We popped the last and passed Rooster in the final 100 yards to win by one and a half lengths, with the rest of the runners a mile back. It was a great feeling, and one Noel enjoyed too.

Later that day I picked up a ride for Paul Nicholls in one of the most competitive King George VI Chases ever run. My good friend Barry Geraghty would go on to win on Kicking King, who was trained by Tom Taaffe. The same partnership would go on to win the Gold Cup at Cheltenham the following year. But the field in that 13-runner King George that day was full of quality, with such horses as Edredon Bleu, Calling Brave, Seebald, Lord Sam and Kingscliff, not to mention Paul Nicholls' first string Azertyuiop, the reigning Queen Mother Champion chaser with Ruby Walsh on board. I was on Paul's second horse Le Roi Miguel, and although we finished fourth a fair distance behind Kicking King, Kingscliff and Azertyuiop, it was a good run and there was still 10 grand in prize money for the fourth placing.

For Harchibald, it was time to put him away for the winter and get him ready for a go at the Champion Hurdle in March. We may have hoped for a prep race before that but the ground was always against us that year and we decided to keep him up for Cheltenham. It was a Cheltenham Festival that we went into with a lot of hope and perhaps my best chance of winning the greatest hurdle race in racing.

CHAPTER 16

Why Didn't You Hit Him?

2004 had been a good year for me. While I didn't have any winners at the Cheltenham Festival, I had a great run in the Gold Cup on Harbour Pilot. Best Mate had won the previous two Gold Cups and was bidding for his historic third and went off odds-on to do so. The previous year he had won easily and while Harbour Pilot had run on to be third that day, he was never near the winner. This time it was much different and coming around the turn I held a slight lead on Harbour Pilot and edged to my left towards the rail to stop Jim Culloty coming up my inside on the favourite. Jim had to switch wide and in fairness, they got up to win by half a length from Sir Rembrandt, with me and Harbour Pilot just a length further back in third. It was a cheeky ride and I don't think Jim Culloty was too happy with me. But I was riding an outsider and my horse was having the race of his life. I wasn't going to surrender ground for anyone.

I wasn't riding much in England at all by then, although I went to Aintree as usual for the Grand National meeting where I had a winner with Lord Of The River in a handicap chase for Nicky Henderson. In the Grand National I thought I had a real chance on Joss Naylor, trained by Jonjo O'Neill. It had been five years since my win on Bobbyjo but from very early on in the race I knew we were beaten. Joss Naylor never travelled at all and I had to pull him up just after halfway. He had broken down and never raced again.

Back in Ireland things were going well, on and off the racetrack. At the Punchestown Festival I won on Definite Spectacle in a valuable two-mile hurdle and Harbour Pilot came good again in the Heineken Gold Cup, just beaten into second by a few lengths to Beef Or Salmon. It was around this time that Beef Or Salmon's jockey Timmy Murphy was spending more and more time riding in England and the horse's trainer Michael Hourigan was looking for a replacement.

I had ridden Beef Or Salmon to win at Clonmel a couple of years beforehand so when I got the call from Michael to ride him in the Lexus Chase at Leopardstown that December I jumped at the chance. It was one of the best rides of my life, but the stewards weren't so impressed.

There were only six runners in the race but all eyes were on Best Mate who had come over from England and was the odds-on favourite. After the previous Gold Cup, there was a bit of history between myself and Jim Culloty on Best Mate so that just added spice to the occasion. Beef Or Salmon was always a better horse around Leopardstown and was loved by the crowd. Because he never did the business in the Gold Cup at Cheltenham, the horse probably never really got the credit it deserved. Leopardstown, however, was where he performed best. That day at the Lexus suited him perfectly, the ground was running very heavy and there were three miles of racing and 17 fences to jump. Even though Jim Culloty was Irish, Best Mate was very much seen as the English raider and it was nice to see his colours lowered a bit. Earlier I had seen Jim walk the track as he often did before racing. I couldn't have been arsed walking the track. Instead, I decided that I'd just keep an eye on Jim in the race and follow him around seeing as how he would know where the better ground was.

I remember Cloudy Bays had bolted off in front, but I took it up from three out and couldn't believe how well Beef Or Salmon jumped and how easily we went clear. Jim tried to get Best Mate to give chase but in the end we won by seven lengths easing down. As I eased Beef Or Salmon down on the run-in I turned around and saw Best Mate flat to the boards. It was then I started waving at him, gesturing with my hand to Culloty to come on and try catch me. The crowd loved it and started singing *'You'll never beat the Irish'* as we went past the winning post. The fun, however, was lost on the stewards who later hauled me in for a caution about my behaviour. Privately, I'm convinced they saw the funny side too but had been forced to act after a complaint by some feckin' eejits who knocked on their door after the race.

In truth, it was all just good fun and even Best Mate's owner Jim Lewis came up to me after the race and gave me a big hug. Once I knew he hadn't been offended I didn't care what the others thought. Sometimes I just think there are people involved in racing who complain just for the sake of complaining. The result is that you can't get away with anything these days, and I definitely think a lot of the fun has gone out of racing in recent years as a result.

****

As I said, away from the racetrack things were going well too, as I met my partner Rachel who I have lived with since.

I've known Rachel Clarke for years, but it wasn't all plain sailing. I had seen her a couple of times with her family at Punchestown and liked the look of her. At that time her family lived down in Kildare so I'd met her a couple of times in Naas through the years before we finally got together properly about six years ago. Rachel is one of four sisters, she has a twin Sarah, a younger sister Lynne while the eldest, Laura is married to top flat jockey Fran Berry. Rachel is a fantastic singer and had been in a band for a short time. She always leads a sing-song at house parties and I guess she shares my love of karaoke, although she can *actually* sing, in sharp contrast to my lame efforts. I had kissed her a couple of times in a nightclub after racing a few years earlier. That was after initially chatting to one of her friends. Rachel was going out with somebody at the time and so I had to be on my best behaviour if I were to have any chance.

Anyway, one time I met her at Fairyhouse with her friend Ciara. I plucked up the courage to ask her what she was doing the next day and pestered her to stay on for the night and come riding with me the next morning. My persistence worked.

That night we hit The Vortex, a nightclub in Dunshaughlin and went back to my friend Willie Murphy's house and were drinking until about four or five in the morning. I was renting a place just across the road at the time but as she was still going out with her boyfriend I was getting nowhere. So I had to bide my time. The hunt was still on, so to speak.

The next day we rode out the horses and in fairness to her she followed me over every jump, every gate, every fence. I was impressed with her skill and bravery on a horse. She wouldn't do it now. I think over time I scared the bravado out of her. I pursued her for a while and when she was single again we got together. I was 32 and she was just 23. Two years later we moved into a rented place in Ratoath before moving in to rent a room in Robbie 'Puppy' Power's house while we saved money to build our own home. At the time we were paying €1,200 a month rent in Ratoath so the room at Puppy's place made sense. The recession had just hit Ireland and while I had some land bought years beforehand in Tara, I was trying to get the money together to build something for myself. It had always been my dream to have my own home with stables, yard and gallops, and some years later I would get it. Rachel has brought great happiness and stability to my life.

****

Back on the racetrack, all was going well in the build-up to the 2005 Cheltenham Festival. I had a nice few rides booked, but the Champion Hurdle in which I was riding Harchibald was the race everyone was talking about.

We had a very strange build-up to the Festival as we didn't run Harchibald at all since Kempton at Christmas. Clearly, he would have been a bit track rusty, although he was working well at home. But in the final days things weren't looking great. Ten days before Cheltenham we did a bit of work with him after Saturday racing on soft ground at Navan with about seven other horses and we tailed off last. The racing TV channel *At The Races* were there filming and after that piece of work Harchibald drifted out in the betting and eventually went off as a joint 7/1 third favourite for the race. In the days up to the big race all the talk was about the battle for the champion hurdle crown. I know Ruby Walsh, AP McCoy and Barry Geraghty were all on a panel on Channel 4's *The Morning Line* and when they were asked who was the most gifted jockey in racing, all three said my name. These things are nice to hear from your fellow jockeys but sometimes these things can backfire, because if I am the *Most Gifted*, well then some will ask why I haven't been Champion Jockey more times. Or why haven't I won a Gold Cup. Or a Champion Chase, or indeed, a Champion Hurdle?

The day had started off well. I'd finished second on Wild Passion in the first race, the Supreme Novices Hurdle behind Arcalis, and then finished fourth in the Arkle on Watson Lake. Next up was the big one.

As we walked around the parade ring for the big race you

could feel the excitement growing. The reigning champion Hardy Eustace was again being ridden by Conor O'Dwyer and was at the head of the betting market alongside the well-backed Edward O'Grady horse Back In Front, being ridden by Ruby. The field was packed with quality hurdlers, with Brave Inca, Macs Joy, Essex, Rooster Booster and Accordion Etoile all lining up.

The race started off well and, keeping Harchibald well covered towards the back, I started to make my move on the back straight. Hardy Eustace had gone off in front as usual with Barry Cash on Brave Inca and AP on Essex leading the rest. Ruby was going well on Back In Front but he weakened from two out and was never really in with a shout after that. Essex fell away around the same time. I was now passing some tired horses and Harchibald was still full of running. When we came to the second last I was lying in third place, cruising behind Hardy and Brave Inca, with both horses being ridden hard. Just then Brave Inca took a swerve to the right going over the second last hurdle and left a gaping gap which Harchibald jumped into, making almost two lengths in air. To another horse this would have been seen as a dream run as he pulled alongside the leader Hardy, but I felt it was too early and would have preferred to have had him covered up until the last. It's a steep hill home at Cheltenham and you don't want to be there too early, especially on a horse like mine. The crowd suddenly went wild when they realised how easily Harchibald was going, with his head still in the air and I hadn't moved a muscle. In running, we would have been probably long, long odds-on to win as Conor was on full drive on Hardy and Barry was pumping away on Brave Inca. I was in between them both, looking all over the winner, and we winged the last.

But it wasn't to be. I cruised past Barry and was eyeball to eyeball with Hardy who as a dour stayer was just about keeping his nose in front. Fifty yards from the line I decided to go for it and get Harchibald to get his head down. When I did there was nothing there and he flattened out in seconds. We flashed past the post in second place, a neck behind the now two-time champion hurdler Hardy Eustace, with Brave Inca back in third.

I was devastated. It was there to be won and we didn't. The first prize was almost £200,000 with second place getting less than half that. But for me right then and there, and I suppose ever since, it's never been about the lost money, it was about winning the race. The horse deserved it, Noel and the owner Des Sharkey deserved it, and the fans deserved it. For God's sake, I think I deserved it too. But the punters weren't exactly in a sympathetic mood as I made the journey from the post to the parade ring. It's a long trek back past the stands and betting area at Cheltenham when you're coming back after a race like that. You have to take the horses down a sand runway past the entire run-in between the stands and the racecourse and then turn left through the crowd and behind the main stand to the parade ring and winners' enclosure. You are within arm's length of the 60,000 crowd who are either saluting you, or in some cases, baying for your blood. While Conor stood up in the irons draped in an Irish tricolor saluting the crowd, I was coming back to jeers and taunting from the crowd. You say that it doesn't get to you, but at times it does and it did then. Punters were roaring *'What the fuck were you at. You should have hit him'* and *'Why didn't you kick on when you could have, you fucking eejit'*. I don't normally listen too much and was lost in my own disappointment as I made my way back to the ring where Noel and the others were.

Noel asked me after the race what I thought would have happened if we had kicked on after the last and I told him straight that I believed we would have finished third. *'That's good enough for me*', he said. But it wasn't good enough for him. I knew that and he knew that.

He had stood beside Dessie Hughes for the race and he was convinced we would win it and he said that even Dessie had thrown the hat in at that stage and was just waiting on Harchibald to pass his horse and win. We had come so close to pulling off one of the greatest Champion Hurdle wins of recent years and no matter how many times you try and leave it behind, the nagging doubts and doubters are still there. There is no way of knowing if we would have won if I had kicked on earlier and I still believe I gave the horse the best chance of winning that I could have. But Noel struggled with it in the weeks after the race. He probably still does. We were getting stick from all sides and the papers were having a field day. Everyone was asking his opinion on it and in fairness, publicly he always backed me as knowing the horse best. But I know privately he was still hurting. He proved that two weeks after the race when he asked me a second time whether I thought we would have won if we kicked on earlier. I gave him the same answer and he left it at that.

I have watched the replays and I know how it looks. I suppose you look at it and say, *'Surely there was some way we could have run the race differently and won the race'.* Kicking on earlier, waiting five yards later, it would drive you mad thinking about what could have been. The truth is that Harchibald did nothing in front and Hardy Eustace, then at his absolute peak, was a tough horse to pass. Noel has watched the replays too but we have never watched it together.

However, then and now, I'm sure that I rode the horse the way he needed to be ridden and I was proved right a few weeks later at the Emo Oil Irish Champion Hurdle at the Punchestown Festival. Hardy wasn't running and on paper we only had Brave Inca to beat and the betting suggested it would be a cake walk as we were long odds-on. Before the race Noel said to me something like *'Now for fuck's sake, let's not have another Cheltenham. If he's going well enough kick him on and go for it. Don't be just sitting on him again trying to prove you were right all along'*. So I just said *'grand so'* and ran the race he wanted me to. There were only five runners in the race with really only Brave Inca and Macs Joy to beat. The other two outsiders made up the numbers. AP was on Brave Inca that day and made all the running. I kept Harchibald well covered, but in touch, and made my move at the last hurdle where I jumped into the lead and kicked for home. We were cruising but as soon as I kicked him on after the last he suddenly came off the bridle and emptied out. Brave Inca passed us by on the run-in. I had made a point but I still felt crap about it, as nobody wanted Harchibald to win that race more than me. I was thick with rage after the line and I was waiting to talk to Noel. I wouldn't normally say a whole lot to him after a race but it was personal this time. I met him in the parade ring and I just said to him *'I hope you're happy now. Don't ever tell me how to ride a fucking horse again'*. I was fuming. I'd put up with so much shit for the previous month about the Champion Hurdle at Cheltenham and now here I was in second place again, when this time I knew we would have hacked up if I'd been allowed ride the horse the way I knew he should be ridden.

This time there were no jeers from the crowd. But with a difference of over 50 grand between the placings, it was still a tough one to swallow. Noel didn't say anything back. He just looked at me blankly, raised his eyes and walked away. Noel has a great way of diffusing situations, and I'm glad the conversation didn't turn into a full-blown argument because I wasn't really in the mood to listen.

I suppose it's mad that one race would cause so much debate in racing circles and it certainly overshadowed the start of the year for me. In hindsight, three placed finishes in the first three races of the Festival at Cheltenham wasn't a bad return and I went on to have two winners later in the week. On the Thursday, St Patrick's Day, I won the Pertemps Hurdle on Oulart at 10/1 for Dessie Hughes and then won the Grand Annual on Fota Island at a nice price for Mouse Morris on the Friday.

There was another silver lining for the Carberry family that year as Nina became the first female amateur rider in over 20 years to win a race against the professionals. Nina was riding a horse called Dabiroun for Paul Nolan in the Fred Winter Juvenile Handicap Hurdle over two miles. I was riding one of Noel's horses, an outsider called Rolling Home, and led for most of the way but the distress signals were going out before the turn. As horses started to pass me, I noticed Nina cruising by on Dabiroun. She may have been on a 20/1 shot, but she was going better than anything in the race. I shouted at her to go win her race, *'Go on Nina, go and win it'*. As I belted my horse up the Cheltenham hill I was watching the big screen to my left which showed Nina hacking up to the winning post. She won by eight lengths and I gave her a massive hug after the line. It was definitely up there as one of my Cheltenham highlights. Nina went on to win the Cross Country race three years in a row on Heads On The Ground in 2007 and twice on Garde Champetre in 2008 and 2009 for Enda Bolger and I'm sure there are plenty more winners still to come. She is an outstanding rider, my little sis.

In the Gold Cup that year, I had the ride on Beef Or Salmon and while we thought he had a chance, he simply didn't run a yard, hit a couple of fences and I had to pull him up as Barry Geraghty won on Kicking King. I was delighted for Barry and we had a great night in Cheltenham after the races. The following day we went to Uttoxeter for the Midlands Grand National which I won on Philson Run. Myself, Barry, Ruby, Davy Russell and a load of other Irish jockeys were coming back on the plane that night and we were in great form. After I sat down one of the stewardesses came down to me and said that while she knew I had won the big race that day, would I mind it if she went on the intercom and congratulated Barry for winning the Gold Cup and Ruby for finishing top jockey at Cheltenham that week. I said no problem, sure I just can't seem to do any right on an airplane these days.

****

I was back in England a few weeks later for the Aintree festival. I had been booked by trainer Paul Nolan to ride Colnel Rayburn in the Grand National but he never really went well and I ended up pulling him up with 13 fences still to jump. But it had been a very good day at the races despite this, as I won the John Smith's Handicap Hurdle on Noel's horse Definate Spectacle at 11/1 and I also had an unlikely third place on a 50/1 outsider called Exotic Dancer for Jonjo O'Neill in the Aintree Hurdle. Exotic Dancer would later prove to be a very good horse over the big fences, winning the Paddy Power Chase at Cheltenham and a Lexus Chase at Leopardstown. He was also second in the Gold Cup behind Kauto Star in 2007 but by that time AP McCoy had long claimed the ride.

I then had four good winners at the March Fairyhouse meeting and another four at the Punchestown Festival as Noel's horses really started firing. The purses at Punchestown were huge, landing over €250,000 in prize money with the best of these being the wins on Wild Passion in the Evening Herald Novice Hurdle and on Asian Maze in the Menolly Homes Champion Novices Hurdle.

****

Harchibald came back to winning ways at Tipperary in October and then went off the 7/4 favourite to follow it up at Punchestown a month later. But in the end we were beaten and I was in trouble with the stewards again for what they regarded as *careless riding*. I was sitting on Harchibald coming around the turn behind AP McCoy on Brave Inca and Essex, being ridden by Ruby Walsh. I was going very well on the rail but was having trouble getting out and when I tried to go up McCoy's inside before the last fence he closed the gap and I was badly squeezed into the railing. I could only finish third and I was later accused of going for a gap that wasn't there. I think Ruby had a right go at me and the stewards hit me with a three-day ban, later reduced to two days on appeal. Was I right or wrong? I'm honestly still not too sure as I'd had a fall off a horse called Father Matt earlier in the day and it was still all a bit hazy for me. Maybe I wasn't at my best but I wouldn't have stood myself down from racing.

Harchibald came back and won the Bula Hurdle handily enough up the other track at Cheltenham that December on what is a tougher track on softish ground, beating Intersky Falcon, but, painfully he was ruled out of the Cheltenham Festival of 2006 when being well-backed for the Champion Hurdle. He suffered an injury when a bit of birch got stuck in his hind leg just over the hoof and missed the rest of the season. He was robbed of a year at his prime and never really got back to his best - although he did win another Fighting Fifth at Newcastle the following year. He was unfortunate with injuries, with niggles ruling him out of both the 2006 and 2007 Cheltenham Festivals. By the time it came around to the 2008 Champion Hurdle he was well past his best and was never in contention as Katchit pulled off a shock result.

Harchibald was just one of those horses that had a quirky nature and a mind of his own. He never liked to be hit with a whip and as long as you could keep him on the bridle the more races he would win. I suppose with better luck and less injuries, Harchibald could have won a couple of Champion Hurdles.

I remember when we lost the Christmas Hurdle at Kempton by a short head to Straw Bear on St Stephen's Day in 2007. Noel, who was at Leopardstown watching the race on TV, rang me afterwards and asked why I hadn't given him a smack. I simply told him that I'd never do that to a horse that was already giving his best. It's not an easy argument to win when you've just been chinned by a nod on the line but that's the way I ride horses. I would never abuse a horse if he wasn't responding positively to demands.

The truth is that for all his flair on the racecourse, Harchibald suffered from a wind problem that handicapped him in a tight finish. That's why he kept his head up and always looked like he was cruising. But when he was pushed and was forced to put his head down under pressure he simply wasn't getting enough air into his lungs and he suffered.

Harchibald is a rare horse, a real character, and he still laps up the attention at various shows when he makes an appearance.

****

The year finished in huge disappointment with the death of Best Mate while I was riding him. As I mentioned earlier, I'd had a bit of history with the horse, beating him when I won the Supreme Novices on Sausalito Bay in 2000; then finishing third twice behind him in Cheltenham Gold Cups; and then the famous *'Come and Catch Me'* controversy when I beat him on Beef Or Salmon in the last Lexus Chase at Leopardstown. While some moaning punters thought I was being unsportsmanlike by taunting Jim Culloty on the run-in, his owner Jim

Lewis thought it was all good fun and I know that Best Mate's trainer Henrietta Knight felt the same way. Otherwise I would never have been considered for the ride on Best Mate when Jim Culloty decided to retire months later.

Best Mate hadn't run since that day at Leopardstown and was being wrapped in cotton wool at Hen's yard as it recovered from a couple of injuries. Having made history winning three Gold Cups, Best Mate had been off the track almost a year and was still highly respected when he took to the Exeter track that fateful day in November 2005 for a Grade Two chase. The race had a quality field, with Paul Nicholls' future two-time Gold Cup winner Kauto Star being ridden by Ruby Walsh and Paddy Brennan riding the favourite Ashley Brook. Monkerhostin eventually won the race for Dickie Johnson but the race that day would be remembered for the sad death of Best Mate.

I got the call the week before and was asked to ride him on the following Tuesday. But that Friday I was out messing on a hunt and I busted my ankle. Not wanting to miss the racing I got the ankle strapped up and I said nothing about it.

The horse had felt fine before the start. He wasn't fancied to win so there was no real pressure as Henrietta was just hopeful of a good run and a clear round. The favourite, Ashley Brook, had gone off in front and was going clear after a couple of fences. I got Best Mate to close up and was travelling quite well as we approached the fifth fence, but over the next couple of fences he just stopped travelling and began to slow up. I knew something wasn't right so I pulled him up before three out and, as I jumped off him, he simply lay down and died. I knew he was gone straight away. My whole life has been horses and I had seen this before. In fact it had happened just a week earlier on a hunter I had on the gallops, but at the track in front of a big crowd it was massively different. My first thoughts were for Hen as she had trained the horse from its very first run and treated Best Mate as the name implied, almost as part of her family.

We had just slowed up and were just about to pass where Hen was standing when he just wobbled a bit and collapsed. Hen ran out to where Best Mate lay and broke into tears. All I could do was try and console her. Sometimes it's very hard to know just what to say to a trainer or owner in those circumstances. It seems strange now, but I found myself telling Hen about my hunter the previous week. Best Mate had been such a huge part of their lives for the past six years and it was a tragic way to end. Best Mate was later honoured in a most fitting fashion, by being buried at the finishing line at the Cheltenham racetrack in recognition of his outstanding achievements.

CHAPTER 17

Crime & Punishment

I had an incredible Christmas meeting at Leopardstown, with seven winners over the four days and almost a quarter of a million in prize money and I finished the week as leading jockey. Beef Or Salmon won another Lexus, completely destroying a decent field with War Of Attrition a long way back in second that day. Mr Nosie also won well in the Deloitte Novice Hurdle and the other winners were Rocket Ship, Rosaker, Sweet Wake, Back To Bid and Zum See.

Sweet Wake won again at Naas in the New Year, and then Nicanor and Mr Nosie won decent races at Leopardstown in February. Both were turning out to be real Cheltenham prospects. The problem was that these two were trained by Noel for different owners and as both were targeting the same race at the Festival, the Sun Alliance Novices Hurdle, a choice would have to be made.

I still hadn't decided which one to ride by the time it came to travelling over and only told Noel the day before the race that I wanted to ride Nicanor even though Mr Nosie had won all of his first five races. Noel tried to get me to change my mind because he thought Mr Nosie had a better chance of winning. But I just thought Nicanor's run, when he absolutely hacked up in the Novice Hurdle at Leopardstown, was too good to ignore.

My decision was confirmed for me the day before at Cheltenham Racecourse when I watched both horses go through some work with other lads in the saddle and I knew Nicanor was travelling the better.

Denis O'Regan got the ride on Mr Nosie and there was nothing between us in the betting ring, as we were both at odds of 9/1 behind the raging hot favourite Denman, a hugely talented Paul Nicholls horse that would go on to win the Cheltenham Gold Cup two years later. But thankfully I made the right choice in the end as Nicanor bounded up the Cheltenham hill, with Denman back in second and Mr Nosie running well in fourth. There had been no real pace in the race and down the back straight Denis took up the lead on Mr Nosie and led into the turn where Ruby Walsh then hit the front. I had been just trying to settle Nicanor into the race, as his jumping could be a bit scatty at times, and I could see that Ruby's horse was going well. So I followed him, passing him out after the last hurdle and getting to the winning line in front. I was relieved to have made the right choice but it was a tough one for Noel. While he was delighted with the result, I don't think the owners of Mr Nosie were too happy and may have thought that Noel may have deliberately sent him off fast to act as a pace-setter for my horse. But that was nonsense, Denis had gone off in front, doing what he believed was right for the horse but Mr Nosie just didn't stay as well up the hill. And the truth is that Noel had asked me at least twice to switch to Mr Nosie before the race.

But the real story was the defeat of English hotpot Denman. He had won all of his previous five races and, in fact, won the next nine after our race. So it turned out that Nicanor was the only horse to beat him in 15 races. But the only person that this meant absolutely nothing to was me. In fact, I didn't even know he was in the race until after I won. I know this sounds ridiculous but it's true. Yes, I had heard the hype about the horse but I didn't know his colours and assumed he was running in some other race. As I've said before, I never look at a racecard or look up form. Sometimes I get owners asking me in the parade ring before a race what I thought of *'such and such'* a horse and I would just tell them that I haven't a clue. I'd tell them what I thought of the horse I was riding if I had ridden him before, but nothing else. This might sound strange but I'm a firm believer that it's hard enough for a jockey to ride his horse to the best of his ability without trying to ride three or four other horses in the race as well. So when Ruby chased me up the Cheltenham hill that day I just stuck my head down and rode to the line. He may as well have been on a 100/1 outsider for all I cared as it wouldn't have made one bit of difference to how I rode my horse.

I finished the day with a memorable Grade One double when I won the Champion Bumper on 33/1 outsider Hairy Molly for trainer Joseph Crowley. But then I had a disappointing result the next day when falling in the Ryanair Chase on Sir Oj.

In the Gold Cup we were confident of a big run from Beef Or Salmon. I know everyone just dismisses him as being unable to handle Cheltenham but people forget that he only ever ran there in Gold Cups and had been placed. That, clearly, doesn't make him a bad horse. Back in Ireland he seemed bomb-proof. He had followed up his Leopardstown Lexus win with a dream run in the Hennessy at the same course in February, hammering Hedgehunter by 12 lengths with everything else a mile back.

By the time we lined up for the Cheltenham Gold Cup, Beef Or Salmon had been backed in to go off the 4/1 favourite. I suppose if you strictly went on form he could have been even shorter as he had beaten nearly all the fancied runners of the 22 in the field and the defending champion Kicking King had been ruled out through injury. So the race was there for the taking, but for some reason I knew after less than a mile that it wasn't going to have a happy ending. He was slow over the second and was further behind than I wanted him. When I tried to pick him up there was very little there and he eventually trailed in 11th well behind the winner, War Of Attrition, with Hedgehunter and Forget The Past next best. These were three horses that Beef Or Salmon had just beaten in his last two races but he just couldn't get it right at the Cheltenham track. Looking back I firmly believe that Beef Or Salmon just didn't like the Cheltenham course. He fell there on his first visit and I think horses remember that when they come back. Even when I'm out hunting and if I try to jump a ditch or a gate where my horse had fallen before, he would remember when he approaches it and would be wary of doing it again. Horses remember when and where they've been hurt and I don't care what anyone else thinks about it.

Aintree turned out to be a bit of a disaster. Beef Or Salmon unseated me in the Betfair Chase and then Sir Oj fell in the Grand National going over Becher's the second time and I ended up breaking my ankle and being out of action for weeks. Sir Oj had been taking liberties the whole way around and I probably should have pulled him up before Bechers but I let him have a go at it and I paid the price.

****

But everything going on at the racecourse was just a distraction for me personally with the trial for the fire on the airplane getting all the nearer. As I said earlier, setting Davy Condon's newspaper alight in Row 18 on Aer Lingus flight 583 back from Spain wasn't the smartest move I'd ever made. I always make a point of not getting worried about things I cannot change but that only gets you so far. Since being arrested on that first day of October 2005 it was fairly regularly on my mind. Just when times were good and all was going well, I'd suddenly remember it, darkening my mood. I knew I could end up in jail but I wanted it dealt with and over. I wasn't going to get myself into a panic over what might happen; I'd deal with it when I had to and that was that.

The day after it happened I was due to ride at Tipperary and having only told my family, I decided that the best thing to do would be to carry on and act as normal as possible. So I went to Tipperary that Sunday as normal where I had three rides for Noel and one for Michael Halford. Bizarrely, in the big race I was to ride Harchibald, the horse that was the subject of the nighttime prank phone messages from Spain to Noel. I hadn't decided yet whether to say anything to Noel about the court case but I wouldn't have much time as I was due in court on the Tuesday. I couldn't help thinking about his last words to me when I told him I was going on holiday with the lads. *'Now don't do anything stupid'*, he said. *'I'll try not to'*, I laughed back.

That day at Tipperary I was all over the place. I tried to just put the last 24 hours behind me but at the track and even in the weigh room I had no idea who knew what had happened and who didn't. I suppose it's one of those times where you imagine people are talking about you but they really aren't at all. I just needed to concentrate on my riding for now and the job in hand.

When the John James McManus Memorial Hurdle came around I had a bit of good fortune on Harchibald. I was just about to finish second when David Casey fell at the last while in the lead on Solerina, so I ended up winning and that gave me a bit of a lift. The rest of the day was a bit of a disaster. I had to pull up the favourite Gortinard when tailed off in the Novice Chase and then finished nowhere in my other two rides. But by now the story of what had happened was spreading like wildfire and I was completely distracted. I was trying to keep it quiet but the newspapers had wind of it and it was being spoken about at the track. Seemingly the *Irish Examiner* had the story and were planning to run it on the Monday morning. There was also word that RTÉ might run it that night. I avoided the parade ring and as soon as my last ride was done I left the track. On the way back I rang Noel and came clean about what had happened and he was great. I dunno, maybe Harchibald's win that day softened him up or something but he was fairly cool about it and so were my close friends and family. My family stuck behind me from day one and I'll never forget Mam sent me a text message that night saying, *'No matter what happens Paul, we'll always still love you,'* which was nice. In fact, anyone who knew me knew I wasn't some kind of lunatic harassing people or trying to kill everyone on a plane. It was more a case of, *'Jaysus Paul, what have you done this time?'* Yes there was slagging too, but I just had to get on with it. The story broke in the Monday newspapers and one even had interviews with some passengers on the flight talking of their *'terror at 12,000 feet'.*

First thing to do was to organise a solicitor and that Monday morning I tried to get hold of a barrister I knew from racing circles but I was unable to track her down and ended up ringing an owner with Noel's yard. He set me up with a firm of solicitors in Dublin. We met within hours and again the following morning before court.

That Tuesday I headed to Swords District Court, the nearest court to Dublin Airport, not really knowing what to expect. My solicitor had already told me that it would be a very short hearing and that it would be adjourned to a later date. There were a good few TV and newspaper reporters and photographers there but I just walked past and got inside as quickly as possible. The Court was in a very old small building at the end of the town and there were people there for all kinds of cases. Occasionally you would get some people looking and pointing at me as it had been in the papers that morning but I don't think most knew who the hell I was. Anyway, I think their minds would have been on their own cases.

When my case was called a garda from the Dublin Airport police station outlined the charge to the court in front of the judge, Patrick Brady. I was to face trial for allegedly 'engaging in threatening, abusive or insulting behaviour', and for breaching the peace. My solicitor said I would be pleading *'Not Guilty'* which was initially a bit of news to me. I know I mightn't have been the most attentive at our meeting but I thought I was going to plead guilty and get it over with. I was told later that, while I wasn't disputing that I had lit the newspaper, I had told my legal team that I hadn't *meant* to do it. So this *'Not Guilty'* plea was the natural course. The case was remanded back for another hearing, where a Judge McDonnell set a trial date for the following May.

I guess that was to give time for the prosecution to present their case and their witnesses, and give me time to prepare my defence. But in the meantime it at least provided some breathing space. Did I think about what would happen if I did end up in prison? ... not a lot if I'm honest about it. As I said, I'm a great believer that if you worry about things you just end up making it worse. People kept telling me that it was the worst possible time to be facing a charge like this because the entire world seemed to be so over the top about behaviour on airplanes. But sure I couldn't go back in time and change things now. Either way, I wouldn't have been able to visualise what it was like behind bars because I'd never spent a night in a cell or even visited somebody in prison. I'd just have to put the whole thing to the back of my mind for now.

They say that sometimes the wait is worse than the actual event but, in my case, I can safely say that the event was worse. Six months later my case and my excuses would be ripped apart

211

by a judge after listening to a room full of witnesses. During the trial, six witnesses would give evidence on my behalf and eight witnesses against. At the time it looked like it was going very, very badly.

I felt sick as I listened to an air hostess tell the court that it had been *'very, very scary'*. *'There were a few passengers who were crying and asking was everything OK and was there a fire. There was a lot of screaming'.* She also added that the fire had been discovered 15 minutes after takeoff and that all passengers from rows 14 to 22 would have noticed the smoke. Some passengers also gave evidence, with one telling how he had been sitting behind me and had seen flames and smoke. It was getting worse by the minute and by the time the flight's captain took the stand I was convinced I was finished. He said: *'In my professional experience, a fire on board a cabin would be catastrophic'*, but added that it was already out by the time he knew about it.

A few of the lads gave evidence on my behalf, including jockeys Davy Condon and Davy Russell as well as my friend Alan 'Horsebox' Egan who was a fireman and who my defence team thought the judge might listen to. I got into the witness box as well, where I claimed that I had lit the newspaper by accident. *'It was a freak accident'*, I said *'I was just flicking my lighter, fidgeting, while talking to someone across the aisle... I was not concentrating'.*

Looking back it was always going to seem worse when you heard the people that were on the airplane. I'm now sure that I should have just held my hands up and apologised to the court. Perhaps the judge would have seen it differently. Two days after the trial we were called back for his decision. It wasn't pretty.

The judge said that my evidence had been *'contrived'* and had varied from the original statement I had given at the time of my arrest. He also said that some of the evidence given by my friends was *'not believable'.* And then the judge added: *'Would* the defendant, an experienced jockey, have acted similarly in a stable or a container with straw and a horse inside? I would say emphatically, no.' He then looked at me and said 'I sentence you to two months imprisonment and a fine of €500'. Two months in jail! I was still in shock as he went on to say that he felt that he had no choice because I had pleaded not guilty and therefore dragged out the trial. My legal team immediately launched an appeal, and after signing a bail form for €1,000 I was free to leave the court while I waited for the date of appeal.

I had decided that morning that regardless of what way the court case went I wasn't going to give a statement to the media. I just thought there were no words that could improve the situation. I had already explained myself to anyone that mattered to me and my family and friends were standing by me. Outside, my pal and fellow jockey Robbie 'Puppy' Power tried to help me out by sending some of the waiting TV and newspaper crews off the scent. Puppy really does look like me and he was always getting confused as a Carberry in the early days. Puppy pulled a tracksuit top over his head and zipped it up to his nose and left the court jogging on foot. About 100 yards down the road with four or five photographers in pursuit he slowed down, unzipped his jacket and turned around. Meanwhile, I had left by car and seemingly Puppy nearly got lynched.

Because of the appeal I was still able to ride but I don't think my head was fully in it. In fact after the trial, and following the broken ankle, I only had a handful of winners all summer. Of course the pressure was starting to build. The conviction and sentence meant I faced not only a stretch behind bars but also the prospect of the Turf Club taking away my riding licence. That would stop me from making a living riding horses: to be perfectly honest I didn't know which I most feared, a prison sentence or a riding ban.

I didn't really know what to think. You would go for a drink to get away from it all and then you would get dragged into a conversation about it. Some lads would tell you that even if you did end up doing time, it could be arranged that you would serve your sentence in a cushy open prison. Others would tell you that you would have to pay some lag to keep you out of harm. I was told that protection money was paid at Timmy Murphy's prison in England when he was jailed for assaulting a stewardess on an airplane. No one really knew if you had to do the same over here. Different people would tell you this and that, but most people were just talking rubbish.

After the court I went back to The Snail Box, a nice pub near my home and tried to get my head around what had just happened. My phone was hopping and there were messages asking if I would go on Joe Duffy's *Liveline* show, Ireland's most popular radio talk show that afternoon. But that was the last thing I needed. I heard later that I got savaged by callers on the show, with one particular caller saying that she had been a passenger on the flight and said that a woman beside her *'had her head in her hands. She thought the plane was going down'.*

The appeal hearing, before a different judge was set for almost five months later, October 15 in the Four Courts, the main court near Dublin's city centre. In the meantime I went back riding and in fairness Noel Meade backed me 100 per cent. It was never mentioned in racing circles either, unless it was by someone expressing support and surprise at the prison sentence. There was one light-hearted moment at Kilbeggan during those months that summed it all up. I was after taking a nasty fall and was holding my battered elbow when I met Noel back in the weigh room. He looked at me and said: *'Perhaps it would have been easier if you had just done the time'.* I replied: *'I'd rather have a sore elbow than a sore arse!'* We both burst out laughing but it was one of the few times it was mentioned between us.

To be honest it wasn't all that funny and as it came nearer the appeal date I started to think the worst. I was even being warned by so-called experts that on appeal the judge could even take a dimmer view and increase the sentence. But this time I just decided to get a senior counsel lawyer, hold my hands up and ask for leniency. This time the plan of attack was much simpler; keep it quiet, avoid the circus of the first trial, don't bring many people with you, go in and plead guilty. So only Rachel, uncle Arthur and Noel came to court and both Arthur and Noel gave character references to the hearing. I suppose we gave a *'I'm mad but not bad'* kind of defence. It worked. This time the judge decided that I suffered more from stupidity than malicious intent. Much to my relief he quashed the conviction and applied the Probation Act which meant that I wouldn't have a criminal conviction recorded against me as long as I obeyed the conditions. These conditions were in the form of community service, and after initially telling me to spend time working at an old folks' home, he decided that my time would be better spent working on a local scheme to help young aspiring jockeys.

It was a great result, like a weight had been lifted from my shoulders. That day I walked from court, hand in hand with Rachel, a relieved man and ready to get on with what I do best, riding horses. Just before I walked out of the court into the sunshine I turned to the others and mimicking the line from the Guildford Four movie In The Name Of The Father I said:

'My name is Paul Carberry. I'm an innocent man... and I'm leaving here through the front door!'

CHAPTER 18

Testing Times

Getting in a double to ring in the New Year is always a good thing and I don't mean at the bar this time. I had a nice start at Fairyhouse, making a few quid with a quick double on the first day of 2007, winning a two-and-a-half mile maiden hurdle very easily on Offaly for Noel, and the Bambury Bookmakers Handicap Hurdle over two miles later that day for Tony Martin on Hearthstead Dream.

It was a fairly quiet after that but at Noel's yard we were getting a great feel off Aran Concerto and believed he had a real chance at Cheltenham. Aran Concerto was owned by John Corr and, while he wasn't the quickest jumper over hurdles, he had a good cruising speed. I had won on him in a bumper at Naas the previous year and then won two races over hurdles, including a nice Grade One at Navan that December. We were looking at the Ballymore Properties Novice Hurdle on the second day of Cheltenham Festival, and had a final prep run at Fairyouse four weeks before. There was a huge prize on offer for the Deliotte Grade One with only four runners and we hacked up. Barry Geraghty was riding the second favourite Catch Me for Edward O'Grady and was going fairly well when he unshipped him at the second last and left me clear to win easing down. It ended up being a nice one-two for Noel as his second string Leading

Run followed me home under Slippers Madden.

So it was all going well until disaster struck once more, this time ruling me out of the Cheltenham Festival.

First the excuse: I had told Noel that a horse stood on my foot in the yard and, should he read this, I'd forgive him for being more than a little annoyed. Now the truth: the real reason how I came to break my foot and miss the biggest festival in racing was because I was out hunting again, despite Noel telling me to take it easy for the few weeks before. I knew straight away it was broken, the blood drained from my body with the sharp pain of it. It's a common enough injury and once you do it the first time it seems to happen fairly often thereafter. I've broken my foot three times since. I was out hunting and came to a simple enough ditch with a tree beside it. But there was a bush at the other side meaning you had to jump straight and then turn left. Unfortunately, the horse took off left from the jump and landed my side straight into the tree and snapped my foot. I knew it was broken but I managed to stay on and finish the hunt. Once I got off the horse later that day I had a look at the foot and tried to tell myself that it was ok, that I'd be fine and I would get it fixed for next week's Cheltenham Festival. But I was only kidding myself. An x-ray confirmed it was a clean break and I would be out for six weeks.

Now came the hard part. It's bad enough having to deal with your own disappointment of missing out on a big race meeting, never mind the pain and hassle of the injury, but I also had to break the news to the trainer. So naturally I thought it would be easier all round if I just made up a story. If I told Noel the truth he'd have a fit and then he would be obliged to tell his owners the truth as well. So I decided to say a horse stood on my foot in the yard. I don't know if he believed it but I suppose he had to at the time.

Anyway, at Cheltenham we were still hopeful of a good run

for Aran Concerto despite my absence. Noel had Timmy Murphy down to ride him but then AP McCoy became available which was unusual for AP, so he was put on him instead. He's a funny sort of horse and he needs to be dropped in and settled. In fact, for that kind of run I thought Timmy would have suited him better than AP. After making a mistake at the first Aran Concerto never really settled and finished back in fifth after hitting almost every hurdle on the way around.

I was out for two months and just got back riding in time for the Fairyhouse Grand National meeting when I rode Mac Three in the big race. But he never travelled well and I had to pull him up. It was no better a week later at Aintree when I had to pull up Tony Martin's Dun Doire in the English National. Tony Martin has a reputation for being able to pull off a nice touch and I thought I might get a good run from him. Dun Doire had won the William Hill at Cheltenham for Ruby the year before and had a quiet build-up to the big race, winning his last outing at Down Royal a few weeks before when all eyes were on the Cotswolds. But on the big day he never ran a yard and we were almost tailed off after a few fences. I kept him going but pulled him up about halfway when the leaders were out of sight. I walked back to the finish in time to see my mate Puppy Power win on Silver Birch for Gordon Elliott. It was an amazing training performance by Gordon who was only 29 years old, working out of a rented stable near Trim, and was having his first ever runner in the Grand National. Silver Birch had won a Welsh National three years before when he was trained by Paul Nicholls but had completely lost his way and hadn't won since. But the move to Gordon's yard obviously suited him and the win put Gordon's name on the training map.

I had known Gordon from years before when he was a young amateur jockey before injuries ended his career. The first time I met him he was only about 16 and he came up to me in a pub when I was about 20 and started in my ear, telling me *'You're the best damn jockey I've ever seen. I love the way you ride with your arse just an inch off the saddle',* and then quickly added, *'Now go up to the bar and get me a drink cos I can't get served'.* He was always that way and fully confident in his ability. He is a top class trainer now and I'm glad to say, a good mate. Not only am I riding many of his horses when I can, he also sends down quite a few horses to my yard for pre-training and assessment or just to give them a fitness check before going back out to race.

Punchestown was fairly quiet with a lot of Noel's horses running below par. We had thought that Iktataf would have a good chance in the Irish Champion Hurdle but he was beaten into sixth when well fancied, a fair distance behind the surprise winner Silent Oscar. Even old Hardy Eustace and Harchibald finished ahead of him that day and it turned out he had picked up an injury and never raced again.

I always enjoyed the Galway Festival in July. With its mix of jump and flat races and mixture of day and evening meetings it always makes for a great week. It gives you a chance to socialise with a lot of jockeys and trainers from the jumps as well as the flat who you wouldn't normally get to see. But that year's Galway Festival would provide another 'first' in my life. And it wasn't a *'first'* that I'm particularly proud of.

Shortly before this random alcohol breath tests for jockeys had been introduced by the Turf Club and as yet no rider had ever failed. At the Galway Festival, all the major races are on earlier in the week with the Galway Plate, which I won in 1997 on Stroll Home, on the Wednesday and the big hurdle on the Thursday which I'd won on Ansar in 2001. I had landed a nice prize on the first day of the week, winning the novice chase on Hovering and then had a great run on a 20/1 outsider Ballyagran for Noel in the Galway Plate, finishing second just behind Sir Frederick. With a couple of other placed horses it was shaping up to be a very profitable week.

I only had one ride on the Friday, and the meeting was on late. I wasn't due to ride a horse called Zum See, owned by the Alex Syndicate, until 6.15pm in the Tony O'Malley Memorial Chase. Zum See had already run on the flat a few days before with Mick Kinane in the saddle but failed to land the gamble finishing in fourth. The owners were hopeful of a better run over fences. Because I only had one late ride the next day a few of us went out and gave it a right lash. I hadn't been drinking all week even though I had been out. But all the big races were over by now and we were out celebrating or commiserating. Either way, we had a mad old night and didn't get to bed until 7.30 or 8 o'clock the next morning. I'd say the alcohol was only getting into my system by then. But, since I still had about 11 hours before race time, I thought I'd be fine. We went to Moran's Of The Weir, a nice spot just at Kilcolgan that afternoon for a bit of grub and everyone was in good spirits with a bit of craic and slagging about the night before. It was then Jason Titley rang me from the course to say that they were testing for alcohol in Galway that day. He said I should watch myself as I had no spleen and because of this alcohol stays longer in your system.

In other sports, like soccer or athletics, random testing means that certain competitors are selected to be tested. In racing, however, it's the meeting that's the random bit. In other words, they select a race meeting, which in this case was the Friday of the Galway Festival, and they test *all* jockeys who are riding that day.

But as I said, I thought I'd be fine, that enough time had elapsed. I rang Noel to check that Zum See was definitely running and sure enough he was. I told him that they were testing and what Jason Titley had said about the alcohol staying in your system for longer if you've lost the spleen. So he asked me what time I had finished up drinking the night before and

I said *'ten past'*. Noel asked, *'ten past what?'* and I replied, *'ten past I dunno'*. But we still thought it would be ok because of the lateness of the race. I wasn't suggesting to Noel that he should withdraw Zum See, even if I was secretly hoping that he wasn't going to run. But once he said that Zum See was taking his chance I was never *not* going to turn up at the racecourse.

When I got to the track I was taken in and asked to blow into the breath test device, much the same as the one used by the police random breath testing at the side of the road or after a road accident. Sure enough I was over the limit and they then asked me to come back in 20 minutes for a second test. What I did next is a lesson in what *not* to do when about to face a breath test. I drank plenty of fluids and went into the sauna for a while to *'sweat it out of me'*. Now I realise that this is exactly what you should not do as it makes things worse. Now I had no chance of passing the second test. When in that situation I know now that I should have eaten something and gone for a walk, but hindsight's a great thing. When the second test posted over the limit, I was stood down from racing for the day and would face the stewards for further punishment.

After the test, I felt rubbish. It was at least better that I'd spoken to Noel earlier and told him there may be a problem and, while he wasn't happy about it, he didn't get on my case too much as he had been pre-warned.

****

Myself and Noel never really spoke about the drink following the introduction of random testing and only once had he seriously suggested that I would give it up altogether. Ironically, it was just after the big Galway Festival the previous summer. I remember I was walking out of the Dublin Horse Show at the RDS on the Wednesday when I got a phone call from Noel.

'Where are you?'

He sounded serious and annoyed about something.

'I'm just coming out of the RDS. Is everything all right?'

'I need to talk to you about something. I'll come down to your house. What time will you be there?'

'I should be there in half an hour.'

'I'll talk to you then.' Click.

I was only at the house a couple of minutes when Noel arrived. He said that I needed to have a serious think about the drinking. He said that every time he saw me at Galway I was pissed.

'You must have been on the lash every night last week. This has to stop. I want you to give it up for the rest of your career. If you don't, I won't put you up on my horses and that's the end of it.'

I had genuinely never considered giving up the drink indefinitely. Yes, I had managed it for the bet with JP McManus seven years beforehand, but now I was being asked to do it for free. And I had at least seven or eight years left in racing. I didn't commit to anything and just said to Noel that I would think about it.

I reacted the way I knew best: I went on the piss even harder. I booked into the Burlington Hotel in Dublin and ended up giving my room to the trainer Paul Nolan who was out drinking with me. After two days of solid drinking and late nights after the RDS, I saw Noel in the Pocket Bar on the Friday night. The Pocket Bar at the RDS was the place to be after the showjumping and Noel was there after having a meal with Puppy Power's father, Capt. Con Power, one of Ireland's greatest ever showjumpers. They were good friends and always met up at the RDS. Worse for wear but in flying form I ran up behind Noel and jumped up on his back. Thankfully he took it well as I pretended to 'ride' him over to the bar to get a drink.

Noel just laughed and said that I could stay in the bar with him that night on condition that it was my last night drinking. He kept saying:

'Now enjoy it. Make the most of it, because it's your last night'.

And I just kept agreeing with him, assuring him that it was. But of course it wasn't. I just didn't drink in front of him too much. He knew I hadn't quit, but knew I had cut back.

In fairness, I always thought there were worse things than drink. I never did drugs, just didn't see the point. If I was ever offered cocaine, or other so-called recreational drugs, I always had the perfect excuse to avoid any peer pressure: that I would be fucked if I got tested for it at the racecourse. When I started in racing there was hardly any of it around. I know some people will say that I'm talking shite but at the beginning of the 90s I saw feck all of it around Meath. In the years since then I heard of the odd guy doing it on the flat, but it largely passed by the jump jockeys. That's not being naive, it's just a fact. To be honest, drugs to us came in the form of a prescription drug known as the *'piss pill'* during my early years. As the quaint description suggests, this was prescribed for patients with trouble passing water. For jockeys, it could help get rid of any excess or unwanted fluids and could take three or four pounds off the weighing scales. That was years ago when I felt pressure to stay light for flat racing, but that's never been an issue for the remainder of my career.

****

But the day of the failed breath test at Galway in 2007 was an absolute sickener. In fairness, the owners of the horse I was meant to ride were fairly sound about it. Finbarr Cahill is a good guy and most of the rest of the syndicate would have known me and they would have known what the craic was. Fortunately for the owners Zum See went on to win with Denis O'Regan in the saddle, meaning it was a missed opportunity for me to bag another winner. He had gone off well-backed at odds of 6/1 second favourite and won a nice prize of over €22,000.

After the failed test I had to appear before the stewards and I really didn't know what to expect. There had already been hundreds of tests carried out over the previous weeks and I was the very first positive. Initially, I thought I would have to appear before the Turf Club at a later date but then I was told that the stewards at the course had the power to deal with it there and then. So my fate was in their hands, and I didn't make much of an effort pleading my case. I just explained that I hadn't been drinking that day, and that the alcohol had obviously remained in my system from the previous night. My medical history had also played a role. It was tougher for my body to break down the alcohol and that it stayed in my system longer than for normal people. After a quick discussion I was called back in and told that I was being stood down for the rest of the day and that I was banned from three further race days the following week.

I left the course disgusted with myself and basically spent the day doing nothing. I had gone there that day with high hopes of riding a valuable winner, but left the track with my tail between my legs and facing a three-day suspension from racing. I would probably have preferred to just head back to Meath but I had rides on the Saturday and Sunday at Galway and there was no way I was just going to leave.

The only silver lining of the entire episode was that the ban was only for three days. I thought it was quite soft at the time and had expected worse. And the three days selected for the ban meant that I only missed travelling to race meetings at Downpatrick and Ballinrobe the following week. My banned days also coincided with the Dublin Horse Show and this meant I could head up to that. It wasn't the worst punishment in the world.

Unfortunately, or some would say stupidly, the next jockey to get done under random breath testing would also be me. And that time, the stewards would not be so lenient.

CHAPTER 19

Off To A Cracker

As it turned out I finished off the week at Galway on a positive note with a Sunday winner on a horse called 'Brave Right'. It wasn't exactly the most appropriate name to sum up the week, but by that time I had decided to try and make light of the whole episode and just get on with the job in hand. In fact, I had even made my mind up that I was going to have some fun about it in the parade ring after the Brave Right race. The story of the failed breath test had been all over the newspapers but I hadn't been asked for a comment by TV or other media. I knew Noel had been quizzed for his reaction but very few people had asked me for mine. I don't know why that was, as it wasn't like I was running away from it. Brave Right was a quirky horse with scatty jumping which was tough to steer and the race was pretty crazy from the start. First of all, the well-backed favourite Breaking Silence, ridden by Barry Geraghty, fell at the very first fence. Then that loose horse pushed out the leader Tully Hill a few fences later and knocked him out of the race. In the meantime, Brave Right was giving me a tough time and he jumped desperately throughout the race. In fact, the horse tried his best to unseat me at the third last but I just about managed to stay on board and won quite comfortably in the end. As I was coming back to the parade ring I prepared myself for the post-race interviews.

I decided that when they ask me the inevitable question about the breath test I'll just laugh and say, *'Well you would need a few drinks to ride a horse like this'* and leave it at that. There was no need for me to hide and be coy about it, I'll give a quote and that will be the end of it. Bizarrely, even though I did all the interviews nobody asked me about the failed breath test at all, which I have to say I was a little bit surprised about. Perhaps, disappointed even.

****

When I got back racing my strike rate was better than ever and I had over 60 winners between Galway and the end of the year, helped by trebles at Gowran Park, Navan and Fairyhouse. In October I went to my friend Mick Foley's wedding in Limerick, but missed the start because I was riding at Naas where I won on a horse called Antipode for Noel. That night I was telling everyone who would listen that I would win the next day at Wexford on a horse called Angels' Share, a horse part-owned by a friend of mine Simon Fay. I think half the wedding was on the horse and we were backed down from 5/1 to 7/2 favourite just before the off. Thankfully, I managed to get up to win by half a length from Andrew McNamara on Marseillais. I went straight back to Limerick after racing and all the wedding guests were in flying form.

The year had finished on a high with almost 30 winners during November and December alone. After the short Christmas break, it was back to business as usual and I enjoyed a rare four-timer at Punchestown in February. Anyone who rides will tell you how difficult it can be to get a winner at times, especially if you or your trainer are going through a bad patch. And to get a double or treble is a fantastic feeling, no matter what the odds are. But to get a four-timer, and in the first four races of the day at that, is priceless. I started off that day by winning the first two hurdle races for Noel Meade aboard Clarnazar and Jered, and then made it three on Moore's Law for Michael Grassick. But the fourth race, the Festival Hurdle, was really the one in which I had really fancied my chances because I was riding a horse called Mourne Rambler for Tony Martin, that had previously won on the flat. I didn't have a moment's worry on the horse as we drew clear just after three out and won to complete a 275/1 four-timer. It was definitely a high point of the season and the troubles of the previous Galway Festival seemed a world away.

So I came into the 2008 Cheltenham Festival three weeks later full of hope. But that Cheltenham said everything about the fickle nature of racing, as I was awarded both the best and the worst ride of the week.

I started off the week with victory in the Fred Winter aboard Emma Lavelle's Crack Away Jack. Timmy Murphy had won on Crack Away Jack last time out at Sandown but was riding the favourite Ashkazar for his boss David Pipe this time around. Murphy was hoping to help land a £75,000 bonus having won the Sunderlands Imperial Cup the previous week and was well fancied to do so. When the tape went up I settled at the back in the last pair with Andrew McNamara on an outsider Indian Spring. We were well covered up for most of the two miles but managed to ease my horse through the field in the final half mile. Approaching the third-last we were still at the back of the main group but going incredibly well and I was always confident of catching the favourite. I jumped up behind Ashkazar at the final hurdle and swept past him on the run-in up the hill to score comfortably in the end by a couple of lengths. I hadn't touched the horse until the final 100 yards and the Festival committee deemed it the ride of the week.

The following day I awoke to the bizarre news that Cheltenham was cancelled for the Wednesday because of high winds. The previous day had been so mild that we could not see this coming at all. But winds had ripped through some of the tenting at the Guinness Village and it was deemed too risky to proceed with racing when there would be over 60,000 punters packed into one side of the racecourse. I watched *The Morning Line* on Channel 4 and could hardly believe my eyes. I had given up the drink for a few months while the major racing was on so I was kind of at a loose end for the rest of the day. Myself and a few other jockeys just went into the town centre for some lunch and kicked our heels for the remainder of the day. At this stage we knew that the Festival organisers had decided to compact the following three days' racing into two, with both Thursday and Friday's cards containing 10 races. They were going to be two tough days' racing, but when you are at a big festival like Cheltenham you would ride 20 times a day just to get a winner.

But the following two days were fruitless as far as winners were concerned. Schindlers Hunt finished fourth in the Queen Mother, but was almost in a different county as Master Minded destroyed the field to win by a distance. In the Gold Cup, I finished last of the seven finishers on Afistfullofdollars as Paul Nicholls had the first three home in the Gold Cup with Denman, Kauto Star and Neptune Collonges, in that order.

Perhaps my best chance of bagging a second winner that week was on a Tony Martin runner called Pyscho, which had been laid out for the Vincent O'Brien County Hurdle. Unfortunately, this was not my finest hour and many would think I completely messed it up. As I said, I was told it was regarded as the worst ride of the week.

The ride came about by chance really. Ruby Walsh had won well on the horse at Leopardstown that January but Ruby had a ride in the race for his gaffer Paul Nicholls on I'msingingtheblues. We were off a low enough weight and Tony Martin was bullish

At home with my partner Rachel and our gorgeous daughter Kacey-Lou

Kacey-Lou with my other daughter Lauryn messing about in the snow

Acting the ass at the Charity Donkey Race at Galway in 2011 **BELOW:** Coming to blows with David Casey in a White Collar Charity Boxing Event in Naas in 2008

- Photo by RAY LOHAN/SPORTSFILE

Hunting has been the love of my life. Here I am out hunting with Juicey

Taking a jump on Mossy at an event in 2010
BELOW: Being tossed in the air by Daiti O Se and rugby stars Ronan O'Gara, Alan Quinlan and Tommy Bowe

- Photo by JIM WALPOLE

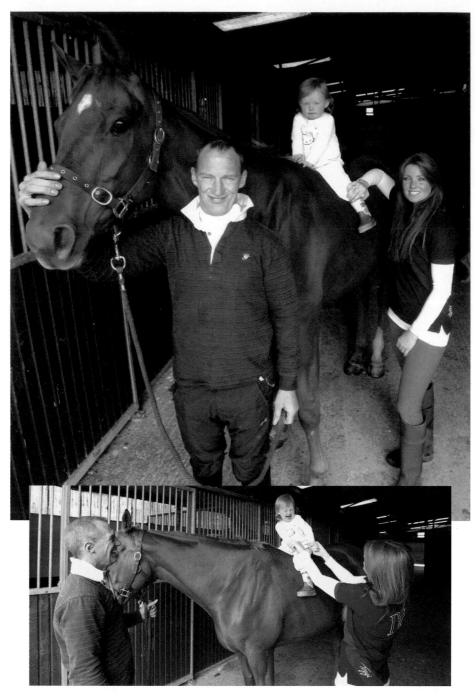

Kacey-Lou is a pure natural aboard a horse in the yard – the real problem is getting her down without her screaming the stables down!

- Photos by GARY ASHE

Back at our new home in Tara with Rachel and Kacey-Lou

- Photos by GARY ASHE

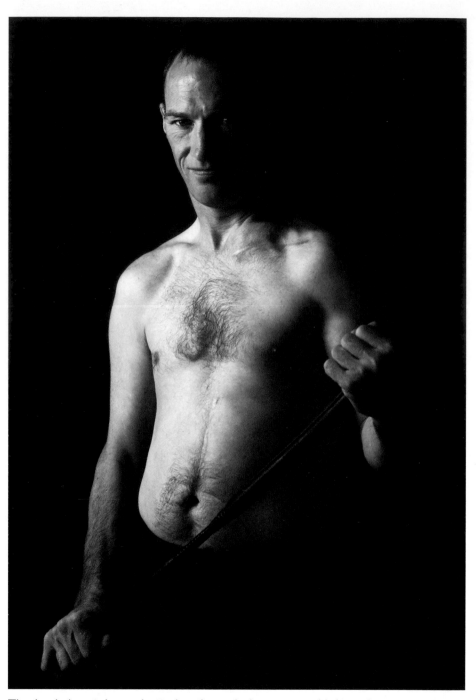

The body has taken a battering through the years, with just about every bone broken

- Photo by GARY ASHE

before the race, in which we went off the 5/1 favourite.

'Just tuck him in behind and don't panic. As long as you're within four lengths of anything at the last hurdle he'll win handy enough. He'll be flying at the finish,' he told me.

But the race didn't go to plan at the finish. He was tough to get going but came back on the bridle and settled in off the pace. I had been cruising for most of the race and passed plenty of tired horses in the 22-runner field when climbing the hill towards the finish. I was still going well when I made my move at the final hurdle but a 50/1 outsider named Silver Jaro had skipped away for Noel Fehily, and as hard as I tried to rein him in, we finished under a length down in second. My horse had been the subject of a massive pre-race gamble, so it's never pleasant when it doesn't come off. A large section of the crowd believed I had left it too late and let their feelings be known as we walked back to the parade ring. And it's hard to argue when you fail to win.

****

The Grand National that year was one of the big points of my career. Nine years previously I had won the greatest race on earth on Bobbyjo, a horse trained by Dad. Now I had a solid chance on a horse trained by Mam's brother Arthur. I was booked to ride King Johns Castle for the first time, a nice grey horse owned by JP McManus and had been ridden by Davy Russell in its last couple of races. But Davy had the ride on Chelsea Harbour and had been quite fancied for the race after winning a National trial nicely at Punchestown that year. AP McCoy had the pick of JP's runners and decided to go for Butlers Cabin, winner of the previous year's Irish Grand National, but I thought King Johns Castle came into the race with quite a bit in hand. Having finished second in five chase starts, he finally got off the mark a few weeks before the big race. But like Bobbyjo had done previously, his win was over hurdles and less than two and a half miles at Naas. So it didn't seem like a great prep race for the Grand National run over four and a half miles and the big fences at Aintree. That said though, it gave him track experience and fitness without serious risk of injury.

The meeting at Aintree had been going just ok up to that point. I hadn't gone there with a great book of rides and had managed to get placed on outsiders Bothar Na in the Topham Chase and Harper Valley in the Grade One Novices Hurdle. Conna Castle finished fourth but was a distance behind the winner Tidal Bay in the Novices Chase, the last test over the fences before the big race.

The betting on the Grand National was, as always, chaotic. My mount, King Johns Castle, was 20/1 in the betting behind the two favourites Comply Or Die and Cloudy Lane, with Simon, Butlers Cabin and Barry Geraghty's ride, Slim Pickings, next best in the market. After the usual pre-race fanfare of the group photograph, the parade and then the bustle around the start, we jumped off nicely. I was able to settle King Johns Castle in about the middle of the field and was able to get him into a good jumping rhythm. The first half of the race went by quite quickly and I remember just trying to keep out of trouble and let the horse pick his stride. We only had two real scares during the race. At Bechers the second time around my horse just kind of dived at the fence and pecked his head on landing. I was up just behind the leaders as McCoy took a fall on Butlers Cabin at that fence, but I managed to sit tight and get King Johns Castle back running. I was then badly hampered three fences later at Valentines when Dominic Elsworth fell on Simon, but from then on the race went like a dream. Coming to the fourth last, Barry was still going well on Slim Pickings but my other good friend Davy Russell was starting to struggle on his horse Chelsea Harbour after leading for a few fences. I was back on the bridle and as I passed Davy, he shouted at me, *'Don't hit the front too soon, wait til the line'*. I still remember that, as it's always nice to hear encouraging words from other jockeys at such a critical time. But as soon as Davy said it, my horse started to wander a bit and I had to push him to keep him up with the leading group. I was still well in contention and tracked the leaders Snowy Morning and Bewleys Berry into the second last before Timmy Murphy kicked for home and went clear on Comply Or Die. Timmy pushed on to the elbow and, even though my horse was flying at the finish, we finished four lengths down in second place. We had travelled four and a half miles and jumped over 30 large obstacles in just over nine minutes. Forty horses had started the race yet only 15 runners completed the course, with 11 fallers, eight unseating their jockeys and the rest pulled up when well beaten. And in the end it came down to just four lengths, probably less than two seconds between ultimate triumph and *almost there*. It was a superb run, but after the race it's hard not to think about what could have been. Especially when you have been there before, in that winner's enclosure. You have tasted that feeling and desperately want to sample it again. Perhaps I will get that chance before my career has ended.

****

I missed the 2008 Galway Festival after taking a heavy fall in a handicap chase at Killarney the week before. I was riding She's Supersonic for Tony Martin but the horse fell at the first fence and gave me a kick in the head knocking me clean out. When I came around I was being taken to the local hospital where I was treated for severe concussion and I was out of racing for three weeks. Ironically, while I was knocked out, the horse was fine and got back to its feet and kept on running. In fact, it was so good that it ran the very next day for Slippers Madden in another chase at Killarney and finished a close second.

But, while I may have missed the big Galway Festival, I was back at that track in October and once again found myself in front of the stewards. This was becoming quite a regular stop-over for me. Last year it was the scene of the failed breath test when I had been suspended for three race days. And at this meeting two years ago I had been fined for refusing to jump off on a horse called Marbeuf when no jockey had wanted to cut out the running. The end result was a farce at the starting line when we all just stayed on the spot after the tape went up and then walked for the first 50 yards or so. After I had finished in third place behind Barry Geraghty and Ruby Walsh all 10 jockeys in the race were called in by the stewards and fined for misconduct.

Now here I was back in front of the stewards again at the same track. This time they were having a go at a few of us for failing to chase a young apprentice jockey Andrew Thornton who had gone off like a scalded cat on an outsider called Ka-huna. The problem was that, despite the heavy ground, Kahuna never stopped and won by a distance with the rest of us trailing in a long way behind. I was on an outsider that day too, a horse called Jaamid, but it was just one of those times where we had misjudged the horse in front.

I finished the year fighting my corner again. But this time lit-erally, as I got 'roped in' to take part in a White Collar Boxing Event at Time Nightclub in Naas to raise funds for two local football clubs. I was supposed to fight Ruby Walsh and I fan-cied my chances. But Ruby was scheduled to ride at Chelten-ham that weekend and had to pull out. I was then phoned and asked to fight flat jockey Johnny Murtagh, but there was no chance I was getting in to a ring with that lunatic. Johnny had been boxing for years at a decent level and I knew he'd fucking kill me. And knowing how competitive Johnny is, he would not be there for the craic. He would be there to fight and knock my head off. So eventually the organisers got David Casey to step in and we had a great laugh as we swung at each other like mad men. We had only trained in the ring for about two minutes before the fight but I think we were both just glad to get the job done. Two years later Robbie 'Puppy' Power was supposed to fight Davy Condon at the same event but Puppy had to pull out because of injury. I put the gloves back on and took a few swings at Condon. It was the least Condon deserved.

****

I had a cracking chance in the first race of the 2009 Cheltenham Festival, the Supreme Novices Hurdle. I was riding a horse called Go Native for Noel which had three hurdle wins under his belt, including a nice win in a Grade Two hurdle at Naas three weeks beforehand. He always jumped very well but he showed lots of gears that day and the decision was made to take him to Cheltenham. We were quietly confident, but he wasn't fancied in the betting ring at Cheltenham. We went off at odds of 12/1 behind one of the Irish hotpots for the week, Cousin Vinny, a horse well fancied to follow up his Bumper win from the previous year. I held Go Native up at the back and eased him through the field, keeping him on the inside in about sixth or seventh before he quickened down the hill to take the lead before the second last. It was a lot earlier than I would have wanted to be in the lead with the full Cheltenham Hill ahead but he kicked on and won well enough in the end from Medermit and Somersby, with Cousin Vinny only managing fifth.

Harchibald had come back into form, after pulling off a surprise win in the Christmas Hurdle at Kempton. He won that race easily on the bridle, despite being bumped by the favourite Punjabi who fell at the second last. Despite this win Harchibald barely had a friend in the betting ring for that year's Smurfit Kappa Champion Hurdle and went off at odds of 33/1, well behind favourite Binocular that eventually finished in third, a couple of lengths off the winner Punjabi. Harchibald never ran a yard that day. I was pushing him after just a few hurdles and we finished tailed off. The ground had gone against us that day, as it had rained that morning and it came up way too soft for Harchibald.

The rest of the week was a bit of a disaster, with Patsy Hall falling at the second last with every chance in the William Hill and then Realt Dubh finished a long way back in the field in the Ballymore Novices Hurdle. But worse was to come on the Thursday as I was unseated off Jaamid and ended up sidelined for months. Jaamid was an outsider in the Jewson, a chase over two miles and five furlongs, and was never going well. When he lost me at the 13th fence I got trampled on the ground and left the course by ambulance. At Cheltenham Hospital the news wasn't good. I had a lacerated liver and a punctured lung. My Cheltenham was over, not to mention the upcoming Grand National at Aintree. The only highlight for me that week was watching my sister Nina grab her third Cheltenham winner on Garde Champetre in the Cross Country Chase, in which I finished fifth on Heads On The Ground.

So I was back on the sidelines. Unfortunately, worse was to come that summer. And this time, I could blame nobody but myself.

CHAPTER 20

It's Racing Or The Booze

Fool me once, shame on you; fool me twice, shame on me ....

2009 was going so well off the racetrack. Rachel gave birth to a gorgeous baby girl and we were finally moving into our dream home that we built at Rathfeigh in Tara in my home county of Meath. I had owned the 40 acres land for almost 10 years but now I was getting my finances in order thanks largely to my personal assistant Joules Lamb, and to my accountant JP Wynne, a Tipperary man who got me back in the right direction, sorted out my taxes, and helped me sort out some property ties that were causing constant headaches. Mam also played a huge part, as she was instrumental in selling the properties. Now I could finally concentrate on getting my land developed. It had always been my ambition to turn the rough land into a home with stables and facilities to either train or pre-train horses. I also wanted a gallops and paddocks and that was all now coming together. In racing you can never really plan too far in advance for when you will retire, or worse, are forced to retire. So I wanted to try and build something for a time when life as a full-time professional jockey would end.

Rachel and I were as tight as ever and I was as happy as I'd been for a long time. Rachel is great and has always has been from the first day we got together. She is just so easy to get on with. She puts up with me and I put up with her. I think that's the simple key to our relationship, and why I can see us being together for the rest of our lives. She's as stubborn and as cranky as I am and I think that's why we clicked. She is such a hard worker at home too, and I would be lost without her down the yard. On top of that she's a super mum, and our daughter is the spit of her, even though it kills her that Kacey-Lou will always run to me first. I guess she's just a Daddy's girl. I was at the birth to watch my gorgeous new baby come into the world and there wasn't a more proud dad in the country that day. Rachel was brilliant there too, and it just felt like everything was coming together. Life was complete. Rachel picked our daughter's name, Kacey-Lou. As I said, Rachel was into her music and particularly loved American Country. I think that's where the name came from. I already had a daughter, Lauryn, 10 years previously and she is now showing great promise as a rider and showjumper. I see her regularly as well as her younger brother Josh.

It was October 30, 2009, and I was due to ride at a fairly typical meeting at Naas Racecourse the next day. I had just ridden Pandorama to win a nice novice chase at Punchestown a couple of days previously and after a short journey to Clonmel for just a single ride, I had a day off before the meeting at Naas. Little did I know that the next day would have a defining moment in my riding career, and perhaps, my life. As Naas in Kildare was so close to home in Meath it meant that myself and Rachel could enjoy a now rare night out together. As long as I didn't overdo it, there would be no problem about riding the next day. Our baby daughter Kacey-Lou had only been born just over a month earlier and it was our first opportunity since then to go out together. A friend of Rachel, Aine who is David Casey's wife, was having a bit of a house party so we went along and had a great night. They are both good friends of ours and there were lots of people there we know very well.

I hadn't tore it as far as booze was concerned and left Rachel there and headed to bed at 1.30am that morning. No bullshit, that's how it happened.

The next day I made my way to the track and after I swiped my card at the jockeys' entrance I was told that there was random breath testing at the course that day. As at Galway, the meeting had been chosen at random for alcohol breath testing and all jockeys were to be tested. At that point I was sure I was grand and I rang David Casey to let him know the craic as he would have been up much later than I was. When I got him he was in his car on the way to the racecourse and had already been told about the tests by another jockey.

Casey had his own testing unit in his car and had already tested himself showing himself to be slightly over. He was confident, however, that he would be under the limit by the time he had to enter the track. To be on the safe side, I told him that I'd meet him in the car park because I wanted to have a go of his machine myself to make sure I was alright. After what happened the last time at Galway, I couldn't afford to be caught again.

If I was done a second time the stewards would throw the book at me, and Noel Meade would probably throw a lot worse at me. Adding to my worries was that I was due to ride Prima Vista, a horse owned by a few good lads including a close friend John O'Meara. John was desperately ill in hospital and I'd just phoned him an hour earlier to see how he was feeling and discuss the horse's chances. Before I ended the call I had told him that I *would* win at Naas that day for him.

I sat into David Casey's car and blew into the test kit. It showed I was marginally over. I was bricking it now. It was Halloween and this was turning into a real-life nightmare. I still had a bit of time so myself and David went for a bit of a walk to try knock off that extra bit of alcohol to get me back under the safety line. Casey wasn't riding until the second race, giving him an extra half hour. But I had the ride in the opening race and I had to go into the track first. I failed the first test. When the light turned red I was told I would have to conduct a second test in front of the stewards a short time later.

I had 20 minutes before the second test but in my heart I knew there would be damn all chance of passing it. After the first time at Galway I realised that because of the spleen injury, it was far tougher for someone like me to break down the alcohol in my system. Since the extra 20 minutes was not going to make much difference I decided to bite the bullet and ring Noel. I only had a couple of minutes to get my head together and think about what to say to him. I decided to just come clean. No small-talk. No bullshit. Just tell him straight out and see if there was anything that could be done. I dialed the number and said *'Look Noel, this isn't looking good. They are testing, and I've failed the first one'.* I asked if he could do something before the second test, perhaps say that I was ill and unfit to ride. But Noel wasn't one bit happy and was having none of it. *'You're on your own this time. I'm not sticking up for you again. Go in and tell them yourself'*, he said, or something to that effect. I knew he was serious, perhaps he had never been more serious in his life. He was in one of his moods and I know when Noel gets like that there's no talking to him and you just have to give him space.

Of course it wasn't Noel's fault; I had let him down again. I suppose I had plenty of past form of staying up all night but on this occasion I had genuinely hit the bed at 1.30 the night before and believed I would be fine. Now I was staring down the barrel of a shotgun. I was in a no-win situation.

I suppose I could have left the track in shame before the second test and face the consequences later. The alternative was to take the second test, inevitably fail it, and probably lose my riding licence forever. I was a lamb to the slaughter. But maybe, just maybe, I might just scrape a pass on the second one. In truth, however, I would never have just done a runner and left the track. Running away would have caused more trouble in the long-term.

I went in and repeated the test which again, as expected, showed I was over the limit and I was stood down from racing for the day. As I took the test, Noel was standing at the door. Clearly he was furious; there was steam coming out of his ears and when the test result was revealed he just shook his head and walked outside. I was fucked. I asked the tester Peter Matthews if I could take the test again before my next ride on the card because I was only 0.1 or something over the limit. He said that there was no going back. That was it; I would not be allowed race at all that day. And unlike the first time I'd failed the test at Galway, the stewards were unable to deal with it that day. I was told that I would get a call to appear before the Turf Club's Referrals Committee in a couple of weeks.

I took my things and walked straight out of the racecourse, got into my car and headed home.

****

After I left the track, I picked up my phone and called the one man who most deserved a direct call in this situation.

Prima Vista's owner John O'Meara was a good friend of both myself and Noel and I'm sad to say that he has since passed away from cancer. John had been an owner with Noel's yard for as long as I could remember and he had given me plenty of winners, well over 20. In my younger days I won a fair few times on his horse Bob Devani and he provided me with my first jump win all those years ago. He was a good decent man and a very good friend.

I felt bad for John as he was in hospital at the time of the race and I certainly didn't want him to hear the news of my failed breath test from anybody but me. So as I left Naas Racecourse I thought he deserved to hear it from myself. I thought about how I had rang him earlier that day trying to cheer him up; this phone call would be much tougher to make. The way I saw it was that if he was ok about it, then I didn't really care what others thought, or what the punishment would be. He was a good friend and I hadn't wanted to let him down. John answered his mobile straightaway and I told him the story, and waited for his response. But John didn't tear into me at all. He just said: *'Look Paul, don't worry about it, there will be other days'*. I got off the phone and just thought about the kind of man John was. I was ringing him to tell him that due to my loss of judgement I would not be able to ride his horse that day, a horse that I told him earlier would win, and he was so good about it.

And he was right, there were other days. The following Sunday I rode his horse Aitmatov to a big win at Navan. A Paul Nolan horse called Noble Prince, that has since won a big race at the Cheltenham Festival, was the hot favourite for the race. I felt huge pressure after what had happened the week before at Naas and gave Aitmatov everything I had. The horse responded and we won the race quite easily at big odds of 10/1. It was a nice Grade 2 winner for Noel as well, and I made it a big race double on the day with another one of Meade's horses, Oscar Looby. At least I felt it had made up in some way for what had happened the previous week. But unfortunately there weren't enough of those good days left. John passed away just seven weeks later. I will never forget the kindness and understanding he showed me. That is why he deserves the Dedication at the start of this book.

On the day of the failed breath test at Naas, Noel got a very good young rider Emmet Mullins to take the ride on Prima

Vista, but unfortunately he could only finish third. I think that made things even worse for Noel. It's hard to say if I would have won on him but I'm certain I knew the horse better and perhaps that may have made the difference on the day.

Later on that night I got a call from Noel as I was due to ride for him at Limerick the next day. He was still fuming. The day before Naas had been the first big hunt of the season and Noel knew I had been riding. So he presumed I had gone straight out with the lads from the hunt and gone on the piss all night. I told him I had gone home and had a quiet night with Rachel at Aine Casey's house but I'm not sure he was convinced. Then the conversation got fairly serious. He said that it was last chance saloon, so to speak.

Noel: *'This is where it ends. The drink has to stop.'*

Me: *'Grand so.'*

Noel: *'No, seriously. We won't fall out about it. You will survive without me and I'll survive without you, and we will still be friends. But you just won't be riding any horses of mine again unless you are off the drink. I'm sure you'll still get plenty of rides from others, but just not from me.'*

Me: *'Grand so.'*

I was never much of a talker in these situations but I did go on to say that I would genuinely give it a try and if I could do it I would. If I couldn't I'd accept what he was saying.

A week later when I rode the double at Navan, Noel called me over after racing and asked how I was getting on. I told him I hadn't had a drink since our chat and I was giving it a good go. I just said, *'Look Noel, I've been off the drink since that day and it's going fine. I'm not making any promises and if I can't fecking do it, well it means I can't fecking do it. But I'm giving it a try and I should be able.'* And he just said something like, *'ok, I'll stand by you so.'* And I don't think Noel's ever asked me about it again.

And that's where it ended for drink and me. It was that sim-

243

ple, but that's not to say it was easy. I suppose I always knew that I'd have to knock it on the head sometime but I guess I got away with it for longer than I should have and I stretched it out for years. Life is there to be enjoyed and if the truth be known I bloody enjoyed drinking. You enjoy the buzz, you enjoy the craic. Whether I was meeting my friends from back home, or going out with other jockeys after racing, drink was always a big part of it. I also liked the effect that it had on me there and then. I was never much of a talker and I wouldn't be great socially among people I didn't know, but drink helped that. It also gave me something to do while listening to other people chatting away. I tended to just take a step back and listen in.

I had reduced the drinking over the previous few years anyway. I know that sounds a bit stupid because I failed the test in Galway just two years earlier, but it's true. During the winter months I was hardly drinking at all except maybe a big session on the Sunday night after racing if there was no Monday meeting. The racing was too important and between travelling and working the horses there was little free time to get into too much trouble. But during the summer there were very few big meetings and there always seemed to be some big festival or dance to go to, meaning I tended to lapse back into the drinking habit.

Did I miss it? Yes of course, but not as much as I thought I would. It's not the big sessions I miss but I suppose it's going for a pint or two with the lads after racing that I miss most. I'm not the kind that can head down the local pub and drink orange juice all night while watching the others get wasted. What I have found strange is that I don't miss the drink at all when I attend big awards nights or point-to-point dances. You just enjoy spending time with people and having the craic. You almost live off their energy on the night. And at these events there doesn't tend to be many sane people in attendance. The night is spent in fits of laughter. I suppose I've come around to not letting the absence of drink bother me anymore and some of that's down to Red Bull. At least it gives a bit of a buzz. Red Bull is my new high and I tend to drink lots of the stuff. I'd be shagged without it.

****

After that day at Naas I would have to wait for a couple of weeks to hear what the Turf Club would throw at me and the newspapers were having a field day in between. I went back racing at Fairyhouse four days after the failed test and tried to dodge endless questions about the upcoming hearing. And it wasn't exactly a dream return, pulling up twice in my four rides and failing to get a winner. Next up was a trip up north to Down Royal but my luck wasn't changing after my two fancied runners Nicanor and Go Native were both beaten into second. But thankfully I did get back into the winners' enclosure later that week with the double at Navan.

In the meantime, I decided that I would get some counselling to help with the absence of alcohol. I must admit, I was very sceptical at first. As far as I was concerned, I'd knocked it on the head and that was that. I didn't know if I could keep off it forever, but I was going to give it a go and I would deal with it myself. To be brutally honest I really only agreed to do the counselling because I was told it would look better for the Turf Club hearing. I would be going in to the hearing, holding my hands up and asking for mercy. I would be going there as someone who not only admitted having a problem, but as someone who was doing something practical to deal with it.

This is a small source of embarrassment for me. Or maybe it's fairer to say that I'm not exactly comfortable talking about it. I was never much of a talker and the thought of going to see someone, a complete stranger, and talking about my troubles made me ill. But, if that's what I had to do, that's what I would do. The risks were too great, and I had no idea what I would do if the Turf Club handed down a lifetime ban. What else would I do? I'm not exactly geared up to do anything else in life, and I certainly hadn't earned anywhere near enough to be able to retire.

In fact, quite the opposite was true. Over the past few years I had completely stretched myself and I was under severe strain financially. I had bought a few houses through the years because it seemed the most financially sound thing to do when I was a young jockey. Obviously things have changed dramatically these days. But when I started riding professionally I seemed to have plenty of cash all at once, and bought my first house when I was only in my early 20s. I bought and sold a couple through the years, mostly renting them out.

By the end of 2009 I still had three properties and was struggling with the repayments. I was building our new home and stables but the building costs were running way, way over budget and I was suffering badly. I had a huge tax bill to pay and the banks were moving in as well. The pressure was immense and some days my head just wasn't where it should have been. Did my riding suffer? I suppose that's for others to judge. But I do know that I was extremely conscious that I needed to avoid injury. If I got 'broke up', as we call it in racing, I would be out injured and unable to earn a living. These are extra pressures that you really could do without in your head as you are riding a charging horse at a fence or hurdle at over 20 miles per hour.

By the time the hearing came around two weeks later I was not in a great place and I feared the worst. I had to appear before the Referrals Committee at the Turf Club's office beside the Curragh Racecourse. There had been plenty of speculation in the Irish and British racing and news pages that I could face a lifetime ban and a fine of between 10 and 20 thousand Euro. I have to say, in all honesty, that I worried greatly about what would become of me if they decided to hammer me. This was new territory for the bosses in Irish racing. Two years earlier I had been the first jockey to fail an alcohol test and now here I was crossing the line a second time. They had never been in this situation before and I guess a message had to be sent to other jockeys that this kind of carry-on would not be tolerated.

The hearing was fairly brief. I had legal representation with me and we asked the Committee to adjourn their decision on my future. My solicitor told them that I had given up alcohol and was attending counseling. He also told them that I would agree to be tested at *every* race meeting for a number of months, to prove my commitment before they handed down the punishment. He also went through the hours before racing. I had not been drinking on the morning. It had been the previous night. My spleen injury had made it difficult to break down alcohol in my system. Everything was thrown in.

But the Committee stood firm. It was in their remit to deal with the flouting of their laws there and then. We were asked to leave the room while they deliberated. They weren't particularly interested in what I would do to avoid breaking the rules in the future; just what I had done in the past. I had already been given a chance at Galway, and they wanted to deal with the failed test at Naas as swiftly as possible. As I stood outside the room I believed they were now going to throw the book at me. I thought that it may have been better had I just gone there on my own that day, held my hands up, and assured them that it wouldn't happen again.

I believe the Turf Club were out to make an example of me. When I was called back in I was told that I would be stood down for 30 race days and fined €5,000. At first I was relieved that they hadn't taken my licence indefinitely. But over the next few days I worried about the months ahead. The recession had been bad enough, but now my only means of earning money had been taken away. And, of course, the bills still had to be paid.

As the ban wouldn't come into effect until November 26 I tried to keep my head down and get some winners on the board. Jered won nicely for me at Punchestown and Watson Lake landed a Grade 2 prize in a two-and-a-half mile chase at Clonmel before the ban took effect. Bizarrely I was able to ride the day after the ban at Thurles as it was a rearranged meeting that was meant to have been run days earlier and I was able to get a final winner on Gordon Elliott's horse Chicago Grey. But that was that as far as my racing year was concerned, as I was banned from the track for the entire month of December and the first half of January.

They were tough times. As I mentioned, I was struggling to make financial ends meet and now I couldn't earn a living for nearly two months. On top of that, I would have to find €5,000 to pay my fine to the Turf Club. In fairness, the Turf Club allowed me to address the fine by paying them €500 a month for 10 months, but it was another bill on top of everything else. I would also miss out on all the valuable December meetings, which always made up for the leaner months. I was drowning in debt, and needed to consolidate all my loans into one large affordable monthly payment. So, on the advice of my accountant JP Wynne, I decided to cut my losses and sell every property I had. There was no way that I could let my family home come under threat, and it was heading that way as the banks zoned in on my assets.

The other three houses were meant to be my nest egg, my pension after racing. One house was now worth what was owed on the mortgage, but the other two did very well on the market and I was able to clear most of the debts. Even with the Capital

Gains Tax, it got me out of trouble. I know many jockeys, and people in all walks of life, have not been so lucky. Many are burdened with 'pension' properties that are actually worth a lot less than they paid for them and have had their life savings wiped out as a result of being caught in negative equity. Thankfully, I was able to clear the boards and eventually ease the burden on the monthly bills.

I also completed the course of alcohol counselling. I was surprised to discover that these sessions did actually help me get through the rough times. During the first couple of sessions, I don't think I hardly said anything at all. But from then on, I got more comfortable with the whole situation and was able to benefit from the entire experience. Noel had encouraged me to complete the course as he believed that it would help. I suppose the very fact that I continued to go to counseling after the Turf Club hearing proved to him that I was serious about staying off the drink.

****

2009 had been a rollercoaster year, both on the track and at home. I'd say that the whole breath test experience had cost me around fifty grand in lost earnings, fines and legal fees. Fifty grand that I could ill afford to lose. But for now, I would just have to kick back, lick my wounds, and hope that 2010 would get off to a better start.

CHAPTER 21

A Matter Of Life And Death

In the end I didn't get back racing until the Naas meeting in the middle of January and it felt like I'd been months away from the track. I didn't go to many race meetings while I was banned, although I did travel over to Kempton for the Christmas Hurdle on St Stephen's Day with Noel to saddle up Go Native, as I had done for the Fighting Fifth at Newcastle the previous month. Davy Condon had taken the ride on both occasions and won well. Instead, I watched a bit of Leopardstown and a few other race meetings on television at home. Meanwhile, there was plenty to keep me occupied at home as I put the finishing touches to the stables, while in the house we enjoyed Kacey-Lou's first Christmas.

The week was great, but by the end of it I was rearing to get back in the saddle and compete. Davy Russell was out of action at the same time as well as he had picked up a ban for use of the whip or something. So when we got together we decided to head off for a couple of days and find some proper action.

We had heard about The Hayes Golden Button Challenge, an old-fashioned point-to-point race run in Gloucestershire on New Year's Eve. This was an open race for professionals and amateurs so it didn't exactly come under rules of racing and, therefore, I was free to take up the ride. The Golden Button was run over three miles cross country, taking in 24 gates, hedges and hay bales, as well as walls, rivers and open ditches. Myself, Davy and flat jockey Eddie Ahern were the pros in the race which, incredibly, had 52 starters. Richard Dunwoody acted as guest starter on the day. This kind of race was right up my street and I managed to get a loan of a horse from trainer Brendan Powell called Blaze Ahead for the race. Davy Russell got to ride Simon, a favourite for a Grand National some years beforehand.

Russell's horse threw him off at only the second or third ditch, and I was going well, leading for most of the race. Coming to halfway I thought I was out of the race as my horse refused, but luckily I managed to give him a turn and he jumped it second time around. I ended up winning the race, with English rider Zoe Gibson back in second. The entire experience was great craic and there was a huge function to celebrate that night where I was presented with my Golden Button. But the most satisfying part was that I was back competing in the saddle and counting down the days for my Irish track suspension to end.

****

Thankfully I started to earn a few quid again on my first day back after the ban at Naas, winning on Oscar Looby, while Muirhead came in a close second in the next race. But then things took a sharp turn for the worse out on the track. With just two winners in Ireland in each of the months of February and March of 2010, I would then ride over 50 runners before my next winner, a double at Punchestown with Cottage Oak and What's Up Gorden at the end of May. This was one of my worst spells in racing, and things weren't much better in England. While I was suspended I had a good day racing in a rearranged meeting at Newcastle which wasn't affected by the ban, riding three winners and three seconds from six runners, but it was a rare highlight of that year.

Both the Cheltenham and Aintree festivals came and went without a winner, and undoubtably the biggest disappointment was the failure of Go Native in the Champion Hurdle. As I've said on many occasions, it's been somewhat of a disappointment to me that I haven't won any of the Big Three at Cheltenham, the Champion Hurdle, the Queen Mother or the Gold Cup. I don't beat myself up over it or anything, but it still rankles with me when I look back on my career. I suppose it's just like the Grand National for AP McCoy. He may have been champion jockey for the best part of a decade, but his failure to win the Grand National was starting to annoy him. He never admitted it too much but when he eventually won the Aintree National on Don't Push It that year, you could tell how much it meant to him. That's the way it has been with me at Cheltenham through the years. Of course it's always nice to have *any* winner at the Cheltenham Festival, but the Big Three are special. Sometimes you look at young jockeys winning big races in their early years and you wonder if they know how important those winners will be to them in their later career. I've been unlucky through the years with those three big races. I never really had a solid chance in the Queen Mother, but I had Gold Cup chances on Florida Pearl, and to a lesser extent, Beef Or Salmon. I also had a golden chance to win the Champion Hurdle on Harchibald and still feel unlucky that I didn't. But going into the 2010 Cheltenham Festival I felt that I could make up for the past by finally landing the Champion Hurdle on Go Native.

Go Native had won the Supreme Novices Hurdle in 2009 and went into the following year's Festival with the best form in the race. He'd won the Grade One Fighting Fifth at Newcastle in November at massive odds of 25/1 in a field that included Binocular, Solwhit, Al Eile and Sublimity. The Fighting Fifth is always a fair marker for the Champion Hurdle, as is the Christmas Hurdle at Kempton on St Stephen's Day. Despite beating Binocular by seven lengths at Newcastle, Nicky Henderson's horse still went off as favourite for the Kempton race; but the result was the same, with Go Native winning to accumulate nearly £120,000 in prize money from the two races. And more significantly, there was a £1 million bonus if Go Native could complete the big race treble by adding the Cheltenham Champion Hurdle to the Fighting Fifth and Christmas Hurdle. The bonus had been put up by an internet betting firm as an incentive to run in all three races. This just added to the expectation as we were looking at the £200,000 prize money for the Champion Hurdle plus the added £1 million. The stakes were extremely high.

Before the race Go Native gave me no impression that all was not well, but as soon as the tape went up, I knew there was something wrong. He jumped way out right at the first hurdle and then hit the second. The distress signals were starting to show very early on in the race and although he came back on the bridle for a while about halfway, he was never in with a shout and finished back in 10th place, a distance behind the winner Binocular. Go Native had in fact broken down and hasn't run since.

Aintree fared little better, with a couple of good placings including finishing second on Muirhead at big odds behind Khyber Kim in the Aintree Hurdle. But the Grand National turned out to be a disaster. It was a unique experience for me and not one that I'd like to repeat any time soon. I again had the ride on Arthur Moore's King Johns Castle owned by JP McManus. JP had a few in the race and all the money was on his other one Don't Push It trained by Jonjo O'Neill. But for me the race was over before it even began.

I had finished second on King Johns Castle in the 2008 but

the race had taken a lot out of the horse and it hadn't recovered well. The horse had been kept off the track for a year but when he came back he still wasn't right and he missed the following year's National. The horse was then lightly raced the following season but had been reluctant to start on a couple of occasions and finished well out of the placings. The Grand National is the greatest race in the world and, for me, it is the ultimate test in jumping and stamina. Some horses relish that and jump and race all the way to the line. For others, it doesn't suit and they may be out of the race fairly quickly. But there's another group of horses that buck the trend; horses that perform incredibly at one Grand National but never want to do it again. And this is the category to which King Johns Castle belongs.

As soon as I mounted King Johns Castle that year I knew that all was not right. Horses remember courses and anyone that disputes this doesn't know what they are talking about. I've ridden horses several times that would suddenly slow into a fence and try to refuse if they had fallen there at on a previous occasion. Likewise, when out hunting, horses would turn away from a ditch or send you flying onto your arse if it was at a point where it had taken a nasty fall before. It is just the nature of horses. The same went for King Johns Castle; he had remembered the 30 fences over four and a half miles from his last visit and had no intention of going through it again. I took the horse down to the start and walked him up to have a look at the first fence, as I would always do before the big race. But I could feel the horse was not right and it wouldn't even walk around the start with the other horses. He just dug his heels in about 50 yards behind the rest and refused to line up. Arthur was watching on the big screen and came down to the start with a bit of birch and tried to help me get the horse moving by hitting it on the hind quarters — something he was later cautioned by the stewards for. The race even had a false start because we weren't at the starting line. I dismounted, tried to calm and walk the horse and then eased back on again. But it was all to no avail and when the tapes went up we were left at the start, stuck on one spot. The race commentary boomed: *'King Johns Castle is proving most uncooperative at the start. So will the starter let the others go who are all lining up patiently waiting for him?... they are walking forward again... And they're off and King Johns Castle has refused to leave the starting area; so a casualty before the race has even begun.'*

Arthur took King Johns Castle back in as I assessed the damage. It was a terrible way for a Grand National to end. If all stays well and I avoid injury, I may get another five or perhaps six shots at the Aintree National. But you want each and every one to count. I stood at the rail and watched as AP won on Don't Push It. I was delighted for both AP and JP McManus, two great servants to racing.

****

On a personal level, that summer wasn't much better, with a treble for Gordon Elliott on days at both Perth and Bellewstown, and a double at the Galway Festival probably the highlights. Between the suspension and injuries I managed just 30 winners for the 2009/2010 season. Things could only get better and in fairness the new season couldn't come fast enough. Thankfully, it kicked off in much better fashion.

I managed almost 50 winners in the second half of 2010 thanks largely to a purple patch in October. That month I rode 17 winners with three valuable successes at the Cheltenham meeting for Gordon Elliott including a first day 66/1 double on Russian War and Chicago Grey. Silverhand won the big hurdle at Thurles and then Punchestown went like a dream, with a treble and then a double over the two-day meeting, as

Noel Meade's horses really began to fire on all cylinders. In fact, it would have been an even more prolific time had I not lost a few weeks of racing after breaking my foot when being brought down on Jetson in a hurdle at Navan at the start of November. But it was the Leopardstown Christmas meeting that really finished off the year in style with two Grade Ones for Noel, Pandorama winning the Lexus Chase and Realt Dubh winning the Bord Na Mona Novice Chase at big odds. I had now ridden almost 35 Grade One winners for my boss over the years, a fair return for any jockey-trainer partnership.

The New Year started as the old one ended, and it's always nice to get a winner on the first day of the year at Fairyhouse. Trendelenburg, trained by Gordon Elliott, won four times for me in the first few months of 2011, but it was the first one that sticks in my mind. It was almost bottomless ground at Fairyhouse, and Trendelenburg had been backed off the boards, going off the 4/6 favourite. I had my horse tucked in at the back and was cruising alongside Andrew McNamara who was riding Energiser for Martin Brassil. As we were turning in there was still about nine or 10 horses in front of us and McNamara said to me *Jaysus I'm starting to struggle here* and I just said, *'Well I'm on the bloody favourite so I better get a move on!'* I gave mine and few slaps and luckily he just got up to win by a neck. People would be surprised just how much jockeys talk during a race, and sometimes a bit of chat can just sharpen you up if your mind starts to wander.

I finished off the January with another Grade One win for Noel on Realt Dubh, by winning the Arkle Novice Chase at Leopardstown in a classic finish with Barry Geraghty on Paul Nolan's Noble Prince. We had both tracked the leaders and then drew well clear of the rest of the field at the last fence. It was a bob of the head and a photograph which separated us in the end.

257

****

But the February meeting at Punchestown in 2011 will remain one of the lowest points of my racing career. Gordon Elliott got a decent horse into his yard called Martin Scruff and asked me to school him over hurdles. He had been trained in England but had unseated his rider twice and finished out of the places on his other starts. He was a lightly raced five year old and his owner Liam Mulryan believed Gordon might be able to turn the horse's fortunes. I go back years with Liam. He had many horses with Dad through the years, and actually had owned Bobbyjo before selling him to Bobby Burke. Within weeks Martin Scruff was jumping fluidly, had a nice few gears and we were pretty confident of a good run when taking him to Thurles that month for the Littleton Handicap Hurdle. Word had obviously got round to punters too as Martin Scruff was subject of a huge gamble which sent us off as the 5/4 favourite despite his dodgy past form. Martin Scruff hosed up that day despite being hampered by a faller at the second hurdle. From then on it was all plain sailing as I took up the lead in the straight and won easily without touching the horse.

It was an impressive winner and the handicapper thought so too, raising its mark by a hefty 19lbs. Since under the rules of racing you only carry a mandatory 4lb extra weight if you run again within a week, Gordon decided to let Martin Scruff have a crack at a handicap hurdle at Punchestown six days later. It was a race I won't easily forget.

There were 22 runners in the field that day, and despite a tough slog through bottomless heavy ground for just under three miles, Martin Scruff was backed down to the odds of 1/2 favourite. Another Gordon Elliott runner, Western Bound, cut out the early pace with an outsider The Three Colleens followed by

Andrea's Answer for Tom Doyle, Dunroe Boy and then Turn-onthegas ridden by Andrew McNamara. I was towards the rear but cruising, and with the heavy ground I was fully sure that all those in front would run out of steam. I had to hold back Martin Scruff because he was the type of horse that you can't put under too much pressure. He finds it difficult to breathe when you stick his head down so you have to keep him on the bridle for as long as possible. I made my way through the field passing tired horses and was still back in sixth coming to the final hurdle. Landing in second place while still on the bridle I gave him a quick breather, but when I went for him he didn't pick up as I expected. Ironically, while all the others ran out of gas, the one in front, Turnonthegas, kept going and while I started to push Martin Scruff to make up the ground, Andrew pushed on his horse to win by a length. I was furious with myself. I had made a bad judgement call. I had let the winner get away assuming he would stop in front and he hadn't. Instead of sweeping into the lead like the previous week, I failed by a length. As far as punters are concerned I may as well have finished stone last.

I had been in that position a couple of times before. You get used to taking stick from punters talking through their pockets when things don't go to plan. But nothing like this. It had been almost 10 years since the abuse at Kilbeggan, but this was worse. That horse had its troubles and wasn't the easiest to ride, and while I should have had him closer to the leader, it wasn't the worst race I had ever ridden. But when you lose on a short-priced favourite, you are never right. Had I got up to win by a nose I would have been a legend. Instead, I was the idiot who got a horse beaten according to a small group of punters at the track. It wasn't my finest moment, but then again I went through years of thinking back over every time I finished second and wondering could I have done something different. But it doesn't change the result; you just have to build a bridge and get the hell over it.

I remember times where I've waited for a bollicking from the trainer for giving a horse a terrible ride, but because I got up on the line to win by a short head nobody else cared. I might be on a really good horse, and just get myself outpaced or take a wrong line and go for a gap that wasn't there. But as long as you get past the line in front nobody else cares; that's just the way it is.

I remember Barry Geraghty was beaten on a favourite at Naas one day where he ended up second in a rough finish. Myself and my good friend Greg Harford were walking past the parade ring where a group of lads were standing at the second spot hurling dogs abuse at Barry while he was talking to the trainer and owners. There was one guy in particular ranting and raving and Greg, who was a very good amateur rider in his day, went over and confronted the punter. He told him he'd knock his block off if he kept shouting abuse and the idiot soon shut up. But that's just one incident in 100s through the years. When people talk through their pockets it's hard to hear sense.

But at Punchestown that day the abuse reached a new level and while you just try and block it out, it was perfectly clear the abuse was becoming more threatening. Gordon led us into the parade ring and we could immediately see a huge crowd gathering around the Number Two spot. I just looked at him and said:

'We're kind of fucked here aren't we?'.. These boys are going to give some amount of abuse here.'

But he was just as cool as always and told me to ignore them. He had sent me out to win, and I had gone out to win. Every time I go out on a horse, I go out to win. In fact we actually had a laugh about it, which made the punters even worse.

'Who the fuck do you think you are Carberry ... is this all a fucking joke to you?'

'Do you think you're too fucking good to hit a horse?'

Some punter then started saying that I had done the same thing the week before in some other race and had got beaten as well. I was being called all the names under the sun, but I didn't react and just walked into the weigh room. I was called in by the stewards to explain the race and I put my case forward. I told them that I had misjudged the horse in front and that I was trying to settle Martin Scruff into the race and had expected the horse to pick up a little quicker. They gave me a severe caution for making an *error of judgement.* Their official verdict was that I *'rode a waiting race and got beaten',* and I suppose it's difficult to dispute that one. Fortunately it was my last race of the day so I put it to the back of my mind and went home. But that wasn't the end of the matter. Not by a long shot.

Later that evening there were a few missed calls on my phone and when I listened to the voicemails there was one from a police sergeant at Navan Garda Station in Meath asking me to give him a call. I immediately thought *'fuck, probably another speeding ticket, or something worse'.* You never want to be getting messages to ring your local cop shop. Anyway the next day I rang him back and he told me that a death threat had been made against me and that they were treating it extremely seriously. He went on to say that I should look after myself and report anything unusual while out racing. Now, I wasn't exactly expecting this. I've put up with plenty of abuse at racetracks in the past. Most punters talk through their pockets; if you win you're a hero, a legend, and if you get beaten you're a jackass. Other times I've been subjected to worse abuse but never before had someone said that they were going to *kill me.* As I listened to the garda it all kind of passed me by. He said the exact threat heard by Turf Club security was that this man was going to *'take me out',* and I don't think he meant for dinner.

I think he asked if I had any questions but since I wouldn't be the best talker on the phone anyway the call was over in minutes. Afterwards I wondered what the hell was I supposed to do. How do you *'Watch yourself'*? Racing is not like any other job. If someone wants to plan an attack on you, it's not exactly rocket science. All they have to do is look at the racing pages of that day's newspaper and they'll see exactly where you will be and from what time.

What can you do in these circumstances, except keep your head up and get on with your job. I admit that the whole experience did play on my mind for a few weeks and at times you start to doubt your ability. You begin to feel that the punters are losing confidence in you. But the only sure thing in racing is this: there is no such thing as a certainty. It took a few winners to get my own confidence back but I never really, deep down, let the death threat affect me. I was riding to the best of my ability and, while punters are entitled to their opinions, making threats was a step too far.

****

The Cheltenham Festival came as a welcome distraction to all that torment, allowing me to put it to the back of my mind. We went there hoping for big shows from Realt Dubh and Pandorama, and while Realt Dubh finished third in a very strong Arkle, Pandorama was outpaced in the Gold Cup and finished a poor seventh, a fair distance behind the winner Long Run. I had other chances that week too, and finished in the places for Gordon on Plan A in the Fred Winter and on Son Amix in the Pertemps. But it was my second successive Cheltenham without a win and I came away from the week a bit deflated.

But Aintree fared a lot better as I opened my account on the first day with Russian War, winning the Silver Cross Handicap Hurdle at a big price, and then I won the Bumper on Steps To

Freedom for Gordon Elliott on Grand National day. I took the ride on Backstage for Gordon in the National but we never really struck a blow. I was at the back of the field for most of the race and were best placed at the finish when completing the course in 10th place, a few places ahead of my little sister Nina who was riding Character Building.

****

Two weeks later Nina won the Irish Grand National at Fairyhouse, steering uncle Arthur's horse Organisedconfusion to victory, while I finished pulled up on Backstage that just seemed to have lost its form. It was the first time Nina had ridden Arthur's horse at a racetrack, and was just another chapter to her incredible career. From a very early age Nina was a pure natural on the back of a horse and a top class jockey. The only difference now is that everyone else knows it too.

But it was another of Nina's wins a few weeks later that provided a lot of laughs and celebration. One of the highlights of the 2011 Galway Festival was the Donkey Derby which had been arranged by a friend Tony Gannon to raise funds for the North Galway Hunt. It had started the previous year, and was run at the Greyhound track after racing on the Thursday. There were eight donkeys, but nine jockeys turned up. Poor Robbie McNamara had to be jocked off. It was some laugh, as Nina came home on the favourite to win by a fair distance. But the real story was the performance of Davy Russell's jackass donkey that was more intent on mounting every other donkey in the race rather than running. The running joke that night was that Davy was the only bloke in Galway that night who was riding something that was riding something else.

But it was a fine end to a turbulent year that in a matter of weeks went from the highs of the Grade Ones to the lows of the

263

death threat at Punchestown. But it also ended with an impressive bottom line of 70 winners for me. I had very little break-ups which is always a good thing. In the entire season I just broke a bone in my foot, putting me out for a few weeks, something I'd gladly take any season. And I fully believe a lot was the result of my being off the drink. My head is more focused than it's ever been and even when I do take a fall, I recover faster than I have for many years. I am now confident that the decision to remain off drink for the remainder of my riding days has extended my professional career for anything up to five years.

CHAPTER 22

What Now Alice?

So where am I going now? I'm not sure if I'm cut out to go into training in the future. I've learned from the very best at close hand and can see the benefits that it can bring. Dad and uncle Arthur both made very successful transitions from riding to training, and Noel Meade is one of the best in the business. Working alongside Noel for so long has given me a real understanding of the dedication and work load involved. And those that I worked with in my early days such as Aidan O'Brien and Gordon Elliott make it look so easy. But it's anything but easy. I suppose I'm just used to doing my talking from the top of a horse. Turn up, do your work, ride the horses to the best of your ability and move on to the next challenge. I'm not sure if I'm cut out for all the management, accountancy, and people skills required to work full-time as a trainer these days. But that doesn't mean either I would rule it out. At the moment I'm doing quite a bit of pre-training and I'm enjoying every minute. I'm breaking horses, getting them race fit and easing them into jumping. And I'm able to do all this from my new home and stables in Meath. It seems the perfect arrangement.

The other business I've been engaged with is a range of race clothing called PC Racewear. In the past I've been unhappy about the quality of clothing available for everyone from beginners to hunters to professional jockeys. It is something I've been passionate about for many years, and with the help of Joules Lamb and my accountant JP Wynne, this clothing project has finally come to fruition and sales are going very well. With other business interests being taken care of, it means that I have more time to concentrate on racing, and getting the very best from the final years of my riding career. The future is looking more positive than ever.

****

I've often been asked what it takes to make it as a jockey. I'm not the greatest at expressing my feelings on such matters because I can't quite remember when exactly it started for me. All my life has been filled with horses and I never once wanted to be anything other than a jockey. I guess I was blessed with natural ability although sometimes it pisses me off that people dismiss my work as just that; as if that is all there ever was. Yes, I've had some good fortune along the way but it's been bloody hard work. Did I have a *'God-given'* talent? Perhaps I did, if there is a God. I've never been overly-religious and haven't gone to Mass in years. The only time I tend to pray is when I'm approaching the last fence of a big race. I struggle with religion at times. Yes, I believe there is a God, but I don't believe in After Life. Incredible I know. But I'm convinced that we only get one shot at this life and we should make the most of it. I'm afraid we're all to spend a long time in a hole in the ground.

Very few jockeys have made it to the level of top-class professional that weren't from a horseracing background. I mean, obviously it helps greatly if you were brought up around horses and were lucky enough to have had stables with your own ponies to practice on. But it is not necessary. As far as I'm aware, AP McCoy's family didn't have horses. His mind was just set on being a jockey so he went down to a local yard and asked for a job doing anything. Flat jockey Robert Winston was brought up in the tough area of Finglas in Dublin and learned how to ride wild horses, while even champion flat jockey Johnny Murtagh got on his first horse for a bet. Seemingly he was walking home from school one day when he was dared by another kid to mount a stray pony. He sat well on the horse and turned out to be a natural. He went on to enter a race in Kildare and ended up as a champion jockey. These things can happen, but it is a lot easier if you were reared around horses.

But being a professional jockey is a damn difficult job. The fall-out ratio is massive. You hear of the rewards for professional soccer players or golfers and it makes you sick. I stand at five feet, eight inches tall and have had to keep my weight under 10 stone all my working life. I currently weigh 9st12lbs, but I have to work at it. You keep your frame small but must be fit enough to survive some horrendous falls. You ride horses at speed, taking on tough fences with everyone else in the race trying to get the better of you. You may not fall, but you could just as easily be brought down by another horse and end up breaking your back. Jockeys regularly break bones, or get *broke up* as we call it. And not just a few bones, but lots of bones. From top to toe, I've broken most bones in my body. The list is endless. I've broken both wrists, my left arm and my collarbone three times. I've broken a bone in my neck, I've snapped a bone in the wing of my spine, and my left leg three times. I've torn numerous ligaments, lost my spleen, lacerated my liver, punctured my lung and have been knocked out and concussed more times than I remember. I've broken my left knee, both ankles, both feet, fingers and toes. And while you take these daily chances, you are doing that for an annual wage that equates to a weekly one for certain Premiership footballers. And a professional tennis player or golfer can win more in one tournament than you would make over the jumps all year. I'm not complaining, I've made between 70 and probably two hundred grand a year for most of my best years, but our travelling and stable costs are huge as well. I guess all I am saying is that you have to really love the job if you are going to make a career out of it.

Going to all the big meetings is easy. You don't have to convince yourself to get out of bed to go to Leopardstown at Christmas. Or to go to Galway or Fairyhouse or to get yourself to Punchestown during Festival week. You would crawl there on your hands and knees just to get the chance of a leg up on a horse. Hell, you would even swim the Irish Sea if there was a chance of a big winner at Cheltenham or Aintree. But it can be tough to motivate yourself to go to a smaller race day in the summer when you know you won't get within an ass's roar of the winners' enclosure.

And when you're young and broken up, you can be forgotten fairly quickly. If you are out, you are out and it can be difficult to get back in. You just get forgotten by the trainers, including some you'd have ridden winners for. They move on and get other jockeys to ride their horses instead. It is a tough, tough job. But, if you truly love riding and love horses, then being a professional jockey is the greatest career on earth.

Being a jockey is my life and I will be involved with horses until the day I die. I know I was lucky because I was good at it and didn't have to work hard to achieve top quality skills, whereas I know a lot of other guys did. It just came naturally to me. For the most part I found it easy, the easiest job in the world. Yes, I was fortunate to live in the shadow of one of the best jockeys to ever sit on a horse. My Dad Tommy is an incredible judge of a horse and I managed to pick up a lot from him along the way. I know I got many breaks in the early stages of my career because of my surname. But it wasn't just the Carberry name that helped me, it was the Carberry gene as well. I know I have Dad's talent and blood running through me and that has helped no end. Nina, Philip and Peterjon have it too, and they have carved out very successful careers out of it as well.

Mam always used to laugh, saying that she has spent her life being just someone to someone else. In her early years, she was Dan Moore's daughter. Then she was Tommy Carberry's wife. She has also been known as Arthur Moore's sister. But then she was tagged as Paul Carberry's mother, and lately she has been known as Nina Carberry's mum. That has happened to me too: when people want to wind me up I'm introduced as Nina Carberry's brother.

But seriously, if you were looking at a career involved in horses, of course it helps if you were surrounded by them growing up. It's like riding a bike. You couldn't just decide at 20 years of age that you were going to learn how to ride a bike and enter the Tour de France. Natural ability counts for almost everything, but you must also work at it and can get there if you persevere.

And if I was going to give advice for any young apprentice jockey it would be simple. Work hard and know what you want to achieve. Enjoy riding because, if horses do not mean everything to you, you are in the wrong business. I have played hard, but worked hard too. It doesn't last forever; be prepared for a more 'normal' life when your time as a professional jockey comes to an end. I have made mistakes through the years by not keeping up to date with taxes and so on. I would advise anyone just get yourself a proper accountant and keep the money in check. When you are earning well, you get in your prize money from the Turf Club on a monthly basis and you can spend like crazy. I was an awful man for buying hunters and whatever the latest gadgets were. I also liked to go on holiday at the drop of a hat, especially if I had just got injured. But the taxman does catch up eventually; I know that for sure.

Young jockeys can get very cocky after a few winners, but you just need to stay loyal to your yard. Sometimes the grass can seem greener on the other side, but believe me, it's always great to have the support of a big yard behind you. It's fairly common for lads to break away from their yard once they start to pick up rides from other trainers. Life, it appears, would be better as a free agent. But you have to remember that these other rides are being offered because your trainer has put faith in you in the first place. He has been the one to give you the leg up on the horse and often the rides can dry up once you go it alone. Other trainers will use you at the start for your claim allowance, thinking it will give their horse the extra edge that it needs. You might be taking three, five or seven pounds off their horse's specified weight and you might be more talented than guys who aren't claiming because they've already notched up 64 winners, having taken them years to do so. But once your claim is gone, you can be gone too. At least if you have a yard behind you that sort of thing cannot happen.

You might not be getting the rides you want at the start, and think you can conquer the world without a trainer. But racing is littered with dreamers and big ideas. So I would always tell lads to stick with what they have and only move if it is to another yard for a job that suits them better.

The other thing about racing is that you never stop learning. Never. I'm still learning whether I'm on a racecourse or hunting out the back fields. You just never stop learning, there's so much to know. Horses are like women, they make liars out of you. You say they'll do one thing and then they can do something completely different, sometimes the complete opposite. The secret of good balance and horsemanship is just not to panic. If your horse makes a mistake, just stay calm and sit tight. If you panic, you're in trouble. You have to adapt to each situation, and experience will tell you the best way to react. It's like jumping into the deep end of a swimming pool when you can't swim. If you panic, you're screwed; if you stay calm, you will get back to the surface. That's what riding is like. You need to stay alert and keep your balance and if things don't go according to plan, you just change the plan. If a horse makes a mistake at a fence, you just have to try and sit as quiet as you can. Sometimes he will come back underneath you, other times he'll leave you and throw you off the back of his arse and you'll end up on the ground thinking, *'How the fuck did I fall off that horse?'.* The quieter you sit, the better it is. Just try not to panic and let it happen naturally. I know it's easier said than done but that's the only way I can describe it. Generally a horse will tell you if he's going well or not going well; you just have to trust yourself and the horse and get on with it. There won't always be good days and you just have to sit tight and enjoy the ride.

I will now share the best advice I ever received from my time as a jockey. Charlie Swan is one of the greatest ever jockeys this country has produced. In fact, he is one of the best jockeys *any* country has ever produced. A great reader of a race, Charlie just instinctively knew when to go for home and when to sit and wait. I had just started at Noel Meade's yard and Charlie was the No.1 jockey in the country. After he watched me win on a horse of Noel's called Random Prince at Fairyhouse he pulled me to one side. It had been one of my very first winners on the track, and even though I was going well, I pushed the horse as hard as I could from before the furlong pole and ran out an easy winner. Charlie then gave me the best advice I've ever got. He said: *'If you are going well, just stay going well'.* In other words, there is no need to start pushing too early; let the horse run his race before you feel the need to hit and push him. I've always ridden that way since, and it has brought me a hell of a lot of winners.

****

271

I hope anyone reading this book will get a better understanding of how tough it is in racing and what makes me tick. I've been honest throughout and I suppose I can be now that I'm off the drink. I know that some people still believe that I could have ridden more winners if I had been off the drink from a young age. Who knows? If I had approached racing differently who is to say that I may have retired years ago? I love what I do and I was still riding a hell of a lot of winners even when I was partying all night.

Some people think I should have done things differently, and maybe they are right. But who hasn't made a mistake or two? No one can be right all the time. It is true that since I stopped drinking I enjoy racing a lot more. I find it is easier to get up and get out in the morning and I don't seem to be getting as many falls. And when I do, I'm recovering a lot quicker. You might look back at my career and say I could have done more, or rode more winners. That's probably true but I can't spend my time looking back with regrets.

I'd like to be remembered for my talent for riding horses and how I get on with them. It's what I love doing more than anything else and it's only when I get on a horse that I feel total freedom. I'd like people to realise that during my riding career I was always out to win, and that I gave every horse one hundred per cent to try and achieve that. I'd also like to be known as someone who worked hard but enjoyed life at the same time. I suppose I'd like the message on my gravestone to read ... 'Here lies Paul Carberry. Born 1974. Died 2074. He lived life to the full'.

****

I know I have a reputation as someone that was wild but, then again, how do you define wild? I'm no wilder than anybody else. I love enjoying myself and being happy and I don't believe that should be a bad thing. People talk about this *new era* of professionalism, as if it was something that was just invented in the last few years. Bullshit. Jockeys have always worked hard to keep fit, maintain their weight and, above all, get better at what they do. I hate to hear about the *new era*, as if jockeys before the last decade just rolled out of bed with a hangover, got a leg up on a horse and hoped for the best. I never had to work at being a good rider as such, I was blessed to have that in my blood. But everything else is damn hard work. You do your years of mucking out, riding out and early mornings on the gallops. You watch what you eat, you watch your weight, and you sweat it out at the gym and the sauna when you need to. You travel hundreds of miles every week to your place of work, where you travel at high speed over dangerous fences with very little protection, with the constant threat of serious injury. You can be the most experienced or the youngest rider in the race and you still have the exact same chance of being trampled on or broke up as the next guy. In every race you have people hoping you win and you have those willing you to fall. And if you break bones as a result, well that's just a sideshow to the main event: who won the race?

With all that going on, I'm surprised every single jockey doesn't need something else to distract them and help make sense of one of the toughest jobs in sport, or any type of professional career. We literally leave for work each day knowing it could be our last if we suffer a career-ending injury or worse. For me, I had my wild nights and endless excess and I'm lucky to be able to look back on them in this book, now that I have come out the other side. I feel like I've been there, done that, and can now take a break from that to go dry for a while until my career reaches its natural end. Two years ago I thought I may have just two seasons left in racing. Now I feel I'm back riding to the best of my ability and I just seem to enjoy it a whole lot more. With luck, I could ride well into my forties, maybe have another five or six years at the top. And I haven't felt that optimistic for a long, long time.

I just don't want this ride to end. Rachel says that I think I'm Peter Pan and that I don't want to grow up. But who wants to grow up? I just want to keep on enjoying what I do and also enjoying myself when I'm not at the track. It's when you start growing up that you start to feel old. Then I'd have to give up riding and I don't want that to happen for a long time. So I keep telling myself that I'm still young, that I can still do it. I guess a lot would depend on the falls over the next few years and how I deal with the pain. At the moment I'm fine in that respect. But when it becomes unbearable I'll know it's time to say goodbye to being a professional jockey.

Should I have done things differently? Given that I've ridden 1,500 winners, it's fair to say I can't have done that much wrong. I've won the Grand National which was always my main goal and I said that I'd retire happy knowing that I had achieved that. That doesn't mean of course that I wouldn't like to win another one, because the hunger is still there. You never lose that. But Cheltenham has always been a marker for top jockeys and it still hurts that I haven't won one of the 'Big Three' at the March Festival. I've had a lot of winners in Ireland but I always feel that we were unlucky when we went to Cheltenham. Horses like Beef Or Salmon and Florida Pearl could and should have won Gold Cups as they had won everything in Ireland in the years leading up to the big festival. Things just didn't go right for them. And I've always felt the same about Harchibald and Go Native in the Champion Hurdle. These were races that could have been won on another day, and they still hurt. Maybe I will get the chance to put that right over my final years.

So was I wild? I think my mother put it best after I won the Grand National at Aintree and people were coming out with all these different stories from my younger days. She simply said: *'Paul isn't wild. He just does things that other people wouldn't do.'* And I guess there's an element of truth in that.

Acknowledgements

I would like to take this opportunity to thank all those from the racing community without whose help and co-operation this book would not have been possible. These included Barry Geraghty, Davy Russell, AP McCoy, Ruby Walsh, Charlie Swan, Howard Johnson, Ferdy Murphy, Richard Hughes, Francis Woods, Davy Condon, Robbie Power, Norman Williamson, Jonjo O'Neill and Gordon Elliott. I also wish to thank Mick Foley, Niall Lord, Adam Lord, Ted Walsh Jnr, Rob Moran, Simon Fay, Gavin Cromwell, DJ Moore and JP Wynne. To the entire Carberry family, in particular Paul's parents, Pamela and Tommy, as well as Paul's partner Rachel, I'd like to say thanks for your help and patience during the research for this book. Also critical in this regard were Martin Murphy, Tamso Doyle and all at Horse Racing Ireland and those at The Turf Club. From Paperweight, I'd like to acknowledge the assistance of Paul Cooke, Gerard Colleran, Ciaran Farren, Gavin O'Leary and Brian Flanagan as well as Ben Blake and Eamonn Gibson in research. A special word of thanks to Noel Meade for his time and assistance, and for providing the Foreword.

- Des Gibson 2011

What They Said

'Paul's talent is unbelievable. Of all the jump jockeys I've used including Norman Williamson, Adrian Maguire, McCoy, Ruby Walsh the lot, based on natural ability and natural talent to see a stride, Paul Carberry had more than the lot of them combined.'
– **Howard Johnson, Trainer**

'From a breeding point of view he was always going to be very good, but he's one of the most natural sportsmen I've ever met. He's like a George Best type of character, and there are many similarities between the two. He has just so much natural talent and he's totally fearless.'
– **AP McCoy, Jockey**

'Without a doubt the most gifted jockey in racing. Nobody, and I mean nobody has more ability than him. He has the full package; an incredible racing brain, fantastic balance and more bottle than Hughes Dairies. But most of all he does it because he loves race riding.' – **Ferdy Murphy, Trainer**

'Paul is unique. You couldn't teach anyone to ride like Paul Carberry because it is not something that can be taught. He has pure natural ability, balance and skill. It's just impossible to replicate. Paul's a brilliant guy, tough but fair. I love to ride with him, and I love to ride against him'
– **Ruby Walsh, Jockey**

'I idolised him. All young jockeys wanted to look like Paul Carberry on a horse but I realised fairly quickly that no-one can look like Carberry on a horse, and that I'd kill myself if kept trying. He is the ultimate jockey of his era. He simply took racing to another level.'
– **Davy Russell, Jockey**

'He's one of the greats; loads of talent, stylish and confident. A brilliant rider, Paul really enjoys his riding and that's why he's been around so long. Any chance I get to use Paul Carberry on one of my horses I give him a call.'
– **Charlie Swan, Trainer**

'He was the jockey that I looked up to and wanted to be like. When I watched him winning the Grand National on Bobbyjo over the big Aintree fences and riding so short like a flat jockey I was just blown away. He was every young jockey's idol. As a person off the racetrack, he's generous and good fun.'
– **Davy Condon, Jockey**

'He's a genius. Pure class. Paul has so much natural ability that he makes it look so easy. He has ridden most of my winners, and will ride any horse for us that he can, simple as.'
– **Gordon Elliott, Trainer**

'Totally fearless, and a great reader of a race. He's a brilliant rider, oozes confidence and has great balance. It's hard to describe it, but horses just seem to run for him and that's why he's always last off the bridle. An artist in the saddle.'
– **Frannie Woods, Jockey**

'Paul was the jockey that everyone wanted to be. Growing up I spent a long time watching Paul, and tried to ride like him but

had more falls trying to do so. He has a unique style and balance that non-one else could handle.'
– **Robert 'Puppy' Power, Jockey**

'He's just a natural. His balance, his judge of pace, his style, he's a great all-rounder. Whether he's riding one of your horses or one for a rival you have to keep an eye on him because he'll always give a horse a chance. You could go on about him all day but he probably has more talent than he even realises himself.'
– **Jonjo O'Neill, Trainer**

'A fantastic jockey and one of the greatest ever. Like his father, Paul's a natural in the saddle and his win on Bobbyjo in the Grand National brought out the best in him. I've been all over the country with him and there's rarely been a dull moment.'
– **Barry Geraghty, Jockey**

'Paul is a special, special rider. A one-off. Whatever a horse has to give, Paul will get it out of him. It's just the rare talent that he has. Any loyalty I have shown him over the years has been paid back in spades.'
– **Noel Meade, Trainer**

'One of the most naturally gifted horsemen we have ever seen. I see it with him all the time, whether it was at the racetrack or when we were out hunting. Basically, he can get a horse to do anything. He can find ability in a horse that no-one else can. When a horse comes off the bridle for Paul, it would rarely go any faster if he hit it. It would have already given its best for him.'
– **Norman Williamson, Jockey**

'I can sum up Paul Carberry in two words: Likeable...and brilliant.' – **Richard Hughes, Jockey**

Complete List Of Winners

DATE	HORSE	TRAINER	RACECOURSE

1990

| 6 August | PETRONELLI | JS Bolger | Leopardstown |

1991

| 10 September | MANY PAWS | JC Hayden | Limerick |
| 16 October | NORDIC DISPLAY | JS Bolger | Navan |

1992

3 June	RETURN JOURNEY	P O'Leary	Curragh
23 June	AMBER KING	N Meade	Sligo
9 July	BEAU BEAUCHAMP	N Meade	Dundalk
6 August	L'ECRIVAIN	D Gillespie	Mallow
12 October	BITOFABANTER	A.L.T. Moore	Dundalk
26 October	KAYFA	N Meade	Leopardstown
29 November	RANDOM PRINCE	N Meade	Fairyhouse
26 December	BOB DEVANI	N Meade	Leopardstown
31 December	PERKNAPP	R Donoghue	Punchestown

1993

20 January	FLYING SOUTH	T Carberry	Fairyhouse
6 February	RANDOM PRINCE	N Meade	Fairyhouse
4 March	GRANADOS	JP Kavanagh	Clonmel
6 March	CASTALINO	J Ryan	Navan
11 March	BALLYVOONEY	J Queally	Wexford
17 March	RHYTHM SECTION	JH Scott	Cheltenham

20 March	FAYDINI	N Meade	Navan
19 April	THE MAIN CHOICE	BV Kelly	Ballinrobe
28 April	BALLYVOONEY	J Queally	Punchestown
1 May	COLOUR PARTY	M Kauntze	Naas
1 May	NEVER BACK DOWN	WP Mullins	Naas
2 May	FAYDINI	N Meade	Gowran Park
8 May	KAYFA	N Meade	Leopardstown
14 May	CLANDOLLY	O Weldon	Leopardstown
28 May	COQ HARDI SMOKEY	N Meade	Dundalk
28 May	LA CENERENTOLA	N Meade	Dundalk
1 June	HOSTETLER	N Meade	Sligo
4 June	LET IT RIDE	EJ O'Grady	Wexford
8 June	BIZANA	N Meade	Leopardstown
15 June	WATERLOO LADY	JJ Mangan	Clonmel
30 June	LORD GLENVARA	DP Kelly	Gowran Park
12 July	COQ HARDI SMOKEY	N Meade	Dundalk
12 July	RELENTLESS BOY	E Lynam	Dundalk
13 July	THE MAN FROM COOKS	EJ O'Grady	Down Royal
17 July	KAYFA	N Meade	Leopardstown
17 July	MUBADIR	N Meade	Leopardstown
28 July	LIFE SAVER	N Meade	Galway
29 July	LA CENERENTOLA	N Meade	Galway
29 July	SHIRLEY'S DELIGHT	N Meade	Galway
4 August	KAYFA	N Meade	Fairyhouse
11 August	OCEAN BLUE	D Gillespie	Sligo
12 August	MORNING NURSE	N Madden	Tramore
13 August	CORTIJA PARK	DT Hughes	Dundalk
16 August	MICKS DELIGHT	N Meade	Roscommon
16 August	BOTHSIDESNOW	N Meade	Roscommon
17 August	PEARL DAWN	N Chance	Laytown
17 August	ARAN EXILE	N Meade	Laytown
17 August	CORAL SOUND	N Meade	Laytown
28 August	LIFE SAVER	N Meade	Tralee
4 September	CLASSIC MATCH	N Meade	Fairyhouse
7 September	MUBADIR	N Meade	Galway
8 September	RUFO'S COUP	N Meade	Galway
12 September	REGAL ACCESS	N Meade	Curragh
13 September	SORRY ABOUT THAT	T Carberry	Roscommon
14 September	BIZANA	N Meade	Roscommon
21 September	LIFE SAVER	N Meade	Listowel
29 September	BIZANA	N Meade	Fairyhouse
30 September	MICKS DELIGHT	N Meade	Fairyhouse
12 October	MAGIC FEELING	AP O'Brien	Navan
15 October	JAZZY REFRAIN	N Meade	Dundalk
1 November	LIFE SAVER	N Meade	Clonmel
11 November	BOB DEVANI	N Meade	Clonmel
2 December	SORRY ABOUT THAT	T Carberry	Thurles
4 December	BOB DEVANI	N Meade	Punchestown
18 December	BOB DEVANI	N Meade	Navan
18 December	HEIST	N Meade	Navan
26 December	COQ HARDI AFFAIR	N Meade	Leopardstown
26 December	SHIRLEY'S DELIGHT	N Meade	Leopardstown

1994

1 January	COQ HARDI AFFAIR	N Meade	Naas
8 January	HEIST	N Meade	Leopardstown
19 January	MUBADIR	N Meade	Fairyhouse
22 January	LASATA	MF Morris	Naas
26 January	IL TROVATORE	N Meade	Down Royal
5 February	DOWHATYOULIKE	K Riordan	Navan
12 February	SADDLESTOWN GLEN	TG McCourt	Fairyhouse

13 February	SHIRLEY'S DELIGHT	N Meade	Leopardstown
5 March	FIDDLERS BOW VI	N Meade	Navan
5 March	GLENCLOUD	N Meade	Navan
24 March	MONKEY AGO	P Mullins	Thurles
27 March	IL TROVATORE	N Meade	Naas
4 April	MICKS DELIGHT	N Meade	Fairyhouse
13 April	FIDDLERS BOW VI	N Meade	Down Royal
26 April	BE MY HOPE	N Meade	Punchestown
27 April	FANE BANKS	N Meade	Punchestown
1 May	RANDOM PRINCE	N Meade	Gowran Park
9 May	COIN MACHINE	P Hughes	Killarney
12 May	DARDJINI	N Meade	Tipperary
12 May	OUT IN THE SUN	A Mullins	Tipperary
20 May	FANE BANKS	N Meade	Dundalk
23 May	MONKEY AGO	P Mullins	Roscommon
27 May	MONKSTOWN MAJOR	N Meade	Dundalk
8 June	CHAMPAGNE HURLEY	D Gillespie	Leopardstown
10 June	STAGE LEFT EVEN	N Meade	Dundalk
19 June	JAMES PIGG	DA Kiely	Gowran Park
20 June	RANDOM PRINCE	N Meade	Kilbeggan
6 July	LA CENERENTOLA	N Meade	Bellewstown
6 July	DASHING ROSE	N Meade	Bellewstown
7 July	COIN MACHINE	P Hughes	Bellewstown
8 July	PARTICULAR	JM Canty	Roscommon
9 July	REGAL ACCESS	N Meade	Curragh
10 July	DISTANT LOVER	N Meade	Dundalk
12 July	OH SO GRUMPY	Mrs J Harrington	Dundalk
14 July	PARTICULAR	JM Canty	Killarney
3 September	WOODY	N Meade	Fairyhouse
5 September	DARDJINI	N Meade	Galway
5 September	FOILACLUG FURRY	DT Hughes	Galway
5 September	JAKDUL	E Lynam	Galway
7 September	SWINGER	N Meade	Galway
17 September	VITAL TRIX	T Matthews	Down Royal
20 September	GALE TOI	TP Mullins	Listowel
23 September	NATALIES FANCY	PG Kelly	Listowel
2 October	DARDJINI	N Meade	Tipperary
6 October	FATHER SKY	N Meade	Punchestown
10 October	DARDJINI	N Meade	Roscommon
13 October	MUBADIR	N Meade	Thurles
16 October	MONKEY AGO	P Mullins	Limerick
20 October	WHO'S TO SAY	P Mullins	Punchestown
20 October	URBAN DANCING	A.L.T. Moore	Punchestown
22 October	MADAME MINISTER	C Collins	Down Royal
26 October	ANNFIELD LADY	W P Mullins	Navan
27 October	OUT IN THE SUN	A Mullins	Tipperary
29 October	SALMON RIVER	D Hanley	Leopardstown
6 November	BART OWEN	P Mullins	Punchestown
13 November	SCRIBBLER	A.L.T. Moore	Leopardstown
16 November	JOHNNY SETASIDE	N Meade	Fairyhouse
17 November	BELLS LIFE	N Meade	Tipperary
19 November	COQ HARDI AFFAIR	N Meade	Navan
24 November	ALL THE RACES	A.L.T. Moore	Navan
27 November	PARSONS TERM	N Meade	Clonmel
3 December	BOB DEVANI	N Meade	Fairyhouse
4 December	GAMBOLLING DOC	P Mullins	Fairyhouse
8 December	DEEP ISLE	S O'Farrell	Clonmel
17 December	GLINT OF EAGLES	DP Kelly	Navan
17 December	COQ HARDI AFFAIR	N Meade	Navan
18 December	BART OWEN	P Mullins	Navan

1995

12 January	OUT IN THE SUN	A Mullins	Gowran Park
28 January	MAJESTIC MAN	P McCreery	Naas
2 February	OFFICIAL PORTRAIT	M Brassil	Clonmel
4 February	BOB DEVANI	N Meade	Fairyhouse
5 February	ADVOCAT	N Meade	Leopardstown
9 February	SAMBARA	WP Mullins	Thurles
19 February	SCRIBBLER	A.L.T Moore	Punchestown
28 February	CLANCY NOSSEL	JG Groome	Gowran Park
4 March	LETHAL COCKTAIL	N Meade	Navan
11 March	JOHNNY SETASIDE	N Meade	Naas
29 March	MILLBROOK LAD	W Patton	Downpatrick
30 March	OFFICIAL PORTRAIT	M Brassil	Clonmel
12 April	TOM SNOUT	SA Kirk	Down Royal
13 April	QUIET CITY	AJ McNamara	Thurles
7 May	BALLY VOONEY	J Queally	Killarney
12 May	MAID OF GLENDURAGH	J.F.C. Maxwell	Downpatrick
15 May	JAZZY REFRAIN	JJ Walsh	Tipperary
18 May	SAMBARA	WP Mullins	Clonmel
21 June	MOBILE MISS	N Meade	Wexford
10 July	DARING STEPS	N Meade	Roscommon
13 July	BISHOPS HALL	H De Bromhead	Down Royal
14 July	TISARA LADY	PG Kelly	Kilbeggan
14 July	BOBBIE MAGEE	JR Bryce-Smith	Kilbeggan
15 July	WESBEST	M McCullagh	Gowran Park
30 August	HANNIES GIRL	D O'Connell	Tralee
1 September	RETURN AGAIN	DT Hughes	Tralee
20 September	MOBILE MISS	N Meade	Downpatrick
1 October	PERSIAN HALO	M Kauntze	Tipperary
15 October	FEATHERED GALE	A.L.T. Moore	Limerick
20 October	BUCKBOARD BOUNCE	G Richards	Newbury
20 October	GENERAL COMMAND	G Richards	Newbury
20 October	SQUIRE SILK	A Turnell	Newbury
30 October	JOHNNY SETASIDE	N Meade	Galway
4 November	PLEASURE SHARED	P Hobbs	Chepstow
10 November	MASTER BEVELED	D Evans	Ayr
14 November	HILL SOCIETY	N Meade	Fairyhouse
20 November	ANDROS GALE	H Johnson	Catterick
23 November	LANSBOROUGH	G Richards	Carlisle
24 November	ACT THE WAG	A Turnell	Newbury
27 November	COLONEL IN CHIEF	F Murphy	Kelso
3 December	JOHNNY SETASIDE	N Meade	Fairyhouse
9 December	GENERAL COMMAND	G Richards	Doncaster
10 December	NATIVE STATUS	T Carberry	Thurles
18 December	NATIVE STATUS	T Carberry	Navan
18 December	PERSIAN HALO	M Kauntze	Navan
20 December	DUKE OF PERTH	H Johnson	Hexham

1996

1 January	EMBELLISHED	N Meade	Fairyhouse
1 January	HILLSON	N Meade	Fairyhouse
3 January	KINGDOM OF SHADES	A Turnell	Lingfield Park
5 January	FIVE TO SEVEN	CW Thornton	Newcastle
5 January	TOM BRODIE	H Johnson	Newcastle
10 January	COLONEL IN CHIEF	F Murphy	Kelso
11 January	FRICKLEY	F Murphy	Wetherby
11 January	LANSBOROUGH	G Richards	Wetherby
12 January	DIRECT ROUTE	H Johnson	Musselburgh
23 January	TARA RAMBLER	S Hall	Market Rasen
30 January	GRAND SCENERY	H Johnson	Musselburgh

Date	Horse	Jockey	Course
1 February	STOP THE WALLER	F Murphy	Sedgefield
5 February	SORRY ABOUT THAT	T Carberry	Navan
10 February	SQUIRE SILK	A Turnell	Newbury
11 February	BOLINO STAR	SJ Treacy	Leopardstown
13 February	ABERCROMBY CHIEF	H Johnson	Kelso
13 February	DIRECT ROUTE	H Johnson	Kelso
14 February	KINGDOM OF SHADES	A Turnell	Ascot
16 February	FRENCH HOLLY	F Murphy	Uttoxeter
18 February	JOHNNY SETASIDE	N Meade	Punchestown
19 February	JOE WHITE	H Johnson	Musselburgh
19 February	MORNING IN MAY	H Johnson	Musselburgh
24 February	MORCELI	H Johnson	Haydock Park
25 February	THE LATVIAN LARK	N Meade	Fairyhouse
25 February	PERSIAN HALO	M Kauntze	Fairyhouse
25 February	SPANKERS HILL	SJ Treacy	Fairyhouse
2 March	ZAMHAREER	W Storey	Doncaster
3 March	PERSIAN HALO	M Kauntze	Leopardstown
3 March	NORTHERN HIDE	A.L.T. Moore	Leopardstown
4 March	REAL TONIC	G Richards	Doncaster
4 March	TARA RAMBLER	S Hall	Doncaster
5 March	ABBEY LAMP	H Johnson	Sedgefield
10 March	QUINTILIANI	P Matthews	Naas
16 March	EDELWEIS DU MOULIN	F Murphy	Newcastle
23 March	OATIS ROSE	M Sheppard	Newbury
28 March	JOE WHITE	H Johnson	Aintree
29 March	PLEASURE SHARED	P Hobbs	Aintree
6 April	COLORFUL AMBITION	A Duffield	Carlisle
8 April	EMBELLISHED	N Meade	Fairyhouse
8 April	HEIST	N Meade	Fairyhouse
9 April	ALASAD	N Meade	Fairyhouse
10 April	DAWN ALERT	N Meade	Fairyhouse
11 April	FIVE TO SEVEN	CW Thornton	Cheltenham
23 April	PROFESSOR STRONG	A.L.T. Moore	Punchestown
24 April	COCKNEY LAD	N Meade	Punchestown
4 May	ALY DALEY	H Johnson	Hexham
8 May	TOM BRODIE	H Johnson	Wetherby
27 May	ADRIEN	F Murphy	Wetherby
27 May	KILLBALLY BOY	H Johnson	Wetherby
28 May	DAISY DAYS	H Johnson	Hexham
28 May	SHELTON ABBEY	J Wade	Hexham
30 May	MINSTREL FIRE	J Brassil	Clonmel
1 June	ABBEYLANDS	H Johnson	Market Rasen
2 June	EARP	N Meade	Sligo
3 June	SPRINGFORT LADY	JJ Walsh	Leopardstown
5 June	BAMAPOUR	M Cunningham	Navan
6 June	BOURDONNER	M Hammond	Perth
13 June	GALAVOTTI	N Meade	Clonmel
13 June	KATES CHOICE	SJ Treacy	Clonmel
16 June	WESPERADA	N Meade	Gowran Park
3 July	WESPERADA	N Meade	Bellewstown
17 July	NOBODYS SON	D O'Connell	Killarney
18 July	JENNYELLEN	F Murphy	Worcester
19 July	THE BOULD VIC	N Meade	Kilbeggan
19 July	LEGITMAN	N Meade	Kilbeggan
25 July	FRENCH IVY	F Murphy	Goodwood
30 July	STROLL HOME	JJ Mangan	Galway
31 July	LIFE SUPPORT	N Meade	Galway
1 August	STROLL HOME	JJ Mangan	Galway
21 December	ALZULU	JG Fitzgerald	Haydock Park
21 December	GENERAL COMMAND	G Richards	Haydock Park

285

1997

13 January	BOBBYJO	T Carberry	Punchestown
14 January	QUANGO	JG Fitzgerald	Carlisle
15 January	FIDDLERS BOW VI	N Meade	Fairyhouse
17 January	ALZULU	JG Fitzgerald	Kelso
17 January	DIRECT ROUTE	H Johnson	Kelso
20 January	CROWN EQUERRY	G Richards	Carlisle
20 January	MISTER ROSS	H Johnson	Carlisle
21 January	CIRCUS LINE	M Easterby	Market Rasen
23 January	WHIP HAND	JG Fitzgerald	Wetherby
25 January	DUAL IMAGE	JG Fitzgerald	Doncaster
25 January	GENERAL COMMAND	G Richards	Doncaster
25 January	WOODBRIDGE	F Murphy	Doncaster
27 January	JERVAULX	G Richards	Ayr
28 January	CHEATER	H Johnson	Musselburgh
28 January	CUSH SUPREME	M Todhunter	Musselburgh
28 January	HEAVENS ABOVE	F Murphy	Musselburgh
1 February	EDELWEIS DU MOULIN	G Richards	Wetherby
3 February	WHIP HAND	JG Fitzgerald	Newcastle
4 February	CROWN EQUERRY	G Richards	Carlisle
6 February	D'ARBLAY STREET	WT Kemp	Kelso
7 February	SQUIRE SILK	A Turnell	Newbury
11 February	COLONEL IN CHIEF	G Richards	Ayr
11 February	MILITARY ACADEMY	G Richards	Ayr
12 February	CUSH SUPREME	M Todhunter	Musselburgh
12 February	DOUBLE AGENT	H Johnson	Musselburgh
13 February	COVER POINT	JG Fitzgerald	Catterick
13 February	MEADOW HYMN	JG Fitzgerald	Catterick
13 February	SIX CLERKS	JG Fitzgerald	Catterick
18 February	BOSTON MAN	R.D.E. Woodhouse	Market Rasen
23 February	BOBBYJO	T Carberry	Fairyhouse
24 February	ACT THE WAG	M Todhunter	Newcastle
25 February	PILKINGTON	H Johnson	Catterick
27 February	RIVER UNSHION	H Johnson	Wetherby
1 March	FRICKLEY	G Richards	Doncaster
2 March	WYLDE HIDE	A.L.T. Moore	Leopardstown
4 March	DISCO DES MOTTES	G Richards	Kelso
4 March	REAL TONIC	G Richards	Kelso
7 March	DISCO DES MOTTES	G Richards	Ayr
8 March	DONJUAN COLLONGES	TA Forster	Chepstow
12 April	ACT THE WAG	M Todhunter	Sedgefield
12 April	MEADOW HYMN	JG Fitzgerald	Sedgefield
15 April	CHIEF MOUSE	F Jordan	Cheltenham
19 April	HOUSE CAPTAIN	JG Fitzgerald	Ayr
23 April	ACAJOU III	G Richards	Perth
23 April	COLONEL IN CHIEF	G Richards	Perth
23 April	PENTLANDS FLYER	H Johnson	Perth
23 April	ROYAL YORK	G Richards	Perth
24 April	GROUSE-N-HEATHER	P Monteith	Perth
7 May	COLONEL IN CHIEF	G Richards	Wetherby
9 May	SHELTON ABBEY	J Wade	Sedgefield
10 May	REAL TONIC	G Richards	Hexham
10 May	TAPATCH	M Easterby	Hexham
15 May	MILITARY ACADEMY	G Richards	Perth
24 May	ACAJOU III	G Richards	Hexham
24 May	ROYAL YORK	G Richards	Hexham
27 May	ROYAL YORK	G Richards	Hexham
28 May	HIGHLAND WAY	M Todhunter	Cartmel
29 May	ACAJOU III	G Richards	Uttoxeter
29 May	EDELWEIS DU MOULIN	G Richards	Uttoxeter
30 May	KILCAR	T Carberry	Down Royal
31 May	LUCY TUFTY	J Pearce	Market Rasen

Date	Horse	Jockey/Trainer	Course
31 May	TAPATCH	M Easterby	Market Rasen
2 June	SARAH SUPREME	GT Hourigan	Tralee
2 June	MERRY PEOPLE	J Queally	Tralee
2 June	LEGITMAN	E Bolger	Tralee
5 June	ACAJOU III	G Richards	Perth
1 July	KILCAR	T Carberry	Bellewstown
3 July	ALAMBAR	N Meade	Bellewstown
4 July	DERRYMOYLE	M Cunningham	Wexford
15 July	STROLL HOME	JJ Mangan	Killarney
16 July	FEATHERED GALE	A.L.T. Moore	Killarney
25 July	ATTACK AT DAWN	SJ Treacy	Wexford
28 July	LANTURN	P Hughes	Galway
30 July	STROLL HOME	JJ Mangan	Galway
30 August	CORAL ISLAND	JG Fitzgerald	Perth
3 September	NOCKSKY	L Browne	Dundalk
5 September	RYHANE	A.L.T. Moore	Kilbeggan
13 September	RANDOM PRINCE	N Meade	Downpatrick
16 September	CORAL ISLAND	JG Fitzgerald	Sedgefield
22 September	HILL SOCIETY	N Meade	Listowel
22 September	BYPHARBEANRI	D Hassett	Listowel
17 October	SIGMA COMMS	N Meade	Downpatrick
18 October	MISTER ROSS	H Johnson	Kelso
22 October	KILCALM KING	N Meade	Navan
25 October	LORD OF THE WEST	J O'Neill	Carlisle
25 October	PENTLANDS FLYER	H Johnson	Carlisle
26 October	GLOBAL DIAMOND	N Meade	Galway
26 October	HILL SOCIETY	N Meade	Galway
31 October	DESERT MOUNTAIN	NA Callaghan	Wetherby
31 October	DIRECT ROUTE	H Johnson	Wetherby
2 November	FIDDLERS BOW VI	N Meade	Navan
2 November	HILL SOCIETY	N Meade	Navan
10 November	ACAJOU III	G Richards	Carlisle
10 November	LIFEBUOY	J Turner	Carlisle
10 November	LORD OF THE WEST	J O'Neill	Carlisle
11 November	CHIPPED OUT	M Todhunter	Sedgefield
11 November	SLIDEOFHILL	J O'Neill	Sedgefield
21 November	EDELWEIS DU MOULIN	G Richards	Aintree
21 November	JUSTIN MAC	JG Fitzgerald	Aintree
21 November	WHIP HAND	JG Fitzgerald	Aintree
24 November	SLIDEOFHILL	J O'Neill	Ludlow
28 November	FORZAIR	J O'Neill	Bangor-On-Dee
29 November	REAL TONIC	G Richards	Newcastle
30 November	WALK ON MIX	N Meade	Fairyhouse
6 December	MAITRE DE MUSIQUE	M Todhunter	Wetherby
7 December	NATIVE ESTATES	N Meade	Fairyhouse
7 December	SPIRIT DANCER	GM Lyons	Fairyhouse
8 December	ROYAL YORK	G Richards	Musselburgh
9 December	AUBURN BOY	I Williams	Huntingdon
10 December	CHIPPED OUT	M Todhunter	Hexham
12 December	CASH FLOW	J O'Neill	Doncaster
12 December	GREEN GREEN DESERT	O Sherwood	Doncaster
13 December	BUDDY MARVEL	O Sherwood	Lingfield Park
13 December	MONKS SOHAM	GA Hubbard	Lingfield Park
15 December	DOUBLE AGENT	H Johnson	Newcastle
16 December	ROYAL YORK	G Richards	Musselburgh
17 December	MINISTER GLORY	M Easterby	Catterick Bridge
18 December	TAKE COVER	MH Tomkins	Catterick Bridge
26 December	JUSTIN MAC	JG Fitzgerald	Wetherby

1998

Date	Horse	Jockey/Trainer	Course
15 January	RIVER MANDATE	TA Forster	Wetherby

Date	Horse	Trainer	Course
16 January	CHINA KING	JG Fitzgerald	Musselburgh
16 January	FORZAIR	J O'Neill	Musselburgh
31 January	BUDDY MARVEL	O Sherwood	Doncaster
3 February	CHINA KING	JG Fitzgerald	Musselburgh
8 February	NATIVE ESTATES	N Meade	Leopardstown
9 February	BALLAD MINSTREL	JG Fitzgerald	Newcastle
9 February	EDELWEIS DU MOULIN	G Richards	Newcastle
10 February	CHIPPED OUT	M Todhunter	Carlisle
11 February	NATIVE STATUS	T Carberry	Navan
11 February	SNOW DRAGON	N Meade	Navan
15 February	MULKEV PRINCE	GM Lyons	Fairyhouse
15 February	BLAZE OF HONOUR	AP O'Brien	Fairyhouse
21 February	LEGAL RIGHT	J O'Neill	Newcastle
22 February	ETON GALE	N Meade	Navan
28 February	EDELWEIS DU MOULIN	G Richards	Haydock Park
1 March	VITUS	DP Kelly	Fairyhouse
1 March	TOMMYS BAND	T Carberry	Fairyhouse
3 March	COUNT KARMUSKI	F Murphy	Catterick
6 March	HERITAGE	Mrs SA Bramall	Kelso
10 March	WOODBRIDGE	F Murphy	Sedgefield
12 March	VITAL ISSUE	J O'Neill	Carlisle
14 March	JOB RAGE	A Bailey	Ayr
17 March	UNGUIDED MISSILE	G Richards	Cheltenham
27 March	MARLBOROUGH	TA Forster	Newbury
28 March	GEORGE BULL	TA Forster	Bangor-On-Dee
28 March	WOODBRIDGE	F Murphy	Bangor-On-Dee
31 March	APACHE RAIDER	F Murphy	Newcastle
31 March	JOE BUZZ	F Murphy	Newcastle
2 April	DIRECT ROUTE	H Johnson	Aintree
6 April	ATTADALE	P Monteith	Kelso
6 April	PREMIER CRU	M Todhunter	Kelso
13 April	FISHIN JOELLA	N Meade	Fairyhouse
13 April	BOBBYJO	T Carberry	Fairyhouse
15 April	JOHNNY BRUSHASIDE	N Meade	Fairyhouse
15 April	MERRY GALE	D.T.R. Dreaper	Fairyhouse
15 April	CEILI QUEEN	AP O'Brien	Fairyhouse
17 April	COLONEL IN CHIEF	G Richards	Ayr
22 April	DR BONES	F Murphy	Perth
23 April	KIT SMARTIE	DM Forster	Perth
24 April	BOLD STATEMENT	TA Forster	Perth
25 April	APACHE RAIDER	F Murphy	Sedgefield
25 April	CYPRSS AVENUE	VC Ward	Sedgefield
25 April	STAGE FRIGHT	F Murphy	Sedgefield
30 April	DIRECT ROUTE	H Johnson	Punchestown
27 July	RATOATH GALE	J Queally	Galway
16 August	MOSCOW EXPRESS	Ms FM Crowley	Tramore
17 August	HEIST	N Meade	Roscommon
17 August	LADY FOR LIFE	GM Lyons	Roscommon
21 August	LARAS GREY	G Cully	Kilbeggan
21 August	LUNA FLEUR	N Meade	Kilbeggan
24 August	JOHNNY BRUSHASIDE	N Meade	Tralee
29 August	CANDY GALE	JG Groome	Tralee
29 August	PERSIAN LIFE	N Meade	Tralee
29 August	BITOFABREEZE	MC Griffin	Tralee
31 August	DISTINCTLY WEST	VT O'Brien	Sligo
31 August	FAIRY MIST	JP Ryan	Sligo
4 September	MARSUL	N Meade	Kilbeggan
14 September	LARAS GREY	G Cully	Roscommon
17 September	FOLLOW THE LEADER	R Hurley	Gowran Park
18 September	DESERT MOUNTAIN	NA Callaghan	Huntingdon
19 September	KID VID	G O'Leary	Down Royal
21 September	PROMALEE	Ms FM Crowley	Listowel
25 September	KINGS BANQUET	N Meade	Listowel
1 October	HILL SOCIETY	N Meade	Punchestown

288

Date	Horse	Jockey/Trainer	Course
4 October	MERRY GALE	D.T.R. Dreaper	Tipperary
7 October	MISS EMER	N Meade	Fairyhouse
16 October	INIS CARA	M Hourigan	Gowran Park
17 October	NOMADIC	N Meade	Down Royal
18 October	LORD HEAVENS	JJ Murphy	Limerick
21 October	NATIVE STATUS	T Carberry	Navan
21 October	CARDINAL HILL	N Meade	Navan
22 October	SNOW DRAGON	N Meade	Punchestown
26 October	STORM CHANCE	N Meade	Galway
1 November	KINGS BANQUET	N Meade	Punchestown
1 November	GREENFLAG PRINCESS	JJ Mangan	Punchestown
4 November	INIS CARA	M Hourigan	Fairyhouse
4 November	HEATHER VILLE	N Meade	Fairyhouse
7 November	SALLIE'S GIRL	N Meade	Naas
9 November	BECCA'S ROSE	F Murphy	Carlisle
12 November	WALT	N Meade	Thurles
12 November	SANDY'S NATIVE	T Doyle	Thurles
12 November	NATIVE DARA	N Meade	Thurles
13 November	LINDEN'S LOTTO	AJ Martin	Cheltenham
14 November	NOMADIC	N Meade	Punchestown
15 November	SALLIE'S GIRL	N Meade	Navan
19 November	HILL SOCIETY	N Meade	Cork
21 November	IMPERIAL CALL	R Hurley	Naas
22 November	STRONG BOOST	S O'Farrell	Clonmel
26 November	NATIVE WIT	WJ Burke	Thurles
26 November	SAVU SEA	P Hughes	Thurles
28 November	SNOW DRAGON	N Meade	Fairyhouse
28 November	SYDNEY TWOTHOUSAND	N Meade	Fairyhouse
28 November	MISS EMER	N Meade	Fairyhouse
6 December	NATIVE DARA	N Meade	Punchestown
6 December	IMPERIAL CALL	R Hurley	Punchestown
6 December	ROSES OF PICARDY	N Meade	Punchestown
8 December	NO PROBLEM	G Cully	Clonmel
13 December	ADVOCAT	N Meade	Thurles
15 December	YOUNG TOMO	H Johnson	Musselburgh
19 December	SALLIE'S GIRL	N Meade	Navan
28 December	DORANS PRIDE	M Hourigan	Leopardstown
29 December	ALMIRA	N Meade	Leopardstown

1999

Date	Horse	Jockey/Trainer	Course
1 January	SUN STRAND	N Meade	Fairyhouse
9 January	NATIVE ESTATES	N Meade	Leopardstown
6 February	NOELS DANCER	M Cunningham	Naas
7 February	LIMESTONE LAD	J Bowe	Leopardstown
11 February	ROSES OF PICARDY	N Meade	Thurles
14 February	COCKNEY LAD	N Meade	Punchestown
18 February	PARIS PIKE	P Mullins	Clonmel
20 February	NOMADIC	N Meade	Gowran Park
21 February	SALLIE'S GIRL	N Meade	Navan
14 March	GREENSTEAD	N Meade	Naas
14 March	SITE-LEADER	P Nolan	Naas
17 March	LOOKS LIKE TROUBLE	N Chance	Cheltenham
20 March	GREENSTEAD	N Meade	Gowran Park
5 April	CARDINAL HILL	N Meade	Fairyhouse
6 April	IRISH LIGHT	MJ McDonagh	Fairyhouse
7 April	WINTER GARDEN	N Meade	Fairyhouse
7 April	STRONG RUN	J.R.H. Fowler	Fairyhouse
10 April	BOBBYJO	T Carberry	Aintree
14 September	VERY TEMPTING	P Hughes	Tramore
8 October	NO PROBLEM	G Cully	Downpatrick
17 October	QUINZE	P Hughes	Fairyhouse
18 October	SUNGAZER	N Meade	Ballinrobe

19 October	NATIVE DARA	N Meade	Navan
20 October	FABLE	N Meade	Navan
20 October	HEIST	N Meade	Navan
20 October	MY NATIVE GIRL	N Meade	Navan
21 October	FROZEN GROOM	N Meade	Punchestown
24 October	QUINZE	P Hughes	Galway
25 October	SLY EMPRESS	M Hourigan	Galway
28 October	THE BONGO MAN	A Mullins	Thurles
28 October	BOLEY LAD	N Meade	Thurles
1 November	TEKNASH	N Madden	Clonmel
3 November	SALLIE'S GIRL	N Meade	Fairyhouse
3 November	OA BALDIXE	N Meade	Fairyhouse
5 November	COQ HARDI DIAMOND	N Meade	Down Royal
6 November	FLORIDA PEARL	WP Mullins	Down Royal
7 November	JIMMY THE LARK	WP Mullins	Cork
11 November	ROSES OF PICARDY	N Meade	Thurles
11 November	BOLEY LAD	N Meade	Thurles
12 November	LINDEN'S LOTTO	AJ Martin	Cheltenham
14 November	OA BALDIXE	N Meade	Navan
18 November	THE BONGO MAN	A Mullins	Tramore
20 November	LISMEENAN	N Meade	Naas
21 November	TRYPHAENA	WP Mullins	Clonmel
27 November	FABLE	N Meade	Fairyhouse
28 November	HILL SOCIETY	N Meade	Fairyhouse
2 December	GARRYDUFF BREEZE	Ms FM Crowley	Thurles
12 December	BOLEY LAD	N Meade	Cork
26 December	TRYPHAENA	WP Mullins	Leopardstown
27 December	COZ HARDI DIAMOND	N Meade	Leopardstown
28 December	OA BALDIXE	N Meade	Leopardstown
28 December	SAUSALITO BAY	N Meade	Leopardstown
29 December	MAGUA	AJ Martin	Leopardstown

2000

1 January	MILL LANE LADY	WP Mullins	Tramore
2 January	GLIN CASTLE	AJ McNamara	Naas
2 January	ROSES OF PICARDY	N Meade	Naas
2 January	ETERNAL NIGHTN	Meade	Naas
5 January	FROZEN GROOM	N Meade	Punchestown
6 January	NATIVE ESTATES	N Meade	Thurles
19 January	BACK TO BAVARIA	FJ Bowles	Down Royal
19 January	CHURCH PLACE	N Meade	Down Royal
23 January	FLORIDA PEARL	WP Mullins	Leopardstown
23 January	FROZEN GROOM	N Meade	Leopardstown
30 January	FANDANGO DE CHASSY	AJ Martin	Naas
6 February	SUNGAZER	N Meade	Leopardstown
6 February	FLORIDA PEARL	WP Mullins	Leopardstown
10 February	ROSES OF PICARDY	N Meade	Thurles
10 February	AMBERLEIGH HOUSE	M Hourigan	Thurles
13 February	STREAMSTOWN	CF Swan	Punchestown
19 February	AIM HIGH	N Meade	Gowran Park
12 March	THE BUNNY BOILER	N Meade	Naas
14 March	SAUSALITO BAY	N Meade	Cheltenham
6 April	ROSS MOFF	AJ Martin	Aintree
23 April	BOLEY LAD	N Meade	Fairyhouse
24 April	ROSS MOFF	AJ Martin	Fairyhouse
25 April	PADDY'S PET	N Meade	Fairyhouse
1 May	SCALLYBUCK	M Hourigan	Down Royal
11 May	DANTE'S BATTLE	N Meade	Tipperary
12 May	MACABEO	N Meade	Dundalk
15 May	MOSCOW RETREAT	M Hourigan	Killarney
16 May	DONICKMORE	GJ O'Keeffe	Killarney
17 May	ARCTIC COPPER	N Meade	Gowran Park

19 May	CLEVER CONSUL	AJ Martin	Downpatrick
19 May	ANDREA COVA	N Meade	Downpatrick
20 May	JUST FOR GER	N Meade	Downpatrick
21 May	FNAN	N Meade	Navan
21 May	CANON CAN	N Meade	Navan
22 May	DANTE'S BATTLE	N Meade	Roscommon
25 May	AJAR	JJ Mangan	Clonmel
31 May	FNAN	N Meade	Fairyhouse
1 June	KATIE FAIRY	MJ Byrne	Tipperary
2 June	DEE-ONE-O-ONE	N Meade	Wexford
13 June	FRANCIS BAY	DK Weld	Ballinrobe
16 June	LUNA FLEUR	N Meade	Wexford
16 June	FNAN	N Meade	Wexford
19 June	CILL BHLEIDIN	L Young	Roscommon
19 June	JOHNNY BRUSHASIDE	N Meade	Roscommon
21 June	LINK HILL	N Meade	Clonmel
21 June	CLANLUCKY	N Meade	Clonmel
3 July	CLASSIC MIX	AJ Martin	Sligo
6 July	MACABEO	N Meade	Bellewstown
14 July	CANON CAN	N Meade	Wexford
14 July	ASHJAR	JG Carr	Wexford
17 July	BERENGARIUS	M Halford	Killarney
18 July	FRANCIS BAY	DK Weld	Killarney
19 July	WOODCHESTER	JJ Mangan	Killarney
20 July	GARRYDUFF BREEZE	Ms FM Crowley	Killarney
21 July	PILLAR ROCK	N Meade	Kilbeggan
2 August	LARIFAARI	J Roche	Galway
4 August	FRANCIS BAY	DK Weld	Galway
6 August	SUN STRAND	N Meade	Galway
7 August	MOLLY-O	M Halford	Naas
8 August	CLANLUCKY	N Meade	Roscommon
9 August	SANDHOLES	E Lynam	Sligo
10 August	MIDNIGHT LOVER	N Meade	Sligo
10 August	RHAPSODY GALE	N Meade	Sligo
11 August	YOUNG WHACK	N Meade	Kilbeggan
15 August	PILLAR ROCK	N Meade	Dundalk
23 August	BILLY BONNIE	N Meade	Tralee
25 August	MICHAEL MOR	N Meade	Kilbeggan
19 September	FEARSOME FACTOR	M Halford	Listowel

2001

19 April	EDEN ROYALE	N Meade	Ballinrobe
26 April	KINGS VALLEY	N Meade	Fairyhouse
30 April	CLASS SOCIETY	M Halford	Sligo
30 April	FINIANS IVY	AJ Martin	Sligo
4 May	BONDI STORM	N Meade	Fairyhouse
4 May	PADDY'S PET	N Meade	Fairyhouse
12 May	O SO BLUE	TJ Taaffe	Navan
12 May	YOUNG WHACK	N Meade	Navan
14 May	CHANOUD	M Halford	Killarney
16 May	KILCASH CASTLE	AP O'Brien	Gowran Park
24 May	LORD GREY	DP Kelly	Tipperary
24 May	YOUNG WHACK	N Meade	Tipperary
25 May	BALLYMOTE	M Halford	Dundalk
28 May	HALFPENNY BRIDGE	N Meade	Kilbeggan
4 June	MORATORIUM	N Meade	Naas
8 June	MIGHTY MANDY	M Halford	Kilbeggan
10 June	HILL SOCIETY	N Meade	Navan
14 June	ROSSWELLAN	M Halford	Tipperary
19 June	EURO FRIENDLY	T Doyle	Laytown
6 July	THE GYPSY BARON	M Halford	Bellewstown
6 July	ASK THE MOON	M Halford	Bellewstown

9 July	SABBATICAL	JA O'Connell	Roscommon
13 July	SADDLERS' MARK	N Meade	Dundalk
13 July	RATOATH GALE	J Queally	Dundalk
18 July	RUD CINNTE	J Brassil	Killarney
23 July	ANNAGHMORE GALE	DT Hughes	Ballinrobe
24 July	GREAT DAYS	DT Hughes	Ballinrobe
2 August	ANSAR	DK Weld	Galway
6 August	MORATORIUM	N Meade	Naas
6 August	GRECO	N Meade	Naas
8 August	DIANEME	T Carberry	Kilbeggan
10 August	ASK THE MOON	M Halford	Kilbeggan
10 August	BACK TO BAVARIA	FJ Bowles	Kilbeggan
10 August	BUTTERSCOTCH	D Hassett	Kilbeggan
13 August	DARIOLE	M Halford	Tramore
13 August	RATOATH GALE	J Queally	Tramore
14 August	PASTEUR	N Meade	Tramore
20 August	SNOB WELLS	N Meade	Roscommon
24 August	BLUE	N Meade	Kilbeggan
24 August	DALE CREEK	H De Bromhead	Kilbeggan
28 August	LORD GREY	DP Kelly	Tralee
29 August	PASTEUR	N Meade	Tralee
1 September	SNOB WELLS	N Meade	Tralee
2 September	GALLILEO STRIKE	T Cooper	Tralee
3 September	CHANOUD	M Halford	Roscommon
5 September	WINTER WHISPER	EJ O'Grady	Dundalk
6 September	LOUGHCREW	M Hourigan	Clonmel
12 September	ROCKHOLM BOY	M Hourigan	Galway
19 September	BLESS 'IM	N Meade	Fairyhouse
20 September	DARIOLE	M Halford	Gowran Park
21 September	DARIALANN	DK Weld	Down Royal
24 September	PASTEUR	N Meade	Listowel
25 September	SNOB WELLS	N Meade	Listowel
26 September	FEARSOME FACTOR	M Halford	Listowel
27 September	BLUE	N Meade	Listowel
29 September	APRIL ALLEGRO	M Hourigan	Listowel
4 October	SATCOSLAM	L Whitmore	Thurles
5 October	MISSING YOU TOO	N Meade	Fairyhouse
7 October	ANSAR	DK Weld	Tipperary
13 October	APRIL ALLEGRO	M Hourigan	Gowran Park
13 October	SIGMA DOTCOMM	N Meade	Gowran Park
18 October	WOODYS BLUE LAGOON	N Meade	Punchestown
3 November	MICKO'S DREAM	WP Mullins	Navan
4 November	MICHAEL MOR	N Meade	Punchestown
4 November	WOODYS BLUE LAGOON	N Meade	Punchestown
10 November	SABRINSKY	N Meade	Down Royal
14 November	GREGORIAN	PJ Rothwell	Tramore
15 November	FALCON DU COTEAU	AJ Martin	Clonmel
17 November	LIMESTONE LAD	J Bowe	Punchestown
17 November	MISSING YOU TOO	N Meade	Punchestown
21 November	SIGMA DOTCOMM	N Meade	Downpatrick
22 November	FRUIT DEFENDU	N Meade	Cork
24 November	GLENS MUSIC	JA O'Connell	Naas
24 November	PIETRO VANNUCCI	N Meade	Naas
2 December	LIMESTONE LAD	J Bowe	Fairyhouse
2 December	HARBOUR PILOT	N Meade	Fairyhouse
6 December	THE BUNNY BOILER	N Meade	Thurles
6 December	NATIVE SESSIONS	N Meade	Thurles
8 December	WILTON BRIDGE	AJ Martin	Clonmel
8 December	SABBATICAL	JP O'Keeffe	Clonmel
9 December	FLORIDA PEARL	WP Mullins	Punchestown
9 December	LINDEN'S LOTTO	AJ Martin	Punchestown
9 December	FALCON DU COTEAU	AJ Martin	Punchestown
12 December	ROYAL JAKE	N Meade	Fairyhouse
14 December	PADDY'S RETURN	F Murphy	Cheltenham

15 December	LIMESTONE LAD	J Bowe	Navan
15 December	WOODENBRIDGE NATIF	N Meade	Navan
26 December	THARI	N Meade	Leopardstown
26 December	WOODENBRIDGE NATIF	N Meade	Leopardstown

2002

3 January	RATHGAR BEAU	E Sheehy	Thurles
20 January	ARCTIC COPPER	N Meade	Fairyhouse
24 January	CRUSSET	A Mullins	Gowran Park
26 January	LIMESTONE LAD	J Bowe	Naas
27 January	FALCON DE COTEAU	AJ Martin	Leopardstown
27 January	PIETRO VANNUCCI	N Meade	Leopardstown
10 February	HARBOUR PILOT	N Meade	Leopardstown
13 February	PASS THE LEADER	AJ Martin	Down Royal
16 February	STAR CLIPPER	N Meade	Gowran Park
16 February	ROOM TO ROOM VALUE	M Halford	Gowran Park
17 February	BEACHCOMBER BAY	N Meade	Navan
21 February	WHATATOUCH	N Meade	Clonmel
3 March	OA BALDIXE	N Meade	Leopardstown
3 March	CHAMPAGNE NATIVE	Miss IT Oakes	Leopardstown
12 March	FRENCHMAN'S CREEK	H Morrison	Cheltenham
31 March	FNAN	N Meade	Fairyhouse
1 April	SCOTTISH MEMORIES	N Meade	Fairyhouse
3 April	THARI	N Meade	Fairyhouse
3 April	STRONG RUN	N Meade	Fairyhouse
10 April	AUGHAWILLAN	N Meade	Gowran Park
11 April	DANAEVE	G Keane	Tipperary
14 April	HANDSOME BOP	M Halford	Listowel
21 April	VICTOR BOY	G Keane	Cork
23 April	STRONG RUN	N Meade	Punchestown
23 April	SCOTTISH MEMORIES	N Meade	Punchestown
24 April	OLD OPRY	N Meade	Punchestown
25 April	MORATORIUM	N Meade	Punchestown
25 April	LIMESTONE LAD	J Bowe	Punchestown
5 May	OLD KILMINCHY	M Hourigan	Gowran Park
7 May	KERGAUL	N Meade	Ballinrobe
9 May	NATIVE SESSIONS	N Meade	Tipperary
12 May	ROYAL JOKE	N Meade	Killarney
12 May	HORNER ROCKS	M Hourigan	Killarney
15 May	BEACHCOMBER BAY	N Meade	Gowran Park
17 May	GIMME GIMME	N Meade	Downpatrick
17 May	YOUNG WHACK	N Meade	Downpatrick
19 May	HEART MIDOLTIAN	N Meade	Navan
2 June	RIDGEWOOD WATER	N Meade	Cork
2 June	MINELLA LEISURE	M Hourigan	Cork
21 June	MULLAHORAN	E Sheehy	Down Royal
21 June	BORN FLYER	JA O'Connell	Down Royal
24 June	CAPPADUFF	L Whitmore	Kilbeggan
24 June	BORORA KING	N Meade	Kilbeggan
24 June	CARLESIMO	N Meade	Kilbeggan
25 June	BRIEF DANCE	P Hughes	Tramore
4 July	CARLESIMO	N Meade	Bellewstown
5 July	GLI GLI	N Meade	Bellewstown
5 July	CAPPADUFF	L Whitmore	Bellewstown
6 July	KNOCKAWAD	M Hourigan	Limerick
16 July	LANTERN LEADER	M Hourigan	Killarney
18 July	SKI JUMP	M Hourigan	Killarney
19 July	TREASURED GUEST	M Halford	Kilbeggan
19 July	SAMASAKHAN	P Hughes	Kilbeggan
22 July	CELTIC FAME	G Keane	Ballinrobe
22 July	DOESHEKNOW	PA Fahy	Ballinrobe
25 July	CARLESIMO	N Meade	Tipperary

293

26 July	FOUR ON THE TROT	M Hourigan	Cork
31 July	DARIALANN	A.L.T. Moore	Galway
1 August	ANSAR	DK Weld	Galway
1 August	LANTERN LEADER	M Hourigan	Galway
3 August	SNOB WELLS	N Meade	Galway
9 August	LAUGHING LESA	T Matthews	Kilbeggan
12 August	HEART MIDOLTIAN	N Meade	Cork
17 August	FNAN	N Meade	Tramore
18 August	MIVEC	N Meade	Tramore
22 August	VANDANTE	L Whitmore	Tipperary
22 August	LORD GREY	DP Kelly	Tipperary
23 August	HARRY THE EAR	M Halford	Kilbeggan
28 August	LOST IN THE	N Meade	Tralee
29 August	BERKELEY BAY	M Halford	Tralee
29 August	FNAN	N Meade	Tralee
30 August	COMPOSTELLO	N Meade	Tralee
1 September	ANSAR	DK Weld	Tralee
3 September	OCTAGONAL	Ms FM Crowley	Roscommon
9 September	THARI	N Meade	Galway
16 September	ASK THE ACCOUNTANT	M Halford	Killarney
23 September	LOST IN THE RAIN	N Meade	Listowel
25 September	LORD GREY	DP Kelly	Listowel
27 September	COOL DANTE	M Hourigan	Listowel
9 October	D JUDGE	T Carberry	Downpatrick
11 October	PARK LEADER	P Nolan	Gowran Park
12 October	GOOD VINTAGE	N Meade	Gowran Park
13 October	PUTSOMETNBY	KF O'Brien	Limerick
14 October	COMPOSTELLO	N Meade	Limerick
20 October	PARK LEADER	P Nolan	Cork
26 October	LORD GRANEY	TJ Kidd	Wexford
28 October	NATIVE SESSIONS	N Meade	Galway
28 October	MONTAYRAL	P Hughes	Galway
3 November	LIMESTONE LAD	J Bowe	Navan
7 November	SOLERINA	J Bowe	Thurles
8 November	SCOTTISH MEMORIES	N Meade	Down Royal
8 November	DASHING HOME	N Meade	Down Royal
15 November	MUTAKARRIM	DK Weld	Cheltenham
17 November	LIMESTONE LAD	J Bowe	Navan
23 November	COPERNICUS	P Hughes	Naas
24 November	BEEF OR SALMON	M Hourigan	Clonmel
5 December	PARTY AIRS	DK Weld	Thurles
5 December	MOSS BAWN	M Hourigan	Thurles
7 December	KINGS GLEN	T Carberry	Punchestown
12 December	KHETAAM	N Meade	Gowran Park
12 December	WOODYS DEEP OCEAN	N Meade	Gowran Park
14 December	HARCHIBALD	N Meade	Fairyhouse
14 December	ROSAKER	N Meade	Fairyhouse
15 December	LIMESTONE LAD	J Bowe	Navan
15 December	THE BUNNY BOILER	N Meade	Navan
15 December	SOLERINA	J Bowe	Navan
22 December	POULAKERRY	N Meade	Thurles
22 December	SHADY LAD	E Bolger	Thurles
26 December	MULLACASH	N Meade	Leopardstown
26 December	RARE OUZEL	AJ Martin	Leopardstown
28 December	LIMESTONE LAD	J Bowe	Leopardstown
31 December	THE GUY	M.J.P. O'Brien	Punchestown
31 December	FANION DE NEULLIAC	A.L.T. Moore	Punchestown
31 December	DEE-ONE-O-ONE	P Martin	Punchestown

2003

4 January	DEE-ONE-O-ONE	P Martin	Cork
4 January	MR SNEAKY BOO	M Hourigan	Cork
15 January	TARQOGAN THYNE	N Meade	Down Royal
15 January	AMMIEANNE	BR Hamilton	Down Royal
18 January	NATIVE COMMANDER	P Morris	Punchestown
18 January	REMINISCER	KF O'Brien	Punchestown
19 January	BORORA KING	N Meade	Fairyhouse
23 January	NOMADIC	N Meade	Gowran Park
26 January	SOLERINA	J Bowe	Leopardstown
8 February	TURN TWO	N Meade	Naas
9 February	SOLERINA	J Bowe	Leopardstown
15 February	BEACHCOMBER BAY	N Meade	Gowran Park
22 February	RINCE RI	TM Walsh	Fairyhouse
23 February	ROSAKER	N Meade	Naas
23 February	ARCTIC COPPER	N Meade	Naas
26 February	HARDRADA	N Meade	Limerick
26 February	KINGS ORCHARD	N Meade	Limerick
1 March	KHETAAM	N Meade	Fairyhouse
2 March	TANDYS BRIDGE	N Meade	Leopardstown
15 March	TAKE THE OATH	M Hourigan	Tramore
16 March	KNIAZ	AJ Martin	Punchestown
10 April	MR SNEAKY BOO	M Hourigan	Thurles
10 April	ROYAL MIRAGE	M Hourigan	Thurles
12 April	YOUNG WHACK	N Meade	Listowel
12 April	MAVERICK DANCER	M Hourigan	Listowel
13 April	SHADE ME SHAUNY	M Hourigan	Listowel
19 April	KING CAREW	M Hourigan	Cork
21 April	DASHING HOME	N Meade	Fairyhouse
21 April	WHATATOUCH	N Meade	Fairyhouse
22 April	THARI	N Meade	Fairyhouse
22 April	SWORDPLAY	M.J.P. O'Brien	Fairyhouse
9 May	AIROLO	M Halford	Wexford
15 May	STAR CLIPPER	N Meade	Gowran Park
17 May	SUPER RUN	N Meade	Downpatrick
18 May	WHATATOUCH	N Meade	Navan
26 May	CORSKEAGH THUNDER	N Meade	Kilbeggan
30 May	RATHNALLY PARK	AJ Martin	Wexford
30 May	ZAMNAH	FJ Bowles	Wexford
31 May	WINDFALL	P Hughes	Tramore
22 June	BROADSTONE ROAD	PJ Gilligan	Navan
23 June	ZAMNAH	FJ Bowles	Kilbeggan
24 June	ITS THE BOSS	AJ Martin	Tipperary
10 July	FNAN	N Meade	Tipperary
13 July	TUNES OF GLORY	N Meade	Sligo
18 July	FABLE	N Meade	Kilbeggan
28 July	JOHNJOE'S EXPRESS	M Hourigan	Galway
30 July	DIRECT BEARING	DK Weld	Galway
4 August	ALPHA RHYTHM	N Meade	Naas
4 August	HARRY THE EAR	M Halford	Naas
5 August	ALWAYS	N Meade	Roscommon
7 August	HAWAIIAN SON	N Meade	Sligo
7 August	FAIRY SECRET	AJ Martin	Sligo
8 August	MOVE THE NEWS	FJ Bowles	Kilbeggan
8 August	RED RED RED	N Meade	Kilbeggan
8 August	GRECO	N Meade	Kilbeggan
11 August	INSTAN	N Meade	Cork
11 August	FABLE	N Meade	Cork
18 August	ALWAYS	N Meade	Roscommon
22 August	MOVE THE NEWS	FJ Bowles	Kilbeggan
22 August	BLUE	N Meade	Kilbeggan
25 August	LOWLANDER	DK Weld	Downpatrick
25 August	MOVE THE NEWS	FJ Bowles	Downpatrick
27 August	MORE RAINBOWS	N Meade	Tralee

30 August	LOWLANDER	DK Weld	Tralee
31 August	FAIRY SECRET	AJ Martin	Ballinrobe
5 September	ACTIVE MEMBER	N Meade	Kilbeggan
20 September	PATTON	N Meade	Fairyhouse
21 September	PATRIZIO	E Griffin	Listowel
25 September	GALWAY BLADE	DJ Ryan	Clonmel
27 September	MOBASHER	DK Weld	Down Royal
2 October	DR TORUS	PJ Rothwell	Thurles
5 October	RUPUNUNI	F Ennis	Tipperary
7 October	QUADCO	PA Fahy	Tipperary
7 October	KHETAAM	N Meade	Tipperary
8 October	SIGMA TECHS	N Meade	Downpatrick
10 October	KERGAUL	N Meade	Gowran Park
11 October	AIROLO	M Halford	Gowran Park
12 October	LOWLANDER	DK Weld	Limerick
12 October	THESEUS	P Hughes	Limerick
12 October	BARNINGHAM	EJ O'Grady	Limerick
19 October	RUPUNUNI	PA Fahy	Cork
19 October	GOOD VINTAGE	N Meade	Cork
22 October	COMPOSTELLO	N Meade	Fairyhouse
22 October	FABLE	N Meade	Fairyhouse
1 November	ZUM SEE	N Meade	Naas
7 November	KHETAAM	N Meade	Down Royal
7 November	KINGS ORCHARD	N Meade	Down Royal
9 November	SAUSALITO BAY	N Meade	Navan
9 November	ROSAKER	N Meade	Navan
12 November	SADDLERS' MARK	N Meade	Fairyhouse
13 November	SMART DESIGN	M Hourigan	Clonmel
16 November	BERKELEY NOTE	M Halford	Punchestown
20 November	SMART DESIGN	M Hourigan	Clonmel
29 November	COMMONCHERO	M.J.P. O'Brien	Fairyhouse
26 December	CENTRAL HOUSE	DT Hughes	Leopardstown
28 December	DEMOPHILOS	DT Hughes	Leopardstown
29 December	DIRECT BEARING	DK Weld	Leopardstown
29 December	AMMIEANNE	BR Hamilton	Leopardstown
31 December	COMMONCHERO	M.J.P. O'Brien	Punchestown
31 December	BAILY MIST	MF Morris	Punchestown

2004

1 January	GOVAMIX	DK Weld	Fairyhouse
3 January	BEECHCOURT	M.J.P. O'Brien	Cork
3 January	MUTAKARRIM	DK Weld	Cork
3 January	REVUE	T Doyle	Cork
17 January	CUPLA CAIRDE	DT Hughes	Punchestown
22 January	ROSAKER	N Meade	Punchestown
24 January	LORD WHO	P.M.J. Doyle	Naas
31 January	DIZZY'S DREAM	N Meade	Fairyhouse
1 February	FIGHTER PILOT	N Meade	Punchestown
7 February	PIETRO VANNUCCI	N Meade	Naas
7 February	SUPERGOOD	I Madden	Naas
8 February	POWER ELITE	N Meade	Leopardstown
15 February	ROSAKER	N Meade	Navan
15 February	SIR OJ	N Meade	Navan
21 February	POWER ELITE	N Meade	Fairyhouse
22 February	STRONG RUN	N Meade	Naas
29 February	HARCHIBALD	N Meade	Leopardstown
6 March	DEFINATE SPECTACLE	N Meade	Navan
6 March	DEANERY NELLIE	G.M. Lyons	Navan
7 March	ZUM SEE	N Meade	Naas
13 March	CAIMIN'S CAPER	J.T.R. Dreaper	Wexford
15 March	CUPLA CAIRDE	DT Hughes	Stratford
21 March	PHILSON-WARRIOR	N Meade	Downpatrick

2 April	LORD OF THE RIVER	N Henderson	Aintree
10 April	HARD SHOULDER	N Meade	Cork
12 April	DAWN INVASION	A Mullins	Fairyhouse
17 April	SUE N WIN	G Keane	Listowel
21 April	RAND	N Meade	Gowran Park
25 April	DEEP RETURN	N Meade	Sligo
28 April	DEFINATE SPECTACLE	N Meade	Punchestown
9 May	NASSARO	M Halford	Killarney
10 May	SIR OJ	N Meade	Killarney
13 May	VICTORIAN LADY	M Hourigan	Fairyhouse
13 May	ALWAYS	N Meade	Fairyhouse
14 May	CARNDALE	N Meade	Downpatrick
15 May	CORPORATE EXPRESS	M Halford	Downpatrick
16 May	MORE RAINBOWS	N Meade	Navan
16 May	BILLY BONNIE	N Meade	Navan
16 May	LANCE	N Meade	Navan
20 May	THREE MIRRORS	A Mullins	Tipperary
20 May	LOUISVILLE	N Meade	Tipperary
21 May	TOP BEN	N Meade	Punchestown
21 May	KNOCKNABROGUE	M Hourigan	Punchestown
28 May	ALWAYS	N Meade	Punchestown
29 May	IKDAM MELODY	M Halford	Wexford
4 June	FABLE	N Meade	Kilbeggan
6 June	SARGON	M Hourigan	Tralee
11 June	YOUNG VINTAGE	N Meade	Wexford
13 June	LOST IN THE RAIN	N Meade	Roscommon
1 July	COMPLETE CIRCLE	M Halford	Bellewstown
1 July	BOUNCING BOWDLER	SJ Mahon	Bellewstown
2 July	QUINTET	JA O'Connell	Bellewstown
5 July	LANCE	N Meade	Roscommon
5 July	WOODY GLEN	AJ Martin	Roscommon
20 August	MAC THREE	N Meade	Kilbeggan
20 August	SNOB WELLS	N Meade	Kilbeggan
22 August	ALWAYS	N Meade	Cork
26 August	VICTOR BOY	G Keane	Tralee
29 August	LAUREL VIEW	N Meade	Ballinrobe
29 August	RUSHNEEYRIVER	RP Burns	Ballinrobe
30 August	LE LEOPARD	DK Weld	Downpatrick
3 September	CLUAIN RUA	LP Cusack	Down Royal
4 September	BOUNCING BOWDLER	SJ Mahon	Down Royal
16 September	RIVERBOATMAN	Ms FM Crowley	Tipperary
16 September	LEOS SHUIL	JE Kiely	Tipperary
22 September	NO HALF SESSION	N Meade	Listowel
23 September	THE SCREAMER	M Hourigan	Listowel
23 September	VICTORIAN LADY	M Hourigan	Listowel
26 September	DIZZY'S DREAM	N Meade	Punchestown
6 October	PAUMAFI	PJ Rothwell	Downpatrick
8 October	RIVERBOATMAN	Ms FM Crowley	Gowran Park
8 October	ATHLUMNEY LAD	N Meade	Gowran Park
8 October	SIR OJ	N Meade	Gowran Park
9 October	NOLEENS MOON	PJ Rothwell	Punchestown
10 October	LAUREL VIEW	N Meade	Limerick
11 October	ALWAYS	N Meade	Roscommon
11 October	MULLACASH	N Meade	Roscommon
17 October	ROCKET SHIP	N Meade	Cork
24 October	SIR OJ	N Meade	Galway
30 October	MARK THE MAN	N Meade	Naas
30 October	RAIKKONEN	WP Mullins	Naas
4 November	WISHWILLOW LORD	L Whitmore	Thurles
6 November	AUGHERSKEA	N Meade	Down Royal
7 November	WILD PASSION	N Meade	Navan
7 November	WATSON LAKE	N Meade	Navan
11 November	MISSED TRIP	J Motherway	Clonmel
11 November	NOLEENS MOON	PJ Rothwell	Clonmel

297

12 November	OPEN RANGE	N Meade	Wexford
13 November	HARD SHOULDER	N Meade	Punchestown
14 November	SIR OJ	N Meade	Punchestown
14 November	HARCHIBALD	N Meade	Punchestown
27 November	HARCHIBALD	N Meade	Newcastle
28 November	WILD PASSION	N Meade	Fairyhouse
28 November	WATSON LAKE	N Meade	Fairyhouse
2 December	THE SCREAMER	M Hourigan	Thurles
2 December	ROLLING HOME	N Meade	Thurles
8 December	TOUS LES TABLES	N Meade	Clonmel
9 December	THE GALWAY MAN	A Mullins	Clonmel
16 December	WISHWILLOW LORD	L Whitmore	Gowran Park
16 December	GUANTAMA BAY	N Meade	Gowran Park
26 December	HARCHIBALD	N Meade	Kempton Park
27 December	CENTRAL HOUSE	DT Hughes	Leopardstown
28 December	BEEF OR SALMON	M Hourigan	Leopardstown
29 December	STRONG PROJECT	CF Swan	Leopardstown
29 December	ALMIER	M Hourigan	Leopardstown
29 December	CARNDALE	N Meade	Leopardstown
31 December	LINCAM	CF Swan	Punchestown
31 December	ASIAN MAZE	P Mullins	Punchestown

2005

2 January	DIZZY'S DREAM	N Meade	Naas
8 January	BOY'S HURRAH	H Johnson	Sandown Park
16 January	CENTRAL HOUSE	DT Hughes	Fairyhouse
23 January	RANSBORO	CF Swan	Leopardstown
29 January	LOYAL FOCUS	DK Weld	Fairyhouse
3 February	THE GALWAY MAN	A Mullins	Clonmel
5 February	CAPTAIN SUNSHINE	N Meade	Naas
13 February	WATSON LAKE	N Meade	Navan
13 February	AFISTFULLOFDOLLARS	N Meade	Navan
14 February	BEAU COLINA	AJ Martin	Navan
17 February	BROGELLA	Ms FM Crowley	Clonmel
20 February	CENTRAL HOUSE	DT Hughes	Naas
13 March	ARTEEA	M Hourigan	Naas
17 March	OULART	DT Hughes	Cheltenham
18 March	FOTA ISLAND	MF Morris	Cheltenham
19 March	PHILSON RUN	N Williams	Uttoxeter
20 March	NO HALF SESSION	N Meade	Limerick
27 March	DUBLIN HUNTER	DT Hughes	Fairyhouse
27 March	ASIAN MAZE	T Mullins	Fairyhouse
28 March	AFISTFULLOFDOLLARS	N Meade	Fairyhouse
28 March	NO HALF SESSION	N Meade	Fairyhouse
9 April	DEFINATE SPECTACLE	N Meade	Aintree
13 April	REINE DES REINES	JE Kiely	Fairyhouse
24 April	FATHER MATT	N Meade	Cork
26 April	DAVIDS LAD	AJ Martin	Punchestown
26 April	WILD PASSION	N Meade	Punchestown
28 April	NO HALF SESSION	N Meade	Punchestown
29 April	ASIAN MAZE	T Mullins	Punchestown
7 May	IKTITAF	N Meade	Kilbeggan
7 May	YARRA MAGUIRE	N Meade	Kilbeggan
8 May	STRONG PROJECT	CF Swan	Killarney
15 May	DASHING HOME	N Meade	Navan
15 May	REGAL SON	P.M.J. Doyle	Navan
8 July	FERGUS VALE	K Purcell	Cork
26 July	ONE MORE MINUTE	CF Swan	Galway
30 July	MY NATIVE LAD	N Meade	Galway
4 August	KING OF FOXROCK	N Meade	Tipperary
15 August	NAPLES	N Meade	Roscommon
17 August	EASE THE WAY	DK Weld	Bellewstown

18 August	BATTLEDRESS	KJ Condon	Bellewstown
19 August	DUNEDEN	N Meade	Kilbeggan
21 August	KHAIRAMBAR	DT Hughes	Cork
23 August	MASTER OF THE CHASE	CF Swan	Tralee
23 August	HAVETOAVIT	T Cooper	Tralee
19 September	SON OF MARY	M Browne	Listowel
2 October	HARCHIBALD	N Meade	Tipperary
3 October	MASRAHI	N Meade	Roscommon
8 October	ALWAYS	N Meade	Gowran Park
9 October	STAR CLIPPER	N Meade	Limerick
9 October	WATSON LAKE	N Meade	Limerick
12 October	POWER ELITE	N Meade	Navan
16 October	MR NOSIE	N Meade	Cork
16 October	BALLYAGRAN	N Meade	Cork
2 November	WILD PASSION	N Meade	Punchestown
4 November	AFISTFULLOFDOLLARS	N Meade	Down Royal
10 November	CAMPANELLA	JE Kiely	Thurles
12 November	WATSON LAKE	N Meade	Naas
12 November	IKTITAF	N Meade	Naas
18 November	COUNTY FINAL	N Meade	Wexford
18 November	AGHADOE HEIGHTS	SJ Mahon	Wexford
18 November	ZUM SEE	N Meade	Wexford
26 November	MARBEUF	N Meade	Gowran Park
1 December	OSCAR NIGHT	A Maguire	Thurles
3 December	FEATHERED LADY	CA Murphy	Fairyhouse
4 December	IKTITAF	N Meade	Fairyhouse
10 December	HARCHIBALD	N Meade	Cheltenham
10 December	SIR OJ	N Meade	Cheltenham
11 December	TOOFARBACK	N Meade	Punchestown
17 December	GOODONYOUPOLLY	AJ Martin	Fairyhouse
18 December	FATHER MATT	N Meade	Navan
18 December	DUN DOIRE	AJ Martin	Navan
26 December	BACK TO BID	N Meade	Leopardstown
26 December	ZUM SEE	N Meade	Leopardstown
27 December	SWEET WAKE	N Meade	Leopardstown
27 December	MR NOSIE	N Meade	Leopardstown
28 December	ROSAKER	N Meade	Leopardstown
28 December	BEEF OR SALMON	M Hourigan	Leopardstown
29 December	ROCKET SHIP	N Meade	Leopardstown

2006

21 January	SWEET WAKE	N Meade	Naas
26 January	DUN DOIRE	AJ Martin	Gowran Park
29 January	NICANOR	N Meade	Leopardstown
9 February	AUGHERSKEA	N Meade	Thurles
12 February	MR	N Meade	Leopardstown
12 February	BEEF OR SALMON	M Hourigan	Leopardstown
16 February	BYE DAY	A Mullins	Clonmel
22 February	HEARTHSTEAD DREAM	AJ Martin	Punchestown
23 February	MATTOCK RANGER	N Meade	Thurles
23 February	CHELSEA HARBOUR	T Mullins	Thurles
26 February	SIR OJ	N Meade	Naas
2 March	ALLEZ PETIT LUIS	CA Murphy	Limerick
15 March	HAIRY MOLLY	J Crowley	Cheltenham
15 March	NICANOR	N Meade	Cheltenham
25 March	WATSON LAKE	N Meade	Navan
25 March	MATTOCK RANGER	N Meade	Navan
23 June	ECOLE D'ART	N Meade	Down Royal
23 August	WHATABOUTYA	N Meade	Bellewstown
25 August	RESTORATION	N Meade	Kilbeggan
25 August	DEEP RETURN	N Meade	Kilbeggan
27 August	KAHUNA	E Sheehy	Ballinrobe

29 August	RESTORATION	N Meade	Tralee
30 August	BILLY BONNIE	N Meade	Tralee
31 August	MANGO CATCHER	P Nolan	Tralee
8 September	DEEP RETURN	N Meade	Kilbeggan
11 September	CLENI BOY	N Meade	Galway
15 September	YARRA MAGUIRE	N Meade	Kilbeggan
15 September	ROCK ON TOM	N Meade	Kilbeggan
20 September	KAHUNA	E Sheehy	Listowel
22 September	OPTIMUS PRIME	WJ Burke	Listowel
23 September	SOME TIMBERING	E Sheehy	Listowel
24 September	BALLYAGRAN	N Meade	Listowel
24 September	WHENEVER WHEREVER	TJ Taaffe	Listowel
2 October	BALLYAGRAN	N Meade	Roscommon
7 October	SIR OJ	N Meade	Gowran Park
15 October	OPTIMUS PRIME	WJ Burke	Cork
15 October	ZUM SEE	N Meade	Cork
18 October	IKTITAF	N Meade	Punchestown
18 October	LEADING RUN	N Meade	Punchestown
19 October	MATTOCK RANGER	N Meade	Punchestown
22 October	DESIGNER GREY	Miss E Doyle	Clonmel
29 October	JAAMID	N Meade	Wexford
29 October	WELL RUN	N Meade	Wexford
30 October	AITMATOV	N Meade	Galway
30 October	KAHUNA	E Sheehy	Galway
3 November	CASEY JONES	N Meade	Down Royal
3 November	IKTITAF	N Meade	Down Royal
5 November	FOOTY FACTS	R Tyner	Cork
5 November	ANOTHERCOPPERCOAST	PA Roche	Cork
8 November	THE ROYAL DUB	AJ Martin	Fairyhouse
11 November	JAAMID	N Meade	Naas
11 November	CAVALLO CLASSICO	N Meade	Naas
12 November	MAJOR STAMPI	N Meade	Navan
12 November	ROSAKER	N Meade	Navan
15 November	ORBIT O'GOLD	N Meade	Downpatrick
16 November	SIR OJ	N Meade	Clonmel
18 November	HOTEL HILAMAR	N Meade	Punchestown
19 November	IKTITAF	N Meade	Punchestown
19 November	WALK OVER	F Flood	Punchestown
26 November	ARAN CONCERTO	N Meade	Navan
30 November	LOUP DU SAUBOUAS	N Meade	Thurles
30 November	THE COLT KING	JJ Coleman	Thurles
7 December	ISLAND LIFE	N Meade	Clonmel
9 December	AITMATOV	N Meade	Navan
10 December	TOOFARBACK	N Meade	Punchestown
15 December	BRIDGE RUN	N Meade	Gowran Park
17 December	ARAN CONCERTO	N Meade	Navan
17 December	ORBIT O'GOLD	N Meade	Navan
26 December	CHARLIE YARDBIRD	N Meade	Leopardstown
27 December	ISLAND LIFE	N Meade	Leopardstown

2007

1 January	OFFALY	N Meade	Fairyhouse
1 January	HEARTHSTEAD	AJ Martin	Fairyhouse
13 January	HERON'S FLIGHT	N Meade	Punchestown
23 January	CLENI BOY	N Meade	Thurles
10 February	ARAN CONCERTO	N Meade	Leopardstown
15 February	GOLDFINGER	N Meade	Thurles
17 February	KHETAAM	N Meade	Gowran Park
17 February	WATSON LAKE	N Meade	Gowran Park
8 April	AITMATOV	N Meade	Fairyhouse
28 April	CASEY JONES	N Meade	Punchestown
18 July	NEWTON BRIDGE	G Elliott	Killarney

300

20 July	WINDY HARBOUR	N Meade	Kilbeggan
20 July	MOSCOW MO CHUISLE	M Hourigan	Kilbeggan
30 July	HOVERING	MG Quinlan	Galway
5 August	BRAVE RIGHT	L Whitmore	Galway
17 August	RING HILL	N Meade	Tramore
23 August	MACS FLAMINGO	PA Fahy	Tralee
23 August	WISHWILLOW LORD	L Whitmore	Tralee
30 August	SALLY'S DREAM	M Hourigan	Bellewstown
31 August	SALFORD CITY	G Elliott	Wexford
1 September	CARLESIMO	N Meade	Kilbeggan
2 September	QUEEN ALTHEA	N Meade	Killarney
2 September	YARRA MAGUIRE	N Meade	Killarney
6 September	MOON AT MIDNIGHT	RJ Osborne	Laytown
29 September	MISTER LUCKY	BR Hamilton	Navan
29 September	MR ROBERT	N Meade	Navan
30 September	BYE THE BEST	A Mullins	Clonmel
30 September	WHATABOUTYA	N Meade	Clonmel
3 October	RINROE	N Meade	Sligo
9 October	WISHWILLOW LORD	L Whitmore	Tipperary
17 October	AITMATOV	N Meade	Punchestown
19 October	THE DOTTED LINE	N Meade	Gowran Park
19 October	SIGNATORY	N Meade	Gowran Park
19 October	SUNSHINE GREAT	MJ Grassick	Gowran Park
21 October	CROOKED STREET	N Meade	Cork
21 October	MR ROBERT	N Meade	Cork
25 October	LUXI RIVER	M McElhone	Thurles
27 October	ANTIPODE	N Meade	Naas
28 October	ANGELS' SHARE	N Meade	Wexford
29 October	RINROE	N Meade	Galway
30 October	NARQUOIS	N Meade	Punchestown
30 October	GEM DALY	N Meade	Punchestown
31 October	JERED	N Meade	Punchestown
1 November	JOYS ISLAND	PA Roche	Clonmel
2 November	AITMATOV	N Meade	Down Royal
2 November	NAPLES	N Meade	Down Royal
3 November	MUIRHEAD	N Meade	Down Royal
4 November	MATTOCK RANGER	N Meade	Cork
8 November	OPTIMUS PRIME	A Maguire	Thurles
10 November	GLENFOLAN	AJ Martin	Naas
12 November	MOON MIX	DK Weld	Limerick
14 November	SON OF MARY	N Meade	Downpatrick
18 November	JAZZ MESSENGER	N Meade	Punchestown
22 November	DARK ARTIST	N Meade	Thurles
22 November	PARSONS PISTOL	N Meade	Thurles
25 November	MR MUJI	N Meade	Navan
25 November	CHARLIE YARDBIRD	N Meade	Navan
29 November	JUDGE DEED	N Meade	Thurles
1 December	HARCHIBALD	N Meade	Newcastle
2 December	MUIRHEAD	N Meade	Fairyhouse
2 December	AITMOTIV	N Meade	Fairyhouse
2 December	SIGMA DIGITAL	N Meade	Fairyhouse
8 December	AFISTFULLOFDOLLARS	N Meade	Navan
14 December	NAQUOIS	N Meade	Gowran Park
15 December	RIGHT OR WRONG	N Meade	Fairyhouse
16 December	JAZZ MESSENGER	N Meade	Navan
16 December	MAJESTIC CONCORDE	DK Weld	Navan
22 December	WELL RUN	N Meade	Navan
22 December	BILLY TO JACK	JP Dempsey	Navan
22 December	SKY HALL	N Meade	Navan

2008

1 January	WELL RUN	N Meade	Fairyhouse
12 January	CLARIFIED	AJ Martin	Punchestown
17 January	COSMO KING	M Halford	Thurles
24 January	PRINCE ERIK	DK Weld	Gowran Park
3 February	DON'T BE BITIN	E Griffin	Punchestown
3 February	MISTER WATZISNAME	H de Bromhead	Punchestown
9 February	DRUMCONVIS	AJ Martin	Naas
20 February	CLARNAZAR	N Meade	Punchestown
20 February	JERED	N Meade	Punchestown
20 February	MOORE'S LAW	MJ Grassick	Punchestown
20 February	MOURNE RAMBLER	AJ Martin	Punchestown
23 February	AFISTFULLOFDOLLARS	N Meade	Fairyhouse
27 February	WELL RUN	N Meade	Downpatrick
1 March	MISS FANCY PANTS	N Meade	Navan
2 March	SAVE THE BACON	AJ Martin	Leopardstown
11 March	CRACK AWAY JACK	E Lavelle	Cheltenham
14 March	HI DENSITY	A McGuinness	Perth
15 March	PARADISE BAY	G Elliott	Perth
18 March	MOURNE RAMBLER	AJ Martin	Naas
23 March	OSCAR REBEL	WJ Burke	Fairyhouse
23 March	CONNA CASTLE	JJ Mangan	Fairyhouse
25 March	JERED	N Meade	Fairyhouse
8 April	HORSE MAN PASS BY	AJ Martin	Fairyhouse
12 April	BALLYAGRAN	N Meade	Fairyhouse
12 April	OFFALY	N Meade	Fairyhouse
30 April	LOCHAN LACHA	AJ Martin	Ballinrobe
3 May	CRY PRESTO	DT Hughes	Kilbeggan
3 May	RING STREET ROLLER	JJ Lambe	Kilbeggan
5 May	CHARMINAMIX	AJ Martin	Down Royal
5 May	NEWTON BRIDGE	G Elliott	Down Royal
7 May	MODEL ATHLETE	N Meade	Punchestown
8 May	CONNEMARA ROSE	G Elliott	Clonmel
9 May	PIPER'S KNOWE	N Meade	Downpatrick
16 May	RING STREET ROLLER	JJ Lambe	Cork
16 May	SALFORD CITY	G Elliott	Cork
17 May	KING RAMA	JE Kiely	Kilbeggan
18 May	DBEST	Ms J Morgan	Navan
19 May	JUBILANT NOTE	MD Murphy	Roscommon
21 May	KING RAMA	JE Kiely	Sligo
22 May	MANTRA LEADER	PP Moloney	Clonmel
29 May	JEWEL OF THE WEST	N Meade	Punchestown
29 May	NOT BROKE YET	T Mullins	Punchestown
1 June	RECOVERY MAN	G Elliott	Perth
8 June	SALFORD CITY	G Elliott	Roscommon
14 June	PICK OF THE PIKE	J.P.A. Kenny	Limerick
20 June	INNER VOICE	JJ Lambe	Down Royal
22 June	KALDERON	T Hogan	Down Royal
23 June	ROSAKER	N Meade	Kilbeggan
23 June	KALELLSHAN	PW Flynn	Kilbeggan
5 July	JEWEL OF THE WEST	N Meade	Bellewstown
6 July	SCHELM	R O'Leary	Limerick
11 July	CONNEMARA ROSE	G Elliott	Wexford
13 July	FRANC VILLEZ	G Elliott	Perth
4 September	SOUTH WING	E Griffin	Clonmel
25 September	BAGUENAUD	G Elliott	Perth
27 September	RINROE	N Meade	Navan
29 September	KALDERON	T Hogan	Roscommon
16 October	FISHER BRIDGE	N Meade	Punchestown
19 October	MYTHICAL PRINCE	N Meade	Cork
25 October	DONNAS PALM	N Meade	Naas
25 October	SIGMA LIFESTYLE	N Meade	Naas

29 October	FISHER BRIDGE	N Meade	Punchestown
30 October	EL JO	M Hourigan	Clonmel
31 October	THE FIST OF GOD	N Meade	Down Royal
31 October	DRUMCONVIS	AJ Martin	Down Royal
5 November	ORPHEUS VALLEY	N Meade	Downpatrick
9 November	PANDORAMA	N Meade	Navan
9 November	WATSON LAKE	N Meade	Navan
9 November	ARAN CONCERTO	N Meade	Navan
12 November	DAN DARE	N Meade	Fairyhouse
16 November	NORTHERN ALLIANCE	AJ Martin	Punchestown
16 November	CASEY JONES	N Meade	Punchestown
22 November	ANOTHER AMBITION	AJ Martin	Gowran Park
22 November	ISLAND LIFE	N Meade	Gowran Park
23 November	PANDORAMA	N Meade	Navan
29 November	BRIDGE RUN	N Meade	Fairyhouse
6 December	OSCAR LOOBY	N Meade	Navan
9 December	GO NATIVE	N Meade	Punchestown
14 December	DONNAS PALM	N Meade	Navan
14 December	LOCHAN LACHA	AJ Martin	Navan
20 December	NEWBAY PROP	AJ Martin	Navan
26 December	HARCHIBALD	N Meade	Kempton Park
27 December	REALT DUBH	N Meade	Leopardstown
28 December	CASEY JONES	N Meade	Leopardstown
29 December	CORSKEAGH ROYAL	N Meade	Leopardstown

2009

1 January	KANDARI	N Meade	Fairyhouse
12 January	THE BOXER ROCHE	A Mullins	Punchestown
17 January	PARSTONS PISTOL	N Meade	Naas
17 January	AITMATOV	N Meade	Naas
25 January	CHATEAU D'EAU	N Meade	Leopardstown
12 February	GO SANDY GO	JJ Mangan	Thurles
15 February	PANDORAMA	N Meade	Leopardstown
18 February	REALT DUBH	N Meade	Punchestown
22 February	GO NATIVE	N Meade	Naas
26 February	EL JO	M Hourigan	Thurles
10 March	GO NATIVE	N Meade	Cheltenham
12 April	ARAN CONCERTO	N Meade	Fairyhouse
14 April	THE FIST OF GOD	N Meade	Fairyhouse
15 April	JAAMID	N Meade	Fairyhouse
25 April	THE GREY FRIEND	AJ Martin	Kilbeggan
17 May	MASSINI MAGIC	OJ Power	Limerick
19 May	AN INNOCENT MAN	N Meade	Punchestown
31 May	ROCHEFORD BRIDGE	N Meade	Kilbeggan
5 June	OSCAR INDIA	H de Bromhead	Cork
29 July	STEVE CAPALL	N Meade	Galway
8 August	CHIP TEA	N Meade	Kilbeggan
21 August	STEVE CAPALL	N Meade	Kilbeggan
27 August	ASIGH PEARL	N Meade	Bellewstown
28 August	STREET LEGAL	N Meade	Down Royal
11 September	FISHER BRIDGE	N Meade	Kilbeggan
4 October	GO NATIVE	N Meade	Tipperary
6 October	HOTEL HILAMAR	N Meade	Tipperary
10 October	DARCEYS DANCER	N Meade	Fairyhouse
11 October	OSCAR LOOBY	N Meade	Limerick
15 October	DONNAS PALM	N Meade	Punchestown
15 October	CASEY JONES	N Meade	Punchestown
27 October	PANDORAMA	N Meade	Punchestown
8 November	OSCAR LOOBY	N Meade	Navan
8 November	AITMATOV	N Meade	Navan
15 November	JERED	N Meade	Punchestown
18 November	WATSON LAKE	N Meade	Clonmel

| 27 November | CHICAGO GREY | G Elliott | Thurles |

2010

19 January	OSCAR LOOBY	N Meade	Naas
20 January	PITTONI	C Byrnes	Punchestown
25 January	BLACKS BRIDGE	H Johnson	Newcastle
25 January	DOOR BOY	H Johnson	Newcastle
25 January	STORMY WEATHER	H Johnson	Newcastle
29 January	BLEAK HOUSE	H Johnson	Doncaster
6 February	ACROSS THE BAY	N Meade	Naas
9 February	WEST OF THE BORDER	N Meade	Fairyhouse
14 March	DREADNOT	N Meade	Navan
20 March	JIM BOWIE	N Meade	Gowran Park
20 March	LADY ROBERTA	G Elliott	Gowran Park
26 May	COTTAGE OAK	N Meade	Punchestown
26 May	WHATS UP GORDEN	A Maguire	Punchestown
7 June	DIRAR	G Elliott	Listowel
17 June	GRACCHUS	N Meade	Tipperary
18 June	RIVERSCAPE	G Elliott	Down Royal
18 June	FINAL DAY	G Elliott	Down Royal
20 June	ABBEY LANE	G Elliott	Gowran Park
20 June	BACHER BOY	G Elliott	Gowran Park
30 June	ABBEY LANE	G Elliott	Perth
30 June	KING ROONAH	G Elliott	Perth
30 June	WIKAALA	G Elliott	Perth
1 July	RIVERSCAPE	G Elliott	Perth
3 July	BACHER BOY	G Elliott	Bellewstown
4 July	HAMALKA	G Elliott	Bellewstown
4 July	RUSSIAN WAR	G Elliott	Bellewstown
4 July	GREY SOLDIER	G Elliott	Bellewstown
6 July	WATERLOO CHATEAU	N Meade	Roscommon
13 July	FINAL DAY	G Elliott	Downpatrick
16 July	MILLROCK LADY	G Elliott	Kilbeggan
28 July	HOOPY	G Elliott	Galway
29 July	CHICAGO GREY	G Elliott	Galway
12 August	WIKAALA	G Elliott	Tramore
15 August	SUPERCEDE	G Elliott	Tramore
20 August	SUPERCEDE	G Elliott	Kilbeggan
25 August	RUSSIAN WAR	G Elliott	Ffos Las
27 August	MAKHAALEB	G Elliott	Down Royal
28 August	DARK PROSPECT	N Meade	Galway
29 August	SILVERHAND	N Meade	Galway
30 August	TARKANI	G Elliott	Downpatrick
30 August	BORAGH PRINCESS	G Elliott	Downpatrick
14 September	DILSHAAN'S PRIZE	N Meade	Listowel
22 September	AL DAFA	G Elliott	Perth
22 September	RIVERSCAPE	G Elliott	Perth
23 September	SUPERCEDE	G Elliott	Perth
27 September	SAVE MY BLUSHES	PW Flynn	Roscommon
2 October	DARCEYS DANCER	N Meade	Gowran Park
3 October	DONNAS PALM	N Meade	Tipperary
5 October	ANSHAN DREAMS	A Maguire	Tipperary
9 October	GALA DANCER	P Nolan	Fairyhouse
10 October	MR CRACKER	M Hourigan	Limerick
13 October	MUIRHEAD	N Meade	Punchestown
15 October	FINAL DAY	G Elliott	Cheltenham
16 October	CHICAGO GREY	G Elliott	Cheltenham
16 October	RUSSIAN WAR	G Elliott	Cheltenham
21 October	SILVERHAND	N Meade	Thurles
23 October	CAPTAIN DECLAN	P Nolan	Wexford
25 October	PRIMA VISTA	N Meade	Galway
26 October	FOOL'S WILDCAT	G Elliott	Punchestown

26 October	PERFECT SMILE	N Meade	Punchestown
26 October	AITMATOV	N Meade	Punchestown
27 October	NOBLE PRINCE	P Nolan	Punchestown
27 October	THEGREATJOHNBROWNE	N Meade	Punchestown
4 November	GRAN TORINO	N Meade	Thurles
6 November	MONASTRELL	N Meade	Down Royal
15 December	ASIGH PEARL	N Meade	Fairyhouse
28 December	FOOL'S WILDCAT	G Elliott	Leopardstown
28 December	PANDORAMA	N Meade	Leopardstown
30 December	REALT DUBH	N Meade	Leopardstown

2011

1 January	TRENDELENBURG	G Elliott	Fairyhouse
6 January	PSYCHO	AJ Martin	Thurles
23 January	REALT DUBH	N Meade	Leopardstown
26 January	TRENDELENBURG	G Elliott	Limerick
27 January	FOR BILL	M Winters	Thurles
28 January	PLAN A	G Elliott	Gowran Park
29 January	CHINO VALDES	G Elliott	Fairyhouse
29 January	MONTAN	AJ Martin	Fairyhouse
10 February	MARTIN SCRUFF	G Elliott	Thurles
23 February	ARABELLA BOY	E Bolger	Fairyhouse
25 February	FINAL VICTORY	G Elliott	Navan
2 March	BRAVE BEAUTY	G Elliott	Downpatrick
6 March	DILSHAAN'S PRIZE	N Meade	Naas
26 March	TRENDELENBURG	G Elliott	Navan
2 April	EIGHT IS THE NUMBER	G Elliott	Gowran Park
7 April	RUSSIAN WAR	G Elliott	Aintree
9 April	STEPS TO FREEDOM	G Elliott	Aintree
15 April	AIBREAN	S.R.B. Crawford	Ayr
16 April	RUSSIAN WAR	G Elliott	Ayr
24 April	REALT DUBH	N Meade	Fairyhouse
24 April	NEAREST THE PIN	AL Martin	Fairyhouse
25 April	PRIMA VISTA	N Meade	Fairyhouse
26 April	ANOTHER PALM	N Meade	Fairyhouse
2 May	COTTAGE OAK	G Elliott	Down Royal
2 May	LIKE THE DA	DM Kelly	Down Royal
20 May	MAGNETIC FORCE	RA Hennessy	Downpatrick
26 May	TOM HORN	N Meade	Clonmel
27 May	JAKROS	N Meade	Cork
27 May	CHINO VALDES	G Elliott	Cork
29 May	ORIGINAL OPTION	N Meade	Downpatrick
29 May	EIRLAND	N Meade	Downpatrick
31 May	JIM WILL FIX IT	S Roche	Ballinrobe
31 May	SUBLIME TALENT	DK Weld	Ballinrobe
10 June	VIRGIL EARP	N Meade	Wexford
20 June	CASEY TOP	L Whitmore	Kilbeggan
20 June	TOM HORN	N Meade	Kilbeggan
2 July	ORIGINAL OPTION	N Meade	Bellewstown
2 July	LONDON BRIDGE	N Meade	Bellewstown
3 July	TOM HORN	N Meade	Bellewstown
15 July	TRENDELENBURG	G Elliott	Kilbeggan
25 July	VIRGIL EARP	N Meade	Galway
8 August	MUIRHEAD	N Meade	Ballinrobe
11 August	TRAFFIC ARTICLE	G Elliott	Tramore
18 August	ORIGINAL OPTION	N Meade	Bellewstown
20 August	COTTAGE OAK	G Elliott	Perth
20 August	SIR WALTER RALEIGH	CA McBratney	Perth
21 August	GALA DANCER	G Elliott	Ballinrobe
25 August	ORIGINAL OPTION	N Meade	Killarney
26 August	NODELAY	CA McBratney	Down Royal
27 August	SAM BASS	N Meade	Galway

29 August	ESPARO	G Elliott	Downpatrick
2 September	LONDON BRIDGE	N Meade	Kilbeggan
11 September	PLAN A	G Elliot	Listowel

Index

D

K

L

316

S

T